A wonderful theme! This surv
warns us against arrogant prid
against spiritual timidity; we 1
Lord, and the blessings of salvation. Such rejoicing is the
path to a healthy spiritual life, and a positive Christ-centred
testimony.

Bill James
Principal, London Seminary, London, UK

Josh Moody takes us on a tour of the scriptures that speak
about boasting. Building on the foundation of Paul's
teaching, especially in Romans but ranging through the
two testaments he carefully shows us how the right kind
of boasting is an excellent Christian virtue. Building his
argument with each text he contrasts the sinful arrogant
self-confident boasting of the unbeliever with the humble,
steadfast trust in the Lord and desire for His glory alone
which marks out the people of God.

Graham Nicholls
Director, Affinity, Cambridge, UK

The intrusion of Christianity into the Roman world, a world
built on a culture of 'boasting', had many consequences. In
this volume of good gospel substance, Pastor Josh Moody
helps us redirect our own propensity for the Roman 'boast'
in ways that fuel a God-honoring life. I commend it to you.

David Helm
Pastor, Holy Trinity Church, Hyde Park,
Chairman, The Charles Simeon Trust

In *Boasting*, Josh Moody has taken his pastor's heart and biblically grounded insight and given the church an important and needed study of a misunderstood and neglected teaching. Everyone knows how ugly it is to be arrogantly boastful. But the Bible also commands us to boast in Christ for the glory of God. This book clearly and powerfully shows us the difference between sinful, self-centered boasting and boasting that pleases God and exalts in God's greatness. Moody does this by using a careful, comprehensively biblical approach to arrive at his conclusions. I pray that this book will be widely read and that God will get more of the glory, worship, and trust He deserves because of it.

Erik Thoennes

Professor of Theology, Chair, Department of Undergraduate
Theological Studies, Talbot School of Theology/Biola University,
Pastor, Grace Evangelical Free Church of La Mirada California,
Author of several books

This book is a great combination of biblical exposition, historical insights and pastoral application. Christians need to grapple with this neglected but important theme of 'boasting', and Josh's exploration of it will certainly help to shape our discipleship. I highly recommend it!

Simon Gathercole

Reader in New Testament, University of Cambridge
Fellow and Director of Studies in Theology, Fitzwilliam College

JOSH MOODY

BOASTING

WHEN WE BOAST RIGHT,
WE LIVE RIGHT,
AND WE BEAR MUCH FRUIT
TO GOD'S HONOUR

Copyright © Josh Moody 2018

paperback ISBN 978-1-5271-0239-2
epub ISBN 978-1-5271-0317-7
mobi ISBN 978-1-5271-0318-4

10 9 8 7 6 5 4 3 2 1

Published in 2018
by
Christian Focus Publications Ltd,
Geanies House, Fearn,
Ross-shire, IV20 1TW, Scotland.
www.christianfocus.com

Cover design by Moose77

Printed by Bell and Bain, Glasgow.

CONTENTS

This one is dedicated to Elijah:

May you never boast in anything except the cross of Christ.

ACKNOWLEDGEMENTS

I wish to acknowledge with gratitude the work of my expert assistant Carolyn Litfin, Steve Laube, Willie MacKenzie, Colin Duriez, John Seward, Stann Leff, and my parents who are an enduring example of glad godliness. I praise God for the sustaining, spiritual, 'uncommon union' with my wife Rochelle.

This book is solely for the glory of God.

At a small consultation of about twenty senior pastors and Christian business leaders in 2010, Billy Graham said he wanted to preach one last time on the text: 'God forbid that I should glory [or, boast], save in the cross of our Lord Jesus Christ' (Gal. 6:14, KJV).

INTRODUCTION

Have you ever felt stuck between trying to be humble while also wanting to be confident? Perhaps someone tells you not to 'push yourself forward' but then someone else tells you to 'stand up for what is right'. What is the difference between the two? How is it possible for you yourself to stand up for what is right if you do not at the same time also (in some way or other) assert yourself?

Or, perhaps you are a preacher, and you have been told that preaching is God's truth mediated through personality. Well, if that is at least one appropriate definition of preaching, then how can you both let God's truth shine through your personality, and also at the same time get out of the way and let the text speak for itself? However hard you try to 'let the text speak for itself', if you are preaching then that voice of the text will still come forward with your own personal voice, your accent, your mode of thinking and operating. How can you preach humbly, when the very act of preaching is to herald the truth?

Or maybe you have noticed the criticism of 'celebrity pastors'. You don't want to be one of those, and you don't want to encourage anyone else to be a 'celebrity pastor' either. And yet, at the same time, how is it possible publicly and boldly to advance God's name if no one even knows your name (if you are the one doing the promotion of God's name)? Where is the line between self-promotion (usually thought to be wrong) and you yourself promoting God (usually thought to be right)? Or, perhaps you wonder how it is possible for someone who is conscious of their own failings and sins to be at the same time rejoicingly confident in their status before God and in their eternal salvation?

I have thought about these questions a lot recently. I have become frustrated by the 'celebrity' culture, and yet also equally frustrated by the lack of standing up for what is right, sharing the gospel, and living lives with holy zeal. I believe the answer lies in grasping the biblical teaching about *boasting*. There is the wrong kind, of course, but also (most strangely and most biblically) there is a right kind. There *is* a kind of boasting that is biblical and healthy, humble and holy: good for society, the church, your family, your relationships; good for your marriage, for your parents, for your children; good for God's glory.

Now, I might as well say it at the outset, but by considering this theme of boasting, the last thing in the world I want to encourage is pride. 'Let me tell you why I am so brilliant and you are not.' There are people who are so puffed up that their heads can hardly fit through the doors of their homes, their churches, or their businesses. Unlike most diseases, pride is often invisible to the person in its captivity.

At some point or other, you will figure out if you have cancer, a bowel disease or a serious infection. You will even at some point or other know whether you are addicted to sex or drugs, depressed, angry, or filled with hate, or stealing from your employer. You may deny these things to yourself, but if you are successful at denying them for any length of time, the reason is because you are using a far greater cloaking mechanism, which is really the sin behind the sin: that is pride.

Arrogance is pride on speed. It is not simply feeling good about yourself beyond all possibility of reasonable self-assessment; it is making sure that others know it and pushing them down at the same time. Arrogant people 'arrogate' (or take) to themselves things that belong to other people: their reputation, goods, or countries. Proud people merely believe they are better than other people, but they haven't yet stepped over the line to shoving their purported superiority down other people's throats.

Those who are proud are usually immune to self-discovery, because the nature of pride is to think that you are fine. I've always loved Charles Spurgeon's famous line about pride, in a paper he wrote on the topic entitled, 'Humility and How I Achieved It.' Woe betide the man who tries to write the book on humility if he does it without a lashing of self-deprecating humour! In fact, in many ways, the best antidote to pride is laughter. Not laughing at other people – that's more pride – but laughing at yourself. We take God seriously; we don't take ourselves seriously. Even that sentence makes us laugh a little.

No, I am not trying to increase the proportion of people who are immune to self-discovery and blind to their own pride – may their tribe decrease. I am trying to show you that there is another way than merely saying: get low, get down, do less, don't be so pushy. Self-denial is important; it is biblical. It is just not the *only* thing the Bible says. If you've never denied yourself, taken up your cross, and followed Jesus, then I encourage you to stop right now and consider this: You are not God. Jesus is God.

But what then? What do we do with the energy that God has given us? What do we do with the gifts that God has given us? How do we use them? How we do make the most of who we are as people, as individuals, as groups? If God is completely and utterly sovereign (as I believe He is), then does that mean that we simply spend our lives getting really low and letting Him get on with running the place? Or is part of His sovereignty expressed in giving us gifts to use for His glory? If the answer is that we are to use our gifts for His glory, then how do we do *that* without self-assertion or pushing ourselves forward – either becoming proud or being accused of being proud?

For me, the answer is in the biblical teaching about boasting.

This book comes out of an experience we had in our congregation when I preached on a verse in Romans 5. I preached through the Letter to the Romans *very* slowly; I will not tell you how long it took me to get to chapter 5 because it's a little embarrassing. All I can say is I'm a slow learner and Romans is hard, and it has taken me a long time to be sure I got various parts of it myself, let alone communicated it to others.

There we were going through Romans at a snail's pace, and we got to chapter 5, verse 2. It was one of the most surprising experiences I have had as a preacher. God seemed to take hold of that message and make it fly. Now, those of us who are preachers will know that sometimes this happens, and we cannot predict always when, and at other times even the same message does not have the same impact. We do our work, we prepare well, God uses His Word, it never returns empty, but sometimes it produces a thirty times harvest, other times a hundredfold. This was definitely of the hundredfold variety: but more than that, not just an 'anointing' of a subjective kind. There was a resonance in my mind, and all of our minds, on the theme of true biblical boasting.

Now this book is not simply a ridiculously elongated version of that sermon. We will look at that key text itself later in the book. But I also want to scan back and put the whole topic of boasting into biblical context.

My thesis is this: *When you boast rightly, you live rightly, and you bear much fruit to God's honour.*

1.
BOASTING IN PAUL

The apostle Paul has this reputation of being angular and difficult, troublesome and overly-zealous. Actually, nothing could be further from the truth. Paul had a lot of friends: the first of a few examples we can take. You can find long lists of these friends at the end of his letters, most particularly at the end of Romans. Person after person was greeted by name. There were details; there was affection. We also know that Paul had key co-workers. It is true he had an argument with one of them (an argument with Barnabas about Mark; see Acts 15:39), but the evidence suggests that by the end Paul had reconciled with this co-worker[1]. Others were dearly beloved, honoured, fellow workers.[2] That kind of affectionate, real relationship cannot happen if the person is angular, difficult, troublesome, or hard-to-get-along-with.

This matter of boasting is strange, however, all things considered. Paul, of course, like all followers of Jesus, was against arrogance, self-centred pride, and the like. He urged Christians not to think more highly of themselves than was related to the grace that they had received (Rom. 12:3), but to consider themselves as debtors to mercy alone (a line from the famous hymn, but echoed in Paul in many places, as in Rom. 12:1, Eph. 4:1); he urged them to consider others

---

1   1 Corinthians 9:6; 2 Timothy 4:11; Colossians 4:10.
2   Look at the beginning of Paul's letters: for instance, Philippians 1:1; Colossians 1:1; 1 Thessalonians 1:1; or the end of his letters, as in, Romans 16:3-16.

as better than themselves (Phil. 2:3). He wanted followers of Jesus to submit to one another out of reverence for Christ (Eph. 5:21). He wanted leaders to lead with grace and humility, focusing on Christ and the gospel (1 Cor. 11:1). No doubt he would have agreed with Peter that leaders are not to be domineering over those in their care, but be examples to them (1 Pet. 5:2-3); and also with the Letter to the Hebrews, that followers are to submit to the leaders, not in a negative, self-loathing way, but honouring the difficult task of leadership, and being the sort of person that is a joy to lead (Heb. 13:17).

But boasting still remained. At one point, he said it was excluded, and excluded from the Christian by being a debtor to mercy alone, saved by grace, not by works, so that no one can boast. Yet at another point, he said that he boasted. He would go on boasting; he boasted in his weakness. Boasting in Paul is a conundrum.

What does it mean to boast in weakness? What does it mean to be so confident, so assured, so exulting that it can be said that you are boasting – while at the same time, in another way, you are not to be boasting at all? Some, of course, would say that Paul was simply inconsistent in his thinking. Those of us who love the Bible will be unlikely to want to admit that solution, however simple and attractive it might be at one level. Why could we not simply say that Paul, at a human level, was not consistent in his thinking in this regard? Sometimes in the very same letter he would at one time speak against pride and boasting, and a little bit later speak in favour of boasting. The most obvious example of that is Romans, chapters 3 to 5. Chapter 3 culminates in a denial of boasting – it was excluded (Rom. 3:27). Chapter 5 begins with a call to boast – in another way, and in a different manner (Rom. 5:2; 'rejoice' or literally 'boast').

'Let the one who boasts, boast in the Lord!'.[3] Yes, but what does that *mean*? What does it mean to 'boast in the

---

3   1 Corinthians 1:31; 2 Corinthians 10:17; Jeremiah 9:23-24, ESV.

Lord'? Does that mean singing songs or going to church? Does it mean doing evangelism or social justice? Is it a disposition of the heart or a kind of psychology? Is it about the orientation of your affections, or is it more about how you think rationally? Or is it more that the 'fear of the Lord is the beginning of wisdom' (Ps. 111:10)?

It is important to ask what Paul meant by 'boasting', because at a surface level, what he meant by it is not consistent. If Paul was a consistent thinker (as we should at least grant any author the possibility before ruling them inconsistent), then his thinking about boasting must be different from ours. What did Paul mean by boasting? His lack of consistency cannot simply be contextualization. He cannot simply be saying this to one audience in this way, and then using the same word in a slightly different way to a different audience. Anyone who is a teacher, an author, or a preacher will know that that kind of variegated communication is more than legitimate. When you use a word in one context, you may use the same word slightly differently in another context. Failure to spot context in communication leads to all sorts of misunderstanding.

A favourite example of this in my own life was a book I wrote with some friends about a rather academic topic. The weight of the book was well-defined in its promotion, and yet the comments on Amazon – which generally are unwise to read, I am told, but strangely compelling, I find nonetheless – ranged from those who loved its content to those who said it was hard to grasp, difficult, or above their heads. Other things I have written have been at a less academic level. But there I was using a similar form of communication (a book) with some similar words to communicate in quite a different way to a different audience! The old story is that Queen Victoria so loved the famous children's story *Alice in Wonderland* that she ordered the next book by the same author as soon as it was published – only to discover that the next book was a very technical treatise on higher mathematics.

But Paul cannot be doing that. He cannot be using the same word in different ways as he communicated to different contexts, because some of the conflict in the meaning of the word (broadly speaking, either meaning something negative or something positive) is found in the same letters written to the same churches, therefore the same audience. It is unlikely that Paul was inconsistent unintentionally in the space of a few hundred words in the same letter. Not if we grant Paul any modicum of intelligence or skill as a writer.

A further possibility, a simple-level answer to the inconsistency in Paul – that lets the inconsistency be, rather than digs for any deeper meaning – is that Paul was *deliberately* inconsistent. A certain form of writing intends to shake up the reader by using words in different ways in the same context in order to create a sort of cognitive dissonance that causes the reader to ask harder questions than appear on the surface. Could Paul have been using this technique? It is not impossible, but it is unlikely because this technique only mirrors parallel developments in other art, the surrealists and other non-literalistic movements of a similar kind that took place hundreds of years after Paul was writing. To call Paul deliberately inconsistent to cause a response as a non-literalistic author is a gross anachronism not too dissimilar to wondering whether Paul wrote on a MacBook or PC laptop.

So what is behind this apparently inconsistent use of boasting in Paul? Or to put it more simply, what on earth did Paul mean by saying that in some way or other it was a good thing to boast (while having also said it was not a good thing to boast)? Boasting in Paul was somehow integral to who he was and what he did and what he represented as a Christian figure in the early church – the great apostle, missionary, author. Something integral to his personality revolved around understanding this matter of boasting.

Paul's story

But if it was so integral to his agenda and his person, then how did that show itself in the story of his life? What did it mean for Paul to boast in practice in the actual decisions of his life? If we can get a handle on how he lived out his idea of boasting in his work and in his living, then it might help us put feet on the idea of boasting in our own lives, too, and apply it to our situations and our lives.

None of us is the Apostle Paul – inspired author of Holy Scripture – and yet all of us face daily challenges when the wrestling with what it means to be humble, and yet also to take initiative, can be very real indeed. How do we honour the growing identity of our teenage son while at the same time continuing to take the appropriate lead over his life? How do we respect our boss while at the same time taking initiative and leadership of our own work area?

This matter of boasting is far more than something for an apostle and far more than something only for a religious person. It is something for us all. If it was so central to Paul's thinking, then perhaps the way it impacted his life could show us that it is potentially central not only to our thinking, but also to our living as well. Certainly, a pastor, minister, vicar, priest, or monk needs to be humble, and yet at the same time also lead and take action, and sometimes risk daringly for Christ. So for a minister or religious leader, then, this matter of boasting could be very real and relevant for their lives, but not only for the religious life. It could also impact all lives – from the bus driver to the astronaut.

How, then, did Paul's *thinking* about boasting impact his actual *living*? To answer that question, we will need to have a clear picture of Paul's life story. Fortunately, we have plenty of material to help us answer that question because Paul's life is described in some detail by his companion Luke in the book of the Bible called the Acts of the Apostles.

That story begins as a description of the pouring out of the Holy Spirit upon the apostles, and then focuses in more and more on one particular apostle, the Apostle Paul. Paul was hardly mentioned at all to begin with. But then the story of the religious persecutor of the early Christian movement – who was converted dramatically on the road to Damascus, and then was sent by the church at Antioch as a missionary – became so dramatically central that it began to dominate the rest of Luke's account of the early days of the New Testament church, so much so that the second half of the Acts of the *Apostles* could also be renamed the Acts of the *Apostle*.

Paul certainly had no problem with pushing himself forward – or at least he apparently had no problem with Luke pushing him forward. I am not for the moment suggesting that Paul was self-serving: that would not do justice to the man who was whipped and beaten, and would give his right eye for the churches that he founded. He literally died for other people – and frequently risked his life for them along the way. It would be absurd to allow ourselves to characterize Paul in any way, shape, or form as self-serving. No doubt he was a sinner, so he was not entirely void of selfishness. (Who could be? Only God is perfect.) But Paul's evident ability to take up the limelight or move to the centre of the stage cannot be interpreted as a self-serving agenda. His vigorous activities were for the good of others, for the founding of churches, for the shepherding of people, and for the preaching of God's gospel (not his own gospel).

But nonetheless, Paul did take up the lion's share of the attention of the Christian movement in the pages of Acts and (arguably) within the New Testament too, or at least certainly as evidenced by the number of letters that he wrote. Paul wrote more letters that are retained in the canon of the New Testament than any other apostle. He did not himself – it is true – write one of the four Gospel accounts of the life of Jesus. But even so, tradition has it that Luke's Gospel (the same Luke who wrote the Acts of the Apostles) was the record of Paul's preaching of Jesus, as well as the careful gathering of all the facts; that Paul's preaching was fuelled by the sort of evidence that he gathered from others and from Luke's work; and that Luke's Gospel was authorized by the apostolic authority of Paul. That, at least, is the tradition. While scholars have debated that since, the very fact that Paul is viewed as somehow or other also behind Luke's Gospel, as well as his own letters, and the way he dominates the second half of Acts, shows what a powerful figure Paul became in the minds of the New Testament church.

This has led some to feel deeply ambivalent about Paul. Some have even suggested that the Christianity we have inherited is as much (if not more) 'Paulinism' as it is 'Christianism'. They view the Gospels, and then they view Paul, and they see a disparity – forgetting, I and many others would argue, the reality that the Gospels were actually written after many of the letters and authorized by the men who wrote the letters. Comparing the tenor and tone of the New Testament Gospel accounts of Jesus to the letters written to the churches about how to follow Jesus as a local church is like comparing chalk with cheese. The one records the preaching of Jesus, the other records preaching about Jesus; the one records the Jesus who preached, the other records the people who preached Jesus. Finding a difference between them is as unsurprising as finding a difference between the autobiographical accounts of a great political leader like Winston Churchill and the records of his speeches in the House of Commons. Neither are untrue, neither are false; they are simply different because they are records of different aspects of his life. Paul's preaching was about Jesus; the Gospel accounts record the life of this Jesus that he preached.

If this is true, then, we would expect to see Paul's life – this life of a particularly unique individual – increasingly wrapped around and enveloped by the other completely and utterly unique and uniquely masterful personality that resonates throughout the Scriptures. You would expect to find, as it were, Jesus and Jesus' cross increasingly bleeding through the personality of Paul. While Paul is still his own person, we would expect to see him increasingly become more and more himself as he becomes more and more the person he was meant to be, as designed by his Creator, and as redeemed by his Saviour. And if boasting was as significant (not central – we would expect Jesus Himself to be central) to Paul's thinking as we have discovered, then in Paul's living we would expect to see that this boasting was somehow connected to his enraptured encounter and following of Christ. In other words, we would expect to find out in practice and in the story of his own life what it meant for Paul to 'boast in the Lord'.

To see whether this is actually the case – whether boasting in the Lord for Paul, in his own life, was integral to his joy in Jesus in a practical and real sense – we will need to do a little bit more than rehearse his well-known story. The basic facts are clear and reasonably familiar. Paul (then known as Saul) was a Pharisee. He trained in Jerusalem under Gamaliel, one of the great famous Rabbinic masters of his age. He was 'top of his class', excelling in his discipleship. He was from Tarsus, and he was a tentmaker.

Paul persecuted the early church, going from house to house dragging Christians off to jail. He approved of the stoning to death of one of the early Christian leaders, a deacon named Stephen. Incensed with religious fervour, Paul was given permission to pursue this persecution agenda yet further and was travelling to Damascus for this purpose when a bright light shone around him and a voice spoke to him. He was blinded, and his companions, while they saw the light, heard no voice. But the voice said to Paul, 'Saul, Saul, why do you persecute me?' A Christian disciple named Ananias was told by the Lord to go visit this Saul. He initially resisted, understandably enough given that Paul was persecuting Christians like Ananias, but then agreed to go and pray for Paul. Paul was again able to see, and from then on went on to serve Jesus in a blaze of passionate commitment.[4]

Paul went down to Jerusalem to meet with the apostles there. He went to Antioch to join the international community of Christians in that city and became one of its leading preachers. He was sent out, along with his friend Barnabas, from that church to plant churches. From then on Paul began first one journey and then others, planting churches and visiting churches he had planted. He confronted the Jerusalem leaders regarding 'Judaizers' who had come out from them claiming their authority, telling the Christians (that Paul had led to Jesus) that, unless they followed the whole law as well, they could not be saved. Paul had nothing against the law per se, but he saw this as a denigration of Jesus' role as sole Saviour and preached passionately against this legalism in his letter to the Galatian churches, and then in the council of Jerusalem when he told how the Gentiles had been converted.

Paul kept on preaching and planting churches. He conceived a vision of collecting money from the wealthier Gentile churches to take to the poorer Jerusalem church. As he went back to Jerusalem to give this gift, Paul was warned by a prophet named Agabus that going to Jerusalem would mean that he would be imprisoned. Paul took this as a warning, but not a divine command, and determined to go anyway. He was duly arrested in Jerusalem, and then when his life was put in danger by followers of the law, he appealed to the highest court in the Empire, namely the personal court of Caesar himself. As a Roman citizen from his birth in Tarsus, Paul was allowed this right. Finally, after a shipwreck (Paul had warned the captain not to sail so late in the season, and when his warning was ignored, spoke to them about their safety through a divine word from God), he arrived in Rome. Luke's account in the Acts of the Apostles left Paul in his own house, under house arrest,

---

4   See Acts 9.

awaiting trial, and doing what Paul did best: preaching, first to the Jewish synagogues of the city before taking the gospel to the Gentiles.

Those are the bare facts. They are colourful, arresting, and well-known. But what do they mean? In particular, what do they mean for this topic of boasting? How did boasting, and Paul's thinking about it, impact his life? Certainly, Paul was no wallflower, no shrinking violet. Paul's life was on a purpose, on a mission: he had something that he was called to accomplish, and, with deep conviction that this was his life's work, he went after it with every bone of his being. This begins to look a little like the kind of boasting that we read about in Paul's letters, and the thinking that we have discerned behind Paul's use of that term starts to percolate through the story of his life.

But we need to do some more digging. There are intriguing holes in the bare facts of the well-known story of Paul's life. Was Paul single? Why? Was he never married, or did he become unmarried for one reason or another? Paul preached against the law and yet circumcised Timothy; he lived in accordance with the law when in Jerusalem, and shaved his head in what was probably a kind of Nazirite vow. Paul had good friends, a team that he worked with. Yet he had a falling out with Barnabas, and his letters are filled with the kind of passionate friction that you would rarely discover in a more peacemaking character. His letters certainly read differently than the other apostles such as John, or even James or Peter, who were equally clear on sin. Paul's determination to cause a church to become Christ-like had an intensity and a burning ardor to it that was quite unlike the kind of emotion you read in the other letters.

Why did Paul go to Jerusalem when warned by the Spirit about what would happen when he got there? What happened to Paul after the story of Acts closed and the narrative discontinued in the text of the Bible with no more information given, at least from the standpoint of Acts?

How do the rest of Paul's letters fit into the narrative of Acts? And (for our purposes) what does all this mean for his understanding of boasting?

Are we reading about someone who was – to use non-medical language – a little screwy at times; who, if not mentally unhinged for sure, was certainly emotionally wrought and passionately engaged; who might have had one or two 'issues' from his childhood if he were put on a counsellor's couch today? To what extent was Paul whole? To what extent was the way he acted inspired by God – brilliant teacher, inspired author, shaped by purpose – and to what extent was it driven by unrecognized needs? To what extent were his ability and willingness to push himself forward in the cause of Christ shaped by his purpose and a mature, deep understanding of boasting? And to what extent was it all just the outworking of a personality desperate to make up for the terrible guilt that he felt about having persecuted Christ's church?

To answer these questions, we need to take seriously not only the obvious facts about Paul's life, but read them in the light of his letters and so discern their meaning, as well as imagine possible backgrounds that will fit into that meaning. We need not colour in the lines to get a picture, certainly not make up or invent anything, but listen carefully to what is being said, why it is being said, and therefore what it could mean. We don't need to put Paul on the couch, but we do need to treat him with the respect he deserves.

We can dispense with the idea that he was driven by guilt very quickly. If any man knew what it was to be free from guilt, it was Paul. He preached grace incessantly. And yet, of course, one wonders why he preached it so incessantly? Perhaps he knew firsthand how important it was to hear that message of grace over and over again. When we read Galatians and find a man who was almost violently opposed to legalism, can we detect someone who knew all too well what it was like to live legalistically? A man who has been in the jaws of a shark is unlikely to recommend the experience to others.

But if Paul was not driven by guilt, could he have been driven by its counterpoint – that is, by the 'zeal of the convert'? Could it be that Paul had discovered in his own experience exactly what it was like to be surrounded by innumerable rules and to try to attain them, and (in his own estimation) actually become legalistically faultless, yet still be empty? Those who say that Paul did not wrestle with a sense of guilt, at least pre-conversion, have not walked in the shoes of a successful legalist. Being a successful legalist is far worse than being an unsuccessful legalist.

An unsuccessful legalist, one who knows that he fails in some regard, at least has the comfort of knowing that there is more left for him to achieve. His gnawing sense of unease can be daily satiated by the thought *if only I did this, or that, or the other, then I would be free!* But the successful legalist is not so fortunate. In his own estimation, he has done all that needs to be done. But he is still driven on; he still feels empty. Yet there is nothing that he can see within his own framework and mental worldview left for him to achieve.

It is a desperate situation, one that Jesus diagnosed in Paul at his conversion when he said that it was hard for Paul to 'kick against the goads'. Jesus has this ability to cut to the chase, pull no punches, and tell it like it is. That is, he saw Paul like a donkey, and a donkey that was not willing to go where his master wanted him to go. He was rebelling against God's true intention through the Scriptures. He was a successful legalist, viewing the law as a series of achievable standards for human beings, rather than understanding its deeper meaning. As Paul said in Romans, it was when he read that he should not covet that he realized that he had not kept the law at all. He was legalistically faultless externally, but internally he was full of brokenness and disappointment. The gnawing sense he had as a successful legalist, refusing the prodding and poking and conviction of God that he was on the wrong path, kept him ceaselessly unhappy, looking for more and more extreme forms of devotion, even to the persecution of his fellow Jews who were now following the Messiah.

So if Paul was not *now* riven by guilt, he certainly had been – even if he had not realized it himself until Christ pointed it out to him. ('It is hard for you to kick against the goads,'[5] or, in other words, 'It is hard for you to constantly be prodded and pushed, and urged and convicted, to go in a certain direction, a place of healing and joy, and to refuse and keep on going down the same old legalistic path.') If Paul certainly had been riven by guilt, and now in Christ was gloriously, marvellously free of that guilt, could it be that Paul was now, as a Christian leader, driven on by the zeal of the convert? That is, was Paul's motivation, the reason behind his concept of boasting, a zeal that came from an over-compensation of what he had been trapped by in the past?

You see this sort of thing all the time. There is the person who *used* to think that sports cars were the best thing ever to own, who *now* realizes that really it is better to have an off-road 4x4 Jeep. He now can be the kind of person who so distances himself from sports cars that he almost cannot prevent himself from sneering at people who still like those silly, small, puny vehicles – when he has a great big, whacking Hummer 4x4. Similarly, the person who *used* to like Superhero movies, and *now* cannot stand them and is bored by them and never wants to see them again, is hard-pressed to avoid saying that the person who still likes Batman is juvenile or immature or 'has not seen the light'.

Paul, quite literally, did see the light. Is it possible that his passionate zeal for grace, and this idea of enthusiastic boasting in that grace, came from the zeal of the convert? That he had seen the light, and to compensate for the years that he spent beforehand, he now was driven to make up for

---

5   Acts 26:14.

it by rescuing as many people as possible from the situation into which he had put himself?

It is certainly possible that Paul was driven by the zeal of the convert. Possible, that is, until you consider Paul's life as a whole: what we know about him before his Damascus Road conversion, as well as what we know about him after his Damascus Road conversion. You see, people who are driven on by a desire to overcompensate for the mistakes of the past tend to act with the kind of passion, a sort of false zeal, that is not true to their own nature and personality. Before they saw the light, they were rather sleepy and disinterested. Now they are running around everywhere, acting out of character by telling people they are going to hell unless they convert – and telling them three times a day before breakfast and their first cup of coffee. They are, in other words, this 'zeal of the convert' kind of people, not being true to themselves. They are driven on by something, not expressing something true of who they really are.

But it was not so with Paul. Paul was always zealous. He told us as much; his zeal before he came to Christ was almost all-consuming. He still had zeal after coming to Christ, though a different kind. Paul was not like a person who has a fake kind of zeal stuck on to his personality by some psychological manipulation of a cult. He was like the person who has always been rather good at doing carpentry, who used to construct handmade rocking chairs to sell in his boss's store, but who is now making them for his own shop and has gone into business by himself. Nothing in his core personality, preferences, or gift-makeup has really changed; on the other hand, everything in his person has changed. It is now being done for a different purpose, a different goal. But he is still recognisably the same person. That picture is much more like Paul. He would have been one of the most zealous Pharisees of his (and any) age. Instead, he became one of the most zealous Christians of his (and any) age. Paul's core person was fundamentally and completely changed from Saul the persecutor of Christians, and yet he was still the same person at the same time. This was no doubt what freaked out the Christians who remembered the Saul who had dragged some of them off to prison.

No, in order to understand Paul's motivations – surely as complex as our own motivations (and who knows the heart but the Lord?) – we need to move beyond the pop-psychology or the simplistic reductionism of late nineteenth-century-theological criticism and embrace a more truly critical, genuinely understanding, insightful approach to the drives of this person we call Paul. Could it be, in other words, that he was not driven on by something, but that he was driving? The difference is all-important. The person who is driven is being driven by something or by someone. But the person who has a purpose, a goal, or an objective is pursuing that purpose, goal, or objective. They are driving; they are not being driven by anyone or anything else.

Of course, Christians would want to say that they are not in the driver's seat of their lives, but that Jesus Himself is sovereign over them. And, of course, that was true for Paul and should be true for each of us: increasingly so as we surrender more of our lives to Jesus. But the strange, wonderful, glorious truth about surrendering your life to Jesus is that, as you lose your life for Him, you find your life. This experience – some would call it paradoxical – is at the core of what is so attractive about the call of discipleship. We find ourselves as we lose ourselves in some bigger purpose. This is different from being driven on by some psychological urge. It is like finding who we are for the first time. Nowhere is this paradox truer – some would say that it is only ever true – than with Jesus Himself.

So Paul had Jesus driving his life, and in that sense he was being driven by his Lord and Master, Christ. But Jesus is not that sort of Master. He does not drive us like a herd of cattle. He calls us to Himself, like an ancient Shepherd, and His sheep hear His voice, and they follow Him.

Each of us may express this paradox in different ways: not truly a paradox, as conventionally understood, meaning a contradiction, but a three-dimensional Trinitarian truth. Each of us will find within our own lives and within our own personalities the call of Christ shaping us: as He wants to shape us to be more who we were meant to be as individuals. The call of Christ is collective; it does come to us all, the whole church, corporeally. But it also comes to us individually, as Christ calls us by name, and we hear His voice and we follow Him. We are driving, but now we have purpose. We are free to live lives as we were designed to live them, no longer being shaped by external forces and expectations or by internal compulsions and drives, but now truly being who we were made to be in relation to the One who made us. And each of us will find our own way of being a child of the Father God.

For Paul, it centred around this idea of boasting. Each time we look at the story of Paul's life, we see this zealous, passionate, committed, emotional (that is, in the sense of affectional), relational, highly intellectual, suffering, devoted, friendly but not weak, educated but not bookish, preacher but not preachy person – and each time running through it is a sort of exuberant exulting. A kind of, well, boasting.

The letters

In several places in Paul's correspondence, this idea of boasting comes across. We need to look at those places and discover what they mean in their context, within the purpose and meaning of each individual letter, and then see if there is a concurrent connection of meaning across the various letters to find ourselves closer to what Paul meant by boasting. We will touch on Paul's use of boasting in Romans (a key text for any understanding of what Paul said, and in particular what he said about boasting), but it will be limited by the desire to look specifically and closely at the key text about boasting in Paul's writings: Romans 5:2. We will do that in a later chapter in this book, but now we will survey, at a higher, less detailed level, the writings of Paul with regard to boasting. Is it possible that this is at least a key to understanding what Paul said, who Paul was as a person, and what that can mean for us as we learn from his example as he followed the example of Christ?

Romans

Let's start with Romans, which is Paul's most famous letter and has been highly praised by its readers ever since it was first read. It is viewed as one of the greatest works of literature, one of the most inspirational pieces of spiritual writing, and also (frankly) as one of the most difficult texts to understand. Questions about the overlying message of Romans abound, but even more surprisingly, there is no clear agreement among scholars as to what exactly made Paul write Romans in the first place. Most of his letters have a reasonably obvious rationale for their writing, even if the precise nature of that rationale is also debated; in other letters, unlike in Romans, the zone of reason for writing is fairly well agreed. But in Romans, some say he wrote it because this was his theological masterpiece; others say he wrote it to deal with a rising tension between Jews and Gentiles in the Roman church. There are others who say he wrote it because he wanted to prepare the way for asking Rome to support his missionary work to Spain. Some say Romans is a theological treatise for its own sake; others that it is written to increase unity and mutual understanding between Jews and Gentile Christians in the church at Rome. There are those who say it was a fundraising letter. Other possibilities also exist: Paul at times appeared to be defending himself against charges of being antinomian, as it is technically known. That is, people were saying that Paul's preaching of grace was giving people licence to live immoral lifestyles. So Romans deals a lot with the law and also with a call to live as obedient to God with what Paul called 'the obedience of faith'. Some others then say that perhaps Romans had several different purposes and ask why we should identify one over against the other.

My own view is that Paul tells us later in the letter precisely why he was writing it when he said that he had written quite boldly at times so that, increasingly from Rome, there would be a gospel movement to all nations. I believe Paul saw Rome as a key epicentre. It is hard for us to imagine again exactly how central Rome was to the ancient world. Rome was everything for many people. 'All roads lead to Rome' – it was the centre of the world. For a missionary, apostle, and church planter like Paul, this was the urban centre to motivate movement towards outward expansionism for the cause of Christ.

I think this overarching purpose is why Paul touched on other things too: defending his own ministry against misunderstandings, looking for money for the gospel purpose, writing a theological treatise that would stand the test of time. Anyone who has been in church planting, missionary work, or leading a church towards a growth mindset for the cause of Christ will know that it is paramount that there is a deep, real, practical, and profound theological superstructure to the whole thing. Paul was trying to put in place foundational building blocks for the church at Rome to have the kind of global impact that indeed it did have, in one way or another.

With that in mind, we find throughout the letter a thread that connects to this idea of boasting; or if not a thread, a see-saw, or even better a switch. In the first half of Romans, Paul's use of boasting was always negative. He talked about religious people who boasted about their relationship to God (Rom. 2:17). He talked about the same sort of religious people who boasted about the law of God (2:23). In each case they were hypocritical, for they did not keep the law that they boasted about. Then he went on to say, most remarkably, that this boasting was entirely 'excluded' (3:27) because actual salvation is by grace, not by works or by law. So in this early part of Romans, the idea of boasting for Paul was negative; it was counterposed to actual religious performance so that it showed the sort of hypocrisy that some religious people can fall into – the Pharisees who were often shown by Jesus to be hypocrites, while boasting about their tithes and their fasting.

But then, the switch in Romans 5. Paul changed how he used boasting: 'we boast in the hope of the glory of God' (verse 2, my translation). So now boasting is positive. It is exulting, exciting, celebratory. It is also something that shows our triumph even over suffering: 'we boast in our sufferings' (5:3, my translation).

Notice that Paul did not say we boast *because* of our sufferings, or even *in spite of* our sufferings. He said we boast *in* our sufferings. Why? Paul's thinking, as he went on to explain, was that for the Christ-follower, suffering has a purpose: it makes us stronger; it does not defeat us; it prepares us; and it strengthens us. Suffering 'produces' something under God's sovereign hand of love in our lives: it produces perseverance, character, and hope (5:3-4). In other words, it makes us strong people who will keep going and always be filled with confident joy about the future that will come under God's mighty power. This is all a very positive view of boasting.

Then, to cap off this top-and-tail pericope in verse 11, he said wait, there's more. Not only is there all this exulting, this boasting, in hope of the glory of God and in sufferings – so nothing need dissuade us from boasting – but we also actually boast 'in God'. That is, we are now able to be so confident in our relationship to God that we boast in God Himself. Nothing can move us therefore. But the switch in Romans is remarkable: in Romans 2:17, boasting in their relationship to God was negative; now in Romans 5:11, boasting in God was positive!

Paul did not return to boasting again in Romans until much later in the book (11:18, NRSV). There he offered a word of warning. 'Do not boast over those branches'; that is, you Gentiles who are now grafted into the vine of God, don't boast about that to the other people, the Jewish people. He said, 'Do not be arrogant, but tremble' (Rom. 11:20). There is a warning that we do not become arrogant in case we too are 'cut off'. So boasting is not without its dangers or limits. And it should not lead to boasting over other people. We are not better than anyone else, for it is all by grace.

But then finally, Paul said that he himself boasts: 'Therefore I boast in Christ Jesus in my service to God' (Rom. 15:17, my translation). This again is a positive view of boasting and one that is modeled by Paul himself. It came at a point in the letter where he was concluding his argument and bringing himself in as an example of what he had been saying. Therefore, because of this purpose of writing the letter, and because of the truth of what he had been saying, 'Therefore I boast in Christ Jesus in my service to God.'

Why this switch from negative to positive? In what sense are we to boast in, towards, and about God, about Jesus, and in what sense are we not to do so? One view is that Paul was simply expressing the salvation-historical reality that had taken place. In other words, because Jesus had now come, then they were no longer to boast in the law (meaning in this case the Mosaic Law of the Old Testament); now instead, they were to boast in Jesus.

This is an attractively simple explanation: simple, not simplistic. Underneath the cover of simplicity are various kinds of complexity. In what sense is circumcision now fulfilled in Christ? How does baptism fit into that framework? (There are many different views on that!) What, most confoundedly difficult, is the nature of the law, which it appears we are to obey, and the law that we are now not to boast in?

The standard explanation of that problem is that there are different types, kinds or usages of the law in Paul. He sometimes by the law meant the *ceremonial* law (that is, the temple rituals of various kinds that were mandated in the Old Testament now no longer necessary). Sometimes he meant the *sacrificial* law (that is, the sacrifice of goats and lambs that was all fulfilled in Christ's once-for-all sacrifice). At other times he meant the *moral* law (that is, the Ten Commandments and God's moral instructions that are fulfilled in those who follow Christ, in the sense that now by God's Spirit they are enabled increasingly to obey God's law from the heart). The difficulty with this extremely helpful categorization is that it is not self-evidently explicit in what Paul was writing. It appears like a useful construct from the outside, rather than an authentic expression of the way Paul himself wrote about the law.

However, that juxtaposition, because it is a framework rather than an expression of what Paul said in his way of saying, is unhelpfully rigid when we consider the matter of boasting. Take, for instance, maps. We use maps all the time. Whether we use Mapquest, GPS navigation, or an atlas, we often use maps when we travel. It would be perfectly possible to argue, in fact impossible to dispute, that maps are not an authentic description of the terrain around us in the actual way that the terrain is formed. How could they be? A one-to-one precise rendition would be an exact copy of what was there, and it would be impossible to carry that around in your pocket or have it come up on your GPS screen in your car. An exact, authentic, full-scale representation of a mountain is an exact copy of that mountain. It's not a map at all; in fact, it's just another mountain. Nice as that is, it doesn't help you understand or navigate your way up a difficult climb.

So the question is whether this well-known map of Paul's use of the law – if certainly not the exact copy of the way Paul himself talked about the law – is a useful map of what

Paul said. That it most certainly is, and most definitely is useful; otherwise, we would not be so familiar with it, or have the ease of understanding it, once it is explained.

However, if it is useful, is it *also* accurate? A map can be useful, in the sense of being relatively easy to follow, but take you to the wrong place when you follow it. That map, while useful in the sense of easy to use, is actually useless in the sense of being helpful for your navigation purposes.

So the question is not really whether this threefold description of Paul's use of the law is an exact copy of the *way* Paul said it. (That it surely is not – but to have that, you should just photocopy the text in the original and be done with it.) Nor is the question only whether this description of Paul's use of the law is useful. (Something can be useful, but not accurate, or not as accurate as would be truly useful, and such maps of thought, while meeting the ease-of-use qualification of being marketable, can actually sometimes be dangerous, because they may lead you off a cliff or into a muddy bog).

The real question is whether using this way of thinking of the law actually leads you, when you follow it, to a better understanding of what Paul was saying in various places. Does it help you arrive at your destination, closer to an understanding of the text? Is it, in other words, a useful and reasonably accurate map?

The answer to that last question – whether dividing the law into ceremonial, sacrificial, and moral is a useful and reasonably accurate map of Paul's thinking – seems to me to be certainly, yes. I remember teaching the Letter to the Galatians to a group of pastors, and pastors-in-training, in a South American city. We were engaged in the text, taking it seriously, and digging into it with humour and joy as we worked together through the passages of Galatians, that rich and controversial book. As we did so and looked at how Paul was talking about circumcision, the law, the way of the Spirit, justification by faith, and all the rest, it became apparent that what was required was a fairly sizeable, but manageable, tool to land on an understanding of the law as a framework in the minds of us all, so that we could get back to hearing from Paul himself. The framework of the three divisions of the law was practical, simple, useful, and certainly reasonably accurate.

It is undeniably not entirely accurate, however. Paul sometimes used the word 'law' as a principle; he talked of the 'law of the Spirit', for instance. There are also many other debates surrounding Paul's use of the law. But for the purposes of understanding what Paul meant by boasting – and whether the switch he made in Romans between boasting as something negative to boasting as something positive, is basically a switch due to the salvation-historical coming of Jesus – this map of the law is accurate enough.

Is it then true that when Paul switched from boasting as a negative to boasting as a positive, he was saying that they were to stop boasting in the ceremonial or ritual law, and to start boasting in Jesus – who not only fulfilled the ceremonial and ritual law, but also by His Spirit enabled them to increasingly fulfill the moral law in their own persons, too?

The difficulty with this view is that when Paul talked about the negative kind of boasting, he did not refer to ceremonial or sacrificial matters. He referred to moral matters: stealing, for instance, or hypocrisy. Plus, Paul did not ever make the argument, that I can detect, along these lines: 'It was okay to boast in the law before Jesus came, but now that Jesus has come, stop boasting in the law and start boasting in Jesus.' Even if we divide up what Paul meant by law into ceremonial and sacrificial and moral, and even if we take seriously that the negative boasting he referenced is the moral, in what sense then did Paul mean that it was okay to boast in their moral performance, but now they were to boast in Jesus (especially as moral performance was plainly still very important to Paul)? Even more confusingly – given his point about the negative kind of boasting is that those who do that kind are hypocritical (they say they do not steal, but really in other ways they do 'rob temples'), also given Paul's point about negative boasting, is that it is not real, authentic, and does not match actual performance – how then can it be said that this is only, or merely, a salvation-historical matter?

Even more, this view of the switch in Paul's boasting in Romans begins to unravel when we realize that in the Old Testament, boasting in God was praised. We will look at that more in another chapter and, in particular, how boasting was praised as a wise life. But if boasting, in some sense, was a good thing in the Old Testament – and if Paul had at least (let's be generous!) a rudimentary understanding of the Scriptures of his heritage in which he was trained, in which he excelled, and in which he was a notable expert – then how could Paul have been arguing that 'boasting in the law used to be okay, but now it is not okay; instead boast in Jesus', if Paul was saying that boasting in the law was hypocritical? If he said 'it used to be okay to boast in the law, but now it is not anymore, now boast in Jesus' that argument would be permissible. But Paul does not say that. What he actually says is: 'boasting in the law is hypocritical because you don't keep the law, but boasting in Jesus is authentic because by God's Spirit you are enabled gradually to fulfil the law.'

So this is not a 'was like that' but 'now is like this' argument. His argument is a 'doing it that way doesn't work' but 'doing it this way does work'. What Paul seemed to be assuming and saying was that *some* (but by no means all) of the Jewish people of his day had got the wrong end of the stick about the law. They had made the law something that was the centre of their religion, when all along the law was *really always* designed to be something that was pointing to 'the one who is to come'. Apparently, in Paul's day, this *misunderstanding* of the law, against which he is teaching, was picking up speed. It was becoming more prevalent, not less, more common not less. Why? Because 'he who is to come' (in Paul's view) *had come* and so those who rejected 'he who is to come' hung on ever more firmly to the law, instead of the One to whom the law is pointing. They were an inch away in their initial navigation from Southampton but by the time they had crossed the Atlantic they had missed New York City altogether and ended up in the Arctic Circle.

Now we come to the really interesting part about this switch regarding boasting in Romans. If this way of understanding it is correct – if Paul was saying that some of the Jewish people of his day were moving further and further away from the true understanding of the Scriptures and the law, and were starting to treat the law as the centre of their religion in a (what we would call) legalistic sense, and he was trying to expose the ridiculous uselessness of this approach because it led to hypocrisy, in order to show his readers the beauty of Jesus as the fulfilment of the law – if that is the right way of interpreting boasting in Paul, then what we have is a brilliant tool for our own use too.

Sometimes it is said that 'religion is the default mode of the human race'. I have used phrases like that on occasion; I think there is truth to it. We tend, as human beings, to become legalistic. But I think it is subtler than that, and more helpful. The reality is that some humans are not legalistic at all. They are vicious and lawless, vile and murderous, and feel little, if any, twinges of conscience about beating down their fellow human beings. Their problem is not (self-evidently) too much law.

For those who begin to be moral, however, who want to care for those around them, and may even want to please the Supreme Being that is traditionally called God in the English language, then there is an immediate trap that is sprung for the unwary. It is what Paul meant by the negative kind of boasting. We begin to think we are better than others; we begin to think we have arrived. We are so desperate, some of us, to please God that we start to psychologically blind ourselves to when we know we are not pleasing God. We advance the case of our moral performance as an argument against our moral failures, to bury them and hide them. This is not a problem for a particular kind of person only, much less a particular kind of ethnic group. This is a problem for all of us *once we start on the journey of trying to please God*.

Jesus discussed this, taught on this, and encountered this a lot. He was living and preaching among the most religious people who had existed. And when He was there, they were especially attuned to their need to be religious. They had been exiled for worshiping false idols. The people returned, and their most recent national heroes, the Maccabees, had been zealots for the law. They began to overreact. Where their forefathers had been slackers, at least some of them, and had been sent into exile as a result, they became zealots. Jesus told stories about them – the Pharisee who went up to pray and thought he was more righteous than the man who prayed and repented; the two sons, one who stayed with his father and was a goody-goody, and the other who went far away, but then returned and was embraced; the two sons, one who said, 'Yes, I'll work in your vineyard,' and did not, and the other who said he would not, and did.

Paul told the same story. It was not just that he was saying that you can never be good enough for God and therefore you need grace (though that is true). Nor was it just that he was saying that the whole of the Old Testament Scriptures was fulfilled in Jesus, therefore stop boasting in the Old Testament law and start boasting in Jesus (though it is certainly true that 'let him who boasts boast in the Lord!'). What Paul was saying is that for the religious, for the man or woman who wants to please God, there is a danger: a danger of trying to please God *the wrong way*. That way is doing good things, but using them as a shield against a deep relationship with God – because you can't admit to yourself, to God, or anyone else that you fail. That way leads to hypocrisy. This however is *not* the only kind of *wrong way* to go about living. There is all the idolatrous, gross evil that Paul also preached against in the early chapters of Romans. But this way, the religious way, is the way that is most likely to be the danger for those who are reading what he wrote!

So by the switch from the negative to the positive boasting in Romans, Paul meant a switch from boasting in your own moral performance (and so hiding yourself from the truth that you need grace and forgiveness, and Jesus), to boasting now in what God has done for you in Christ (and so increasingly opening yourself up to God's grace and power, and His Spirit, that you might live for Him and become like Him more and more and more).

We took the longest time surveying Romans – no doubt Paul's most influential piece of writing. We will take less time on his other letters.

1 Corinthians

The background to the Corinthian correspondence is usually described as follows. Corinth had been planted by Paul. Apollos had come along afterwards. The Corinthians interpreted Apollos' speaking gifts as more in line with their expectation of a public speaker in the classical sense. The Corinthians were very pleased with their spiritual giftedness, especially the gift of speaking in tongues. The Corinthian church began to divide along the lines of their most influential teachers. In addition, the Corinthian church had a well-known case of scandalous sexual immorality about which no one had done anything decisive. There were other questions as well that came to Paul which he dealt with and which we have recorded in our two surviving letters.

In the midst of all this, in 1 Corinthians, as well as 2 Corinthians, there is a theme of boasting. Unlike in Romans, there is not a clear switch from the negative to the positive, but both elements are present. The negative elements of boasting – hubris, pride, arrogance – are more obvious and familiar. But the positive elements of boasting in 1 Corinthians are less often noted. For instance, after Paul said that the gospel of Jesus Christ excluded boasting because God chose the foolish things of this world to shame the wise so that no one can boast before Him (1 Cor. 1:27-29), he concluded with a quotation from the prophet Jeremiah when he said, 'Let the one who boasts, boast in the Lord' (1:31). So Paul was not against boasting *per se*; not all boasting is wrong. Some boasting is good, the kind of boasting that is 'in the Lord' (whatever that may mean – and that question is what we are seeking to answer).

Again, later in the letter, after Paul had talked in various places about how the Corinthians had become puffed up, and described his ultimate antidote to their hubris/pride, which was love (in his justly famous 1 Corinthians 13), Paul then at the end had a highly enigmatic – apparently throwaway – line about boasting. It again suggested there is a positive element to boasting. He said (in word-for-word transliteration), 'Each day I die, by your boasting, brothers, which I have in Christ Jesus our Lord' (15:31). What did Paul mean by that? The NIV translates, 'I face death every day – yes, just as surely as I boast about you in Christ Jesus our Lord.' Which suggests that the NIV thinks that Paul meant that the boasting here was in the positive sense and referred entirely to Paul's boasting in Jesus Christ (see the earlier quotation from Jeremiah, 'Let the one who boasts boast in the Lord'). The ESV translates, 'I protest, brothers, by my pride in you, which I have in Christ Jesus our Lord, I die every day!' Which suggests that the ESV also thinks the word boast here (translated 'pride') was positive, but in this case, thinks that it referred to Paul's attitude towards the Corinthian Christians, which was also somehow an expression of his personal relationship to Jesus Christ, and so modified the 'pride' in them in an acceptable, even admirable way. The Authorized Version (known also as the King James Version), translates, 'I protest by your rejoicing which I have in Christ Jesus our Lord, I die daily.' This suggests that the translators thought Paul was also talking about boasting (translated 'rejoicing') in a positive sense, but in this case, they thought the people doing the boasting/rejoicing were the Corinthians (not Paul as ESV suggests), though at the same time this boasting/rejoicing was something that he had somehow concurrently in his own relationship to Jesus.

Whenever there is a tricky verse to understand, it is often because there is an important truth that we find hard to grasp in our own current set of presuppositions, attitudes, worldviews, and assumptions. There is a cognitive dissonance generated by the words because we assume one thing about what is being said, and the text is saying something else, or at variance to what we assume, and therefore we don't get it. Sometimes there are other reasons, but this cognitive dissonance reason is common – and therefore when a text is hard to understand, the best thing is to push into it more and try to grasp it more, until light shines.

What then did Paul mean in 1 Corinthians 15:31? My own view is that Paul was summarizing, in highly condensed form, both the positive and the negative aspects of boasting that he held to be true at different times in different ways.

On the one hand, he was dismayed, utterly distraught, undone, and at the point of actual physical death – and not just once or occasionally, but every single day; he died daily. He had suicidal ideation, or at least he had 'cidal' ideation – he felt like he was dying. Something inside him died daily when he thought of the Corinthians boasting; it was just killing him. So (to put it mildly) there is that negative aspect of the verse.

On the other hand, there is also the positive. Paul also said here that he does, though, boast himself, but his boasting was quite different from that of the Corinthians. His boasting was not thinking he was better than the Corinthians, the other apostles, or any other person; rather, he boasted in

Christ Jesus. The tension in the verse – exploding out like a volcano suddenly erupting – is encapsulated in the phrase, 'I die every day.' The source of this tension was that the Corinthians had got it so badly wrong. It was not that they were boasting that was wrong. They certainly had a lot to boast about! But what they had to boast about was not themselves, or their teachers, or their gifts – that boasting was always complete nonsense and ridiculous, divisive, unloving, as well as dangerous to the whole community of the church. What they *did* have to boast about – and this was massive, and in this boasting Paul 'rejoiced' himself – was this boasting 'in Christ Jesus our Lord'.

2 Corinthians

Boasting is everywhere in 2 Corinthians. It is a highly dominant theme in this letter to the Corinthians, a follow-up to the previous letter, and in which at least some of the problems that Paul had identified earlier had been addressed. However, not all was perfect by any means, and Paul now addressed the matter of boasting head-on. In fact, he used the word 'boast' twenty-three times, and each time, not as a side matter, but as central or as close to central as the point being made. Unlike in Romans, there was no switch from the negative to the positive. And unlike in 1 Corinthians, the positive boasting was not confined almost entirely to a personal relationship to the Lord. It is clear in 2 Corinthians that Paul thought that positive boasting might legitimately include boasting about other people, boasting about their own ministry – as long as that ministry was assigned to them by the Lord.

One example will suffice – 2 Corinthians 1:12 – 'Now this is our boast: Our conscience testifies that we have conducted ourselves in the world, and especially in our relations with you, with integrity and godly sincerity. We have done so, relying not on worldly wisdom but on God's grace.' So it is evident that for Paul, positive boasting included not just a personal relationship to God, but things that we do – things we do in the church, and things we do in the world – as long as they are done with sincerity and with God's grace. This boasting in one sense is about 'the heart' (5:12), but it is also something that can be visible in another way: 'Therefore show these men the proof of your love and the reason for our pride [boast] in you, so that the churches can see it' (8:24). Paul seemed aware that his boasting could be misinterpreted, but he pushed on regardless: 'So even if I boast somewhat freely about the authority the Lord gave us for building you up rather than tearing you down, I will not be ashamed of it' (10:8).

With that kind of boasting going on, Paul though – and most famously – at the end started to recalibrate. What did he really *mean* by boasting? Is this *actually* the same as hubris, pride, arrogance, over-self-confidence? He grounded the idea of boasting in the same text from Jeremiah that he used in the previous letter: 'But, "Let the one who boasts boast in the Lord." For it is not the one who commends himself who is approved, but the one whom the Lord commends.' (10:17-18). And what does that mean? Most astonishingly of all, for Paul, it meant weakness. 'If I must boast, I will boast of the things that show my weakness' (11:30). And by weakness what did he mean? He meant suffering. Beatings. Shipwreck. Being lowered from a basket over a wall to escape persecution.

Then, in 2 Corinthians 12, Paul identified an area of weakness that he did not specify (and which has caused endless, fruitless speculation) when he said that 'a thorn in my flesh, a messenger of Satan' was given to him to 'torment' him (verse 7). Despite his pleading with the Lord three times that it be removed (verse 8), God refused, saying, 'My grace is sufficient for you, for my power is made perfect in weakness,' to which Paul immediately concluded about boasting: 'Therefore I will boast all the more gladly about my weaknesses, so that Christ's power may rest on me' (verse 9).

It is apparent, then, that by boasting Paul meant something counter-intuitive. Not only can it mean something negative as well as something positive, depending on what kind of boasting we are talking about, it can also mean (even when positive) something broadly related to our concept of success, as long as that effectiveness is by God's grace. However, at the same time, the real boasting, and where Paul landed that discussion, is intimately related to a boasting about weakness, by which Paul evidently meant specifically suffering for Jesus and especially for His church. 'Besides everything else, I face daily the pressure of my concern for all the churches' (11:28).

On top of this, there is this mysterious element for Paul, that he does not entirely reveal, some personal pain, suffering or spiritual attack, through which he learnt directly by a word from Jesus, that 'my grace is sufficient for you, for my power is made perfect in weakness.'From that word Paul concluded that he would 'boast all the more gladly about my weaknesses, so that Christ's power may rest on me' (12:9).

Before we go on, let us recap. Boasting may be positive or negative. When positive, it is rooted in a boasting in the Lord. It can be related to spiritual effectiveness in ministry, church planting, preaching, 'fruit'/success, as long as that is by the grace of God, and it can also be related to activities outside of the specifically religious ('in the world'). However, this boasting, when properly grounded in the Lord, is only truly powerful when it is a boasting about weaknesses, which are not moral weaknesses, but weaknesses related to sufferings for the church. Is this basic framework one that continues in the rest of Paul's letters?

Galatians

As usual, there is both a positive and negative use of the word 'boast' in Paul's letter to the Galatians, but there is an extra dimension too. Whereas before, we have seen a range of application of the core meaning of the word – negative and positive, along a more binary axis – there is at the end of Galatians a dual negative/positive. So in Galatians 6:4 (ESV), boasting in oneself was *positive*, whereas boasting in someone else was *negative*: 'But let each one test his own work, and then his reason to boast will be in himself alone and not in his neighbor.'

Then in 6:13-14, boasting in the law was negative, whereas boasting in the cross of Jesus was positive: 'Not even those who are circumcised keep the law, yet they want you to be circumcised that they may boast about your circumcision in the flesh. May I never boast except in the cross of our Lord Jesus Christ, through which the world has been crucified to me, and I to the world.' How is this dual element introduced? What is its significance in Galatians, and for us?

Paul, in Galatians, was countering a false teaching from 'certain men [who] came from James' (2:12), who were infiltrating the Galatian churches, teaching them: 'Unless you are circumcised, according to the custom taught by Moses, you cannot be saved' (Acts 15:1). The problem in Galatians was about salvation and whether it was purely by grace through faith, or whether some extra additional activity, ceremony or religious practice was required (in their case, circumcision). Given that the false teachers were claiming that Paul's teaching about grace would lead to bad behaviour and ungodly lifestyles, in the second half of Galatians Paul showed that actually it was the work of the Spirit (not the works of the law) through whom they were, and we are, enabled to become Christ-like.

This background helps us tease out what Paul was saying about boasting as he came to the concluding part of

Galatians. Paul was saying that a grace-orientated approach to life gives what we would call appropriate self-confidence, rather than insecurity or constantly comparing ourselves with the achievements of other people. Then he said that the law – which had been his bête noire throughout the letter – was not to be boasted in, but the cross of Jesus was the only appropriate boast. So we are to boast in ourselves (that is, have the right kind of self-confidence) due to grace, not compare ourselves to other people. We are to boast in Christ, not boast in self-attained moral improvement through a wrong use of the law. Good boasting (as opposed to negative) in Galatians then functions as a result of the good news.

Ephesians

The word 'boast' only appears once in the letter to the Ephesians. Here it is entirely negative: 'For it is by grace you have been saved, through faith – and this is not from yourselves, it is the gift of God – not by works, so that no one can boast' (Eph. 2:8-9). Boasting then here was something that was entirely excluded from everyone because we are saved only by grace. How that is consistent with Paul's teaching at the end of Galatians, that we can and should boast in ourselves as opposed to comparing ourselves to other people, is not immediately obvious. Perhaps there is a right kind of boasting in ourselves, self-confidence, and a wrong kind of boasting in ourselves, arrogance.

Philippians

The letter to the Philippians has three occurrences of boasting. Each case is some variant of a positive use of boasting, though the last has an implicit comparison with negative boasting.

In the first instance, Paul was certain that he would not yet die – because it would be good for the Philippians to see him again so that they could boast in Christ Jesus on account of Paul, when he visited them (Phil. 1:25-26). This seems to be an expression of the specially close relationship that Paul enjoyed with the Philippian church: they clicked together. When they were together, he knew they would rejoice [boast] in Christ Jesus because he was with them. This suggests two things about Paul's use of boasting: first, it suggests that boasting, when positive, is always somehow rooted in the real person of Jesus; but, second, it also suggests that such boasting in another human being is also possible and delightful.

The second instance of boasting is similar. Paul (in Phil. 2:15-16) wanted the Philippians to shine like stars in the sky, by holding on to God's Word and holding that Word out in gracious witness to those around them, shining like a star, so that he 'will be able to boast on the day of Christ that I did not run or labor in vain'. So part of the reason why he wanted them to be excellent Christians was so that he could boast about them to Jesus! We are probably, most of us, tempted to think that boasting, whenever good, can only be spiritual. Also, by 'spiritual', most of us will tend to think ethereal, insubstantial, and certainly invisible. But Paul's boasting was rooted in real flesh-and-blood people – albeit ultimately grounded in Christ.

Again, in Philippians 3:3, Paul used the positive way of describing boasting in a mode that was more typical in other letters. Those who received grace and trusted Christ were the real circumcision, whereas those who were trying to distort that grace were not able to boast in any real sense about their relationship to God. We 'boast in Christ Jesus' and 'put no confidence in the flesh', meaning in the legalistic and improper use of the law that was so prevalent in Paul's day among the Pharisees that he knew so well.

1 and 2 Thessalonians

Finally, Paul used boasting once in 1 Thessalonians and again once in 2 Thessalonians. In 1 Thessalonians 2:19,

Paul described boasting as what he will do in the presence of Jesus when He returns, on account of the Thessalonian church. This boasting was future-looking, but also rooted strongly in the present reality of this particular Christian church. Then in 2 Thessalonians 1:4, the boasting was more *now* (and less *then*), and instead of being only in one church, it was a kind of boasting that was comparative! 'Therefore, among God's churches we boast about your perseverance and faith in all the persecutions and trials you are enduring.' The Thessalonians are not just being held up as an example to other churches. When Paul was talking to other churches, he was consciously, verbally, explicitly boasting about the Thessalonians. And the topic of his boasting? Perseverance. He boasted about them because, despite their suffering and persecution, they kept on going.

Summary

Types of boasting

	Negative	Positive
Romans 2:17	Moral Performance	
Romans 2:23	Hypocrisy	
Romans 3:27	Excluded by Faith	
Romans 4:2	Moral Performance	
Romans 5:2		Hope/Glory/God
Romans 5:3		Sufferings
Romans 5:11		God through Jesus
Romans 11:18	Spiritual Superiority	
Romans 15:17		In Christ Jesus in Ministry to God

1 Corinthians 1:29	Excluded by Election	
1 Corinthians 1:31		In the Lord
1 Corinthians 3:21	About Men	
1 Corinthians 4:7	About Men	
1 Corinthians 5:6	Moral Libertarianism	
1 Corinthians 9:15		Not Being Paid Voluntarily
1 Corinthians 9:16	Excluded by the Gospel	
1 Corinthians 13:3	Physical Sacrifice	
1 Corinthians 15:31		Over Church in Christ Jesus
2 Corinthians 1:12		About Holiness
2 Corinthians 1:14		About Other Christians
2 Corinthians 5:12		About What is in the Heart
2 Corinthians 7:4		In Church
2 Corinthians 7:14		In Church
2 Corinthians 8:24		In Church
2 Corinthians 9:2		About Church's Generosity
2 Corinthians 9:3		About Church's Generosity
2 Corinthians 10:8		Authority to Build Church
2 Corinthians 10:13		About Own Ministry
2 Corinthians 10:15		About Own Ministry
2 Corinthians 10:16		About Own Ministry

2 Corinthians 10:17		In the Lord
2 Corinthians 11:10		Not Being Paid Voluntarily
2 Corinthians 11:12		Not Being Paid Voluntarily
2 Corinthians 11:16	Foolish Boasting	
2 Corinthians 11:17	Foolish Boasting	
2 Corinthians 11:18	Foolish Boasting	
2 Corinthians 11:30		In Weakness
2 Corinthians 12:1		Visions from Lord
2 Corinthians 12:5		In Weakness
2 Corinthians 12:6		Visions from Lord
2 Corinthians 12:9		In Weaknesses
Galatians 6:4		In Oneself
Galatians 6:13	In the Flesh	
Galatians 6:14		In the Cross of Jesus
Ephesians 2:9	Excluded by Grace	
Philippians 1:26		In Christ Jesus because of Paul
Philippians 2:16		In Ministry Effectiveness
Philippians 3:3		In Christ Jesus
1 Thessalonians 2:19		In Ministry
2 Thessalonians 1:4		In Perseverance/ Faith

So, in summary, across Paul's letters we find the word 'boasting' employed in both negative and positive ways – the positive being surprising for English readers, who are used to the word 'boast' only being utilized in a negative sense. But the word Paul used can have both a negative and a positive sense, and Paul employed both in his writings. There is not an apparent, total consistency to his use of the word; there is significant variegation according to context, ministry need, the people to whom he was writing, and the theological or spiritual situation which he was encountering.

But while there is not a total consistency, there are some remarkable patterns. For instance, Paul used the word 'boast' in a broadly speaking, positive sense about twice as often as in a negative sense. By my count, Paul used the word 'boast' as a negative, 15 times. On the other hand, he used the word positively, 34 times – over twice as often as in the negative. That by no means necessarily means that Paul tended to think of boasting more frequently in the positive, because there are other reasons for the disparity of word count. For instance, the word is used largely in the negative in 1 Corinthians, but then (after the Corinthian church had changed some of its ways) the word 'boast' is used largely in the positive in 2 Corinthians, and it is used frequently in 2 Corinthians. In addition, in Romans – very often the place where Paul established his intended balance and framing to his thinking – we find an almost precise balance to the use of the word 'boast'. It is used in the negative in the first major section of Romans, before switching to its being used mainly in the positive thereafter (with one return to the negative at the end of Romans).

This pattern does not establish a clear preference from Paul regarding boasting, that boasting was for him mainly a positive, or that it was twice as often a positive as a negative: because such word counts don't give sufficient subtlety to the context or intention of the individual letters and paragraphs and sentences in which the word is found. But what it does establish is that it is very clear that Paul believed that boasting *could*, under certain circumstances, be a positive. It shows that he thought of boasting as something to embrace, and to do so confidently, certainly, boldly. It shows that his thinking of this positive side of boasting was not only limited to the more numinal, spiritual matters – about a relationship to God and the way we tend to think of that in terms of our prayer lives or personal Bible studies – but also about his own ministry; about other Christians; about giving money to a worthy Christian cause; about his own refusal to take a salary when it was his right to receive one; and perhaps most remarkably about sufferings and, most counter-intuitively, about weaknesses.

Can we boast too?

Is boasting, like pride, something to avoid at all costs, and from which we are never entirely free? Or is boasting like confidence, something which is healthy in certain situations when well-grounded, but dangerous when not being confident about the right things? It seems from this survey of Paul that boasting is much more like our word 'confidence'. We can be self-confident and wrongly so.

I remember someone once telling me that he was borderline genius, that he was certainly going to go to an elite university, and that he hardly needed to try or work hard to get there. This seemed unlikely to me, but mathematical superstars do exist, and we could have unearthed another John Nash of the movie, *A Beautiful Mind*, fame. As it turned out, this individual had wildly overestimated his ability to assess his own gifts. He did not even come close to succeeding in the goals that he assumed he would easily attain.

If anything, you would think that people who tend to overestimate themselves are more common. But even this is complicated. When people overestimate their own abilities, it may be because they genuinely are big-headed and ludicrously out of sync with reality. Or it may be that they know just as well as you do their own talents (or lack thereof) and are painfully aware of the fact that actually they find basic arithmetic challenging. What they are doing is kidding themselves in the hope that they can kid you and thereby be accepted, do well, succeed, and prove themselves. In short, what they may need is not to be told to grow up, or that they are actually nowhere near as good as they think they are, but instead to be helped to see who they really are and be confident in that.

Confidence may then not be a sufficiently accurate way of looking at this idea of positive boasting which we find in Paul. Confidence often has the sense of 'gearing yourself up' or 'psyching yourself up' to do something. It may well be something that you really, truly can do, but before you go out to play the game, you get into a huddle and focus your mind on the success you hope to achieve, and before the big deal goes down, you remind yourself of all your achievements so far so that you carry appropriate confidence to the table. None of this is bad, but this doesn't seem sufficiently accurate to describe all that Paul was saying about the positive side of boasting. Or at least not by itself.

It also misses some of the joy of it. The word, as Paul used it positively, seems to have a sense of fun, almost mischievousness (especially in those famous chapters in 2 Corinthians where he started to play with the idea of foolish boasting to show those who were doing it just how foolish it really was). There is an exulting (to use an old word), a rejoicing, a thrill. It is not dogged determination, which the word 'confident' can suggest, but thrilling wonder at how great something is. It pulls you on; it does not drive you from behind. It is magnetic, not willing yourself to do 'better and better every day in every way'.

No, I think we are going to have to settle with 'boast' – and let the uneasiness of the word unsettle us. You can boast in a good way. Really. Paul did. Did Jesus?

2.

DID JESUS BOAST?

The simplest answer to this question would be 'No'. The word for 'boast' is entirely absent from the words of Jesus as recorded in the Gospels. Matthew, Mark, Luke, and John do not have any record of Jesus talking about boasting – whether in the negative or the positive sense. If by the question 'Did Jesus boast?' we mean 'Did Jesus used the word "boast" in a recorded sentence in one of the four Gospels?' then the answer is definitely that Jesus did not boast.

However, the simplest answer may not be the right answer. To begin with, if we take the traditional approach to the Bible (which is that the whole Bible is God's Word), and we take the orthodox approach to Jesus (which is that Jesus is fully God, as well as fully man), then when we read the word 'boast' anywhere else in the Bible, we are in a certain sense also reading what Jesus said. When Paul talked about boasting, we are then, in this way, also reading what God says about boasting, and because Jesus is also fully God, we are reading what Jesus says about boasting. Those who study the texts in the original historical context balk at such a one-step-removed theology, but it hangs together at a straightforward, consistent level. Jesus is God; God speaks in all the Bible; and the Bible does talk about boasting: therefore, Jesus talks about boasting.

That said, though, most people, when they ask whether Jesus said or did this or that, they are asking whether Jesus in His incarnate state said or did something of which we have a record in the Gospels. If that is what is meant by 'Did Jesus boast?' then it seems fairly straightforward to answer that He did not. But is that what is meant by 'Did Jesus boast?' Can someone be said only to be talking about the same idea as someone else if they use the precise same word as someone else?

For instance, in Canada, it is normal to describe those sweet fizzy drinks of coloured water as pop. In many parts of America (though not all), it is normal to describe those drinks as soda. So, if someone asks, 'Do you want a soda?' and someone from Canada replies, 'I'd like a pop,' are they talking about something different, or are they talking about the same thing? The obvious answer is that they are talking about the same thing even though they are using different words for it.

Let's then make the question more precise. By 'Did Jesus boast?' we mean 'Did Jesus, in His incarnate state, as recorded in one of the four Gospels in the Bible, speak or act in a way that equates to the same idea that Paul used in his letters about boasting, whether in its negative sense or its positive sense?' That is, 'Did Jesus boast?' means 'Did Jesus talk or speak in a way that meant the same or similar to what Paul meant by boasting?'

To answer that question – whether Jesus boasted in a way that is similar to how Paul boasted without using the exact same word – requires not only a good understanding of what Paul meant by boasting (see previous chapter), but also a good understanding of the kind of person Jesus was as revealed in the Gospels, and a good grasp of what He said in various contexts.

By boasting, Paul meant both the negative and positive. That is, boasting, for Paul, can mean hubris and therefore spiritual pride or even arrogance, and can lead thereby to hypocrisy. On the other hand, boasting can also mean exuberant and exulting confidence in what Christ has done, what He is doing in you, and what He is doing through you to other people and churches. It can mean exulting, or it can mean arrogance, depending on the context and the situation. On the positive side, there is an exuberant, confident, thrilling shout of joyful bravery. Did Jesus speak in either of these terms about boasting, whether in the negative or the positive?

Negative boasting in Jesus

Did Jesus speak about anything else? So common is this idea of religious hubris being dangerous that it is arguable that it is one of the standard tropes or themes of the whole ministry of Jesus. There were people who got Jesus, and there were people who didn't. In the Gospels, the people who didn't get Jesus were very frequently the religious people – whereas the tax collectors and sinners flocked to follow Jesus. It is possible then to make the case that this idea of boasting in a negative sense is one of the key ideas, thoughts, and themes of Jesus' ministry.

Luke

Consider Jesus' famous story of the Pharisee and the tax collector in Luke 18:9-14. The Pharisee thought he was righteous, far more righteous than the tax collector who was also praying. The Pharisee listed before God all his good deeds and was certain that he had every right, therefore, to be addressing the Almighty. The tax collector, on the other hand, did not boast (in this negative sense) at all. He was mortified by his own sinfulness and asked God to have mercy on him, a sinner. Jesus concluded that it was the tax collector, not the Pharisee, who went home justified before God.

In this one short, brilliant parable, we see the boasting idea of Paul's filled out and taught by Jesus through one of the most alarming (to the religious) stories ever told. Self-confident, self-righteous boasting is not going to make you justified before God. Only humble, contrite repentance will lead you to being justified. Because we are all sinners and no one is righteous, it is God who must have mercy on us all. Or as Jesus Himself concludes, 'For all those who exalt themselves will be humbled, and those who humble themselves will be exalted' (Luke 18:14).

This may not be the best example for some, though, because there are those who view this parable as a particularly 'Pauline' parable – that is, reflecting the kind of teaching that you find in Paul's writings. Traditionally, Luke (whose close association with Paul is recorded in the Book of Acts) is seen as representing Paul's theological emphases, and this parable is sometimes seen as an epicentre of such close association. Nonetheless, even if that close association in this particular parable is granted, the parable itself still stands as clear, strong evidence of the kind of negative boasting (without using that term) that is present in Jesus' recorded words and actions in the Gospels. It may not be the best example, but it is one of the strongest examples, and it stands as highly relevant to discovering what Jesus may (or may not) have meant by boasting.

Matthew

Are there other examples of negative boasting? Oh, yes, many. Remember, again, that the word boasting is itself absent from the recorded lips of Jesus in the Gospels. But the concept of negative boasting is present. It came across frequently in Jesus' interactions with the Pharisees. They were confident in their own righteousness and looked down at others' moral standing before God. Not all Pharisees were like this; some followed Jesus (like Nicodemus, it seems). But taken as a large, general impression, many of the Pharisees fell into this trap of negative boasting or being mistakenly confident in their own righteousness.

For instance, take Jesus' stinging rebuke of the Pharisees and the teachers of the law in Matthew 23. The kind of negative boasting that He reacted against there was the kind that led to the hypocrisy that was so rampant among them (and against which Paul himself also taught in Romans 2). Jesus said, with sizzling sarcasm, 'The teachers of the law and the Pharisees sit in Moses' seat. So you must be careful to do everything they tell you. But do not do what they do, for they do not practice what they preach. They tie up heavy, cumbersome loads and put them on other people's shoulders, but they themselves are not willing to lift a finger to move them' (Matt. 23:2-4). He carried on, 'Everything they do is done for people to see: They make their phylacteries wide and the tassels on their garments long; they love the place of honour at banquets and the most important seats in the synagogues; they love to be greeted with respect in the marketplaces and to be called "Rabbi" by others' (Matthew 23:5-7). They were 'hypocrites' (Jesus says several times), and their boasting was in the wrong place and for the wrong thing. 'Woe to you, teachers of the law and Pharisees, you hypocrites! You give a tenth of your spices – mint, dill and cumin. But you have neglected the more important matters of the law – justice, mercy and faithfulness. You should have practiced the latter, without neglecting the former. You blind guides! You strain out a gnat but swallow a camel' (Matt. 23:23-24). That is, their boasting was misguided – not that they should not have had any zeal, enthusiasm, or passion. Jesus was not asking them to stop being so excited or to get less hot about God. He was telling them that they had put their enthusiasm in show and exhibition, keeping relatively minor parts of the law, rather than sticking to the big point of God's law: justice, mercy, and faith. They had negative boasting – and they had it in spades!

Mark

In another instance in another Gospel – this time Mark's – Jesus was confronted by the Pharisees and some of the teachers of the law because they saw His disciples eating food with ceremonially unclean hands. Mark then explained this fact for his non-Jewish readers (one of the indicators in Mark's Gospel that his primary audience was Gentile) before recounting this conflict between Jesus and the Pharisees. The Pharisees asked Jesus why His disciples didn't live 'according to the tradition of the elders' (Mark 7:5). Jesus, in typical bullish fashion, at least when confronted by religious hypocrisy, replied: 'Isaiah was right when he prophesied about you hypocrites; as it is written: "These people honor me with their lips, but their hearts are far from me. They worship me in vain; their teachings are merely human rules"' (Mark 7:6-7). Quite a strong verse to pluck out and apply to them immediately! Jesus then exposited that verse for their context and made the application crystal clear: 'You have let go of the commands of God and are holding on to human traditions' (Mark 7:8).

How could that be the case? How could their boasting have been so misguided, so focused upon traditions handed down from their forefathers rather than on the actual Word of God, which, of course, they professed to be following according to the interpretation of their tradition? Jesus explained in two ways.

First, He gave an example, one among many He could have chosen. He indicated how they were doing this in practice, how they were nullifying the Word of God for the sake of their tradition (Mark 7:13). Suppose, Jesus said, someone has a father or mother who needs care and help, and suppose this person wants to get out of that duty, then he can say 'Corban' (that is, Mark explains, a gift devoted to God), thus avoiding his filial responsibilities. So part of it is financial.

But second, this boasting in tradition – in such a way that God's Word is nullified in the end – was not only financially motivated: it was a misunderstanding about how God works. 'Are you so dull?' Jesus asked His disciples, as He further explained: 'Don't you see that nothing that enters a person from the outside can defile them? ... What comes out of a person is what defiles them. For it is from within, out of a person's heart, that evil thoughts come ...' (Mark 7:18-21). That is, Jesus was saying that the nullifying of the Word of God for the sake of tradition was also a matter of misunderstanding the cause of human behaviour: how it is that people's hearts – their thinking, their feeling, their wills – affect their actions; and how it is the heart's intentions that go on to make someone unclean or clean; not whether they have washed their hands!

In other words, negative boasting (in this case boasting in traditions rather than in God's Word) was fundamentally attractive to people because, first, it was easier. It made things easier to achieve, for instance. As in Jesus' example, it could give specially and religiously sanctioned excuses to get out of uncomfortable and inconvenient duties: like taking care of an elderly parent. Second, it was all about the externals: the show; the boasting; the more easily achieved external cleanness that looked impressive (negative boasting). But it was really not getting to the root of the problem: the problem of the human heart.

John

John's Gospel has a subtly different trajectory of Jesus' interactions with the religious leaders of His age, but the end result was pretty similar. One notable example is the story of the man who was born blind. Jesus came across this man in the company of His disciples, who asked Him whether the blind man or his parents sinned – assuming that his blindness could be nothing but the result of individual, direct sin. But, while it is true that sin in general is the cause of suffering in general (there would be no suffering if there had been no sin), and while it is also sometimes true that suffering is the direct result of a particular sin (sin has consequences in our own lives, and sometimes we suffer because we do things that lead to suffering), it is not true that someone's suffering is always the direct result of a particular sin. In this case, this man's suffering had nothing to do with a direct sin, but was actually part of God's plan to reveal more of who Jesus was: 'Neither this man nor his parents sinned ... but this happened so that the works of God might be displayed in him' (John 9:3).

Jesus then healed the blind man in a slightly unusual way, and those around began to be amazed at what had taken place. Now the Pharisees were not pleased, for the healing had taken place on a 'Sabbath', meaning that according to their own traditional interpretation of the Bible, it was illegitimate for Jesus to have helped him. So the Pharisees interviewed the man, the parents of the man, and then the man again. The man replied confidently, and a little snarkily, 'Why do you want to hear it again? Do you want to become his disciples too?' (John 9:27). And they threw him out of the synagogue fellowship (John 9:34).

Jesus found the man once more and asked him whether he believed in the 'Son of Man' (Jesus' special designation of Himself drawn from Daniel's vision of a divine 'Son of Man' figure in the Old Testament). The man ended up believing and worshiping Jesus (John 9:35, 38).

But the Pharisees were now incensed; some were overhearing what Jesus was doing and saying to the man. In particular, Jesus had said, 'For judgment I have come into this world, so that the blind will see and those who see will become blind' (John 9:39). Jesus' point was His original point: that the physical healing of the blind man was for a spiritual purpose of glorifying God. It showed that Jesus was there to heal those who knew they needed healing, and those who refused to 'see' Jesus would remain blind. The Pharisees asked Jesus, 'What? Are we blind too?' And Jesus replied in His famous aphorism: 'If you were blind, you would not be guilty of sin; but now that you claim you can see, your guilt remains' (John 9:40-41).

Again, the Pharisees had their boasting (in Paul's terminology) in the wrong place. It was negative boasting.

They claimed that they could see. Really, they were spiritually blind. If they had acknowledged that they were spiritually blind, Jesus would have healed them. But because they were confident that they could see and they were boasting in their religious position, attainment, and authority, they were unable to see the one person who could help them see. Their negative boasting made them proud, arrogant, and conceited in a spiritual sense that blinded them to the doctor who could not only diagnose their disease but heal it too.

Here are some examples, then, from each of the four Gospels in the Bible of what we have called negative boasting. The term 'boasting' is, as we have said, not found literally in any of the Gospels. But is the concept, the idea, the meaning of that boasting language, as used by Paul, found in the Gospels? Is there a common idea that we can trace in Jesus' own interaction with people and in situations that helps us understand more of what the Bible (and therefore God) means by boasting?

Well, first, we are discovering that negative boasting is present in the Gospels. In particular, the Pharisees and the religious leaders were liable to the critique of negative boasting. They were confident in their own righteousness, and looked down at the righteousness of others. They were blind when they thought they could see because they were the spiritual elite. They held on to their own traditions while rejecting the Word of God in order to get what they wanted – financially, even – while ignoring the real heart matters that were the source of all human conduct, good and bad. They were 'blind guides' whose negative boasting left them open to the charge of fundamental hypocrisy; they said good things, but they did not do good things. They neglected the weightier matters of the law, but kept the relatively minor matters. They had their boasting in the wrong place; they were marked by what we could call negative boasting. It was not that they did or said nothing. Their zeal itself was not the problem; it was their zeal without knowledge. Their wrong kind of enthusiasm for the wrong kind of thing was what led to hubris, pride, arrogance, and conceit of a spiritual and religious kind; it was therefore similar, if not identical, to what Paul meant in basic concept by the word 'boasting' as it related to the negative kind of boasting.

Positive boasting in Jesus

What about positive boasting? Can we find in the Gospels the positive boasting that we also see in Paul's writings – the exultation, rejoicing, and confidence in the right kind of thing; a humility about oneself; and a brave, audacious celebration of God which does not lead to hubris but to lovingkindness?

Luke

One instance is when Jesus sent out the seventy-two (Luke 10). Jesus told them to go ahead of Him in pairs to the villages and towns as a preparation for His arrival, like an advance team, and instructed them how to do this mission work. They were to go without money and instead depend on the kindness of a person of peace who, in each of the towns, would take them in, and they were to stay with that person and not move around. They were to heal the sick and proclaim, 'The kingdom of God has come near to you' (Luke 10:9). If they were not welcomed, then they were literally to shake the dust off their sandals as a sign to that village or town that they were under the judgment of God for refusing to accept their message about the coming kingdom of God in the person of Jesus (Luke 10:10-11).

After this mission trip the seventy-two returned with 'joy'. They told Jesus, 'Lord, even the demons submit to us in your name' (Luke 10:17). You would have thought this was a fine case of positive boasting. They had gone about Jesus' work in Jesus' way and had achieved Jesus-like miraculous results. But no. This was not the kind of exulting, rejoicing or boasting that Jesus wanted from them – or at least not the highest kind of positive boasting. Jesus commended them by saying that in a spiritual vision He saw Satan being defeated, perhaps referencing the original battle with Satan in the heavens or the disciples' part in the ongoing battle, and then told them that He had given them spiritual authority to overcome the spiritual forces of darkness. 'However,' He said, 'do not rejoice that the spirits submit to you, but rejoice that your names are written in heaven' (Luke 10:20).

In other words, the kind of rejoicing that Jesus viewed as positive was not finally about ministry effectiveness, even if that was in the name of Jesus and achieved impressive results. The kind of positive boasting, rejoicing or exulting that Jesus wanted was one that had an eternal focus. 'Rejoice that your names are written in heaven' (Luke 10:20).

Matthew

This focus on the eternal locus of boasting is found also in Matthew's Gospel. In Jesus' famous Sermon on the Mount (Matthew chapters 5 through 7), He began with the equally famous Beatitudes (Matt. 5:3-12). These are a series of pithy statements that summarize the foundational blessings of the Gospel of the kingdom of heaven – in a ladder-like ascent towards conversion and then descent towards living as a follower of Jesus. 'The kingdom of heaven' is the top and tail of the central portion of the blessings. Jesus began with, 'Blessed are the poor in spirit, for theirs is the kingdom of heaven' (Matt. 5:3), and then concluded this central section with, 'Blessed are those who are persecuted because of righteousness, for theirs is the kingdom of heaven' (Matt. 5:10). So the 'kingdom of heaven' frames the Beatitudes in a way that indicates that the *kingdom of heaven* is the central proposition of the Beatitudes.

An example in contemporary English might be the following. 'On this day in history a great event occurred that had a dramatic impact on the future direction of the city in which you live, and that event took place on this day in history.' The emphasis of the sentence is on 'this day in history', which is indicated by the repetition of the phrase at the beginning and end of the sentence. It's a device not frequently used in English, but it is sometimes. One famous example would be the 'St Crispin's day speech' in Shakespeare's *Henry V*.[1] The king begins the key part of the speech by saying,

> This day is called the feast of Crispian.

Then, after a passionate call to arms based on the fact that those back home would want to be with them for this famous day, the king ends his speech by repeating,

> And gentlemen in England now a-bed
> Shall think themselves accursed they were not here,
> And hold their manhoods cheap whiles any speaks
> That fought with us upon Saint Crispin's day.

Again, the emphasis is indicated and affirmed by the repetition at the beginning and end – in Shakespeare's case often in the middle of that speech too!

The pinnacle of conversion is found in Matthew 5:6 where those who 'hunger and thirst for righteousness,' who are repentant and believing, and long for God and for His godliness, are 'filled' with God and His righteousness and are what Christians often call 'saved'. Thereafter, these regenerate Christ-followers become people who were living in a way that was counter-intuitive to the world around them, exemplary of what it meant to be a Christian and liable to receive opposition as a result. They were 'merciful'; they were 'pure in heart'; they were 'peacemakers'; and because of this counter-cultural lifestyle, they were likely, in one way or another, to be 'persecuted'. This too was a

---

1   In Act IV, scene III.

blessing – even persecution – particularly when it focused on the eternal aspect of positive boasting that the end of the Beatitudes lands on.

Scholars disagree as to how to structure the final Beatitude. Is it a part of the blessing of verse 10 (for it also focuses on persecution)? Or is it another blessing (because while it is focused similarly on persecution, it ramps up the blessing to an eternal level)? My view is that it was an amplification of the final blessing because it also focused on persecution, but that it also landed in a way that showed this positive boasting (in Paul's language) in high and exalted terms. Jesus said, 'Blessed are you' (turning to those around Him and addressing them directly) 'when people insult you, persecute you and falsely say all kinds of evil against you because of me' (Matt. 5:11). This was an amplification of the final blessing, now directed personally at His hearers and extended to include 'all kinds of evil', and the aspect He had in mind was 'because of me', that is, because of being Christ-followers. Then He concluded these Beatitudes with an exultant, rejoicing, positive-boasting celebration. 'Rejoice and be glad, because great is your reward in heaven, for in the same way they persecuted the prophets who were before you' (Matt. 5:12).

What is this rejoicing? Is it the same sort of idea that Paul expressed (when positive) by his term 'boasting'? Or is it something different? It is a celebratory, exultant shout of acclamation, a joy that is confident, bold, and audacious, in spite of what is happening to those who are rejoicing. Compare Paul's teaching about suffering in Romans 5:3-5, 'Not only so, but we also glory in our sufferings, because we know that suffering produces perseverance; perseverance, character; and character, hope. And hope does not put us to shame, because God's love has been poured out into our hearts through the Holy Spirit, who has been given to us.'

Do you see the connection of idea? Paul was saying that we rejoice, not because of, or even in spite of, but 'in' our sufferings, because we know that under God's sovereign care such sufferings are designed for an eternal purpose. Once we grasp that, eternal hope comes, and that hope will not disappoint us in the end, and so it causes rejoicing right now. Jesus was saying, 'Rejoice and be glad' – a double emphasis that sounds like it is the same idea of exultant celebration, positive boasting – because when you are suffering for Jesus' sake, it shows that you are a Christ-follower. This then means that you know that you have an eternal destiny, and indeed one that means you will have 'great reward in heaven'.

Why? Because they treated the 'prophets' in the same way. In other words, the way that you are being opposed is the same template, type, and kind as the way the prophets beforehand were opposed. Therefore, you, like them, are genuine God-followers, and so you can be sure that you have great reward in heaven. Hence, 'rejoice and be glad'. Exult, have positive boasting.

Mark

This kind of positive boasting seems less prominent in Mark's Gospel. In Mark, the focus in the first part of the Gospel is on who Jesus is, and then in the second part of the Gospel on what Jesus did. Mark was interested in matters of identity and then of mission, all connected to the person of Jesus. As such, on top of his well-known predilection for punchy, short, to-the-point sentences, Mark was also threading a theme of the Suffering Servant. The resonance throughout the Gospel is with this Jesus who 'did not come to be served, but to serve, and to give his life as a ransom for many' (Mark 10:45).

That said, there is one element – and perhaps others, but at least one. This element is particularly striking in terms of positive boasting because it connects to the theme in Mark's Gospel of Christ's identity, and it is also a sort of positive boasting that is specifically and literally God-centred. That is, the exultant boasting is centred in God Himself, from God the Father Himself, and about God the Son Himself. We gain a little peek and can peer through the window into the celebratory, audacious boasting that is a very part of the nature of God Himself.

You find this at the beginning of Mark's Gospel when Jesus was baptized. Mark recorded this extraordinary 'voice ... from heaven' (Mark 1:11), which surely must have astonished all who heard it, and he told us specifically what the voice said. 'You are my Son,' addressing Jesus, 'whom I love; with you I am well pleased.' There we have God the Father exulting, celebrating, praising, in positive boasting about God the Son. The voice did not say, 'This is my Son; now Son, go do this task for me.' It was a celebration of not just the identity of Jesus in a cold, formal, clinical way, but also the affection and celebration that comes with that identity. He was not just God's Son; He was God's Son who was loved by God the Father and about whom God the Father was 'well pleased.' There was pleasure, enjoyment, satisfaction, celebration, exultation: positive boasting about who Jesus is. It took place in public before others, and it showcased how the eternal Father, Son, and Holy Spirit are shrouded not only in mystery, but also in love.

To emphasize how important this celebration was of who Jesus is *and* how much He is loved by God the Father, the same event happened again. It is amazing to think that one supernatural rupture of regular events, to cause a burst of divine positive boasting about the Son, was not enough; there must be a repeat occurrence, and this time to even greater fanfare, though less public. Jesus was transfigured – 'His clothes became dazzling white, whiter than anyone in the world could bleach them' (Mark 9:3). Something of the true power and glory of Jesus was revealed, the kingdom of God in power in at least a small aspect, and the two great heroes of the Old Testament who were thought specifically and concretely to come or point to the Messiah (Elijah and Moses) appeared with Him. Peter lost his head, not for the first time, and tried to think of something to do to make the most of the situation; he immediately considered something practical, like building some shelters so everyone had a comfortable place (verse 5). This time a voice from a 'cloud' enveloped them (instead of the Spirit descending like a dove) (verse 7). Peter had addressed Jesus as 'Rabbi' (verse 5). The voice corrected. This is no Rabbi. 'This is my Son' (verse 7). But again, the voice did not merely give attestation to the identity of Jesus in a cold, formal, clinical way. The voice said, 'This is my Son, whom I love. Listen to him!' (verse 7). This time instead of the final words being 'with him I am well pleased', they were a specific instruction to 'listen to him'. The voice was celebrating and exulting in positive boasting about Jesus. And the voice told others to do so as well; at the very least to begin by listening to Jesus. To put it simply, the voice was saying, 'This is my boy, isn't He amazing? I love Him; now listen to Him!'

John

John's Gospel records two instances of what in Paul's terminology we might call boasting (in a positive sense), though neither of them are *by* Jesus, but *about* Jesus. The first was John the Baptist's testimony about Jesus (John 3:22-36). People noticed that John's ministry was beginning to get overshadowed by Jesus'. In particular, they noticed that Jesus' disciples (not Jesus Himself, John 3:22, 4:2) were baptizing more people than John was baptizing. They realized that 'everyone is going to him' (John 3:26), that is to Jesus.

John the Baptist was then presented with a reality, and a verbal confirmation of that reality, which could have caused him to feel jealous, insecure, upset, miffed, or disappointed that what he was doing was no longer the centre of attention or as appreciated by the people as it had been. It would have been easy for John to feel a little bitter towards this new movement that was taking over the limelight, making him play second fiddle, presumably for the first time in his entire ministry. He was the rock star, the celebrity, the go-to guy for radical, cutting edge, drawing-a-crowd preaching and baptizing. In fact, 'baptizing' was John 'the Baptist's' calling card. It was what made him stick out from the crowd and gave him the 'stickiness' to draw people to him. He came preaching 'a baptism of repentance for the forgiveness of sins' (Mark 1:4). So it was not just that Jesus was getting a bigger crowd than John (difficult enough to handle on its own for an insecure preacher). It was that Jesus' disciples were apparently using the very same technique that John the Baptist had 'trademarked' as his own.

Would John begin to denounce Jesus as a stealer of his thunder? Would he start to undermine Jesus with carefully nuanced attacks, cleverly disguised behind theologically sophisticated verbiage, but nonetheless deliberate? That, as many a leader knows, is one way to draw a crowd. Go on the offensive. Go 'negative', as politicians call it, and your campaign will at least get a momentary blip of renewed attention.

But John the Baptist did none of that. Instead, he launched into what must have been one of the most amazing sermons ever given (John 3:27-36). For it was not only not about him, it was not for him or advancing his ministry in any way, shape, or form. He used a metaphor, a picture, a story. He talked about a wedding.

Everyone knows what happens at a wedding. There is only one focus for everyone's attention – the bride and the bridegroom. It doesn't matter who else turns up or how important they are, the wedding is about the two people getting married. If a head of state, a celebrity musician, or a New York Times bestselling author turns up, it doesn't matter when it comes to the ceremony. No one, not even a president, would stand at the altar blocking the view of the happy couple and say, 'Now I've just got a few words to say about my campaign, and thank you all for coming to listen to me.' It would be ridiculous, outrageous, and it would backfire and hurt the celebrity trying to advance his own cause (however worthy). The unwritten rule of every wedding is that there are only two stars of the show – the bride and the bridegroom. Everything is about them. The guests gather, they are honoured, recognized if need be, and if they are particularly noteworthy, but the more noteworthy they are, the more they are honouring the two people who are at the centre of attention.

That's the image that John the Baptist used to describe what was going on in this moment in his ministry, and the image that launched him into what (in Paul's language) we could call a version of 'positive boasting'. Except it was not about John the Baptist at all – it was about the bridegroom, not the guest, and not even the best man who was getting everything ready for the bridegroom. John the Baptist put it like this, 'The bride belongs to the bridegroom. The friend who attends the bridegroom waits and listens for him, and is full of joy when he hears the bridegroom's voice. That joy is mine, and it is now complete' (John 3:29).

'Full of joy' can sound a little distant. But let the metaphor carry the exclamation, the exulting. Imagine that the friend who has been waiting for the bridegroom has been waiting for quite some time. Everyone's beginning quietly to wonder whether the bridegroom has 'done a runner', skipped out of the service, let his nerves get the better of him. The best man, the friend, is waiting and waiting, and all eyes are on him because everyone assumes that he knows what's going on. He tries to keep smiling, keep the crowd happy, keep them in line and waiting appropriately and getting ready to acclaim the wedded couple. At the last moment, the bridegroom arrives! Yeah! 'Full of joy.' Big hug. Fist bump. High five. A smile so wide that it hurts the corners of your mouth. That joy was John the Baptist's, and that joy was complete; in other words, this was now exactly what was going on.

Jesus, the bridegroom, had arrived, and He was coming for His bride, the people of God. John the Baptist was exulting over this. He was not in any way, shape, or form disappointed by the fact that Jesus was getting more attention than he was now, in the same way that a best man would not be disappointed that the guests' eyes are no longer on him but have turned to the happy couple at the wedding. John the Baptist was overjoyed that they were now focusing on the bridegroom! That was the whole point. He could not have been happier. In fact, he was exultant about it, full of joy, having 'positive boasting'.

The other instance of positive boasting in John's Gospel is later, after Jesus had been anointed at Bethany, when he came back to Jerusalem for the Passover (and for the crucifixion), and there was a great crowd that gathered. This triumphal entry is almost a trope, a standard theme repeated – if not to cliché, then at least to familiarity – and an echo that reverberates in most people's minds when they read the story. It is a trope, in particular, of how at one moment people acclaim you, and then a few days later the crowd can turn against you.

Now, whether or not all the people in the crowd were the same people who shouted 'Crucify him!' a few days later is in many ways beside the point. As far as I know, no one has ever done a head count, traced the names of each of the individuals, and matched who was where when. It is quite possible there was some overlap. Crowds draw all sorts. Perhaps some were not quite sure that what they were saying was true and were caught up in the moment, as they were likewise caught up in the moment when they shouted 'Crucify him!' (instead of 'Hosanna!') later.

On the other hand, there were a lot of people in Jerusalem for the feast. It would be possible that there was very little literal overlap between the two groups. What is certain, however – and this is the point that the poetry is attempting to make when it talks of this shift from 'Hosanna' to 'Crucify,' and the point of the familiar trope about the same idea – is that the same city of people one moment embraced Him and the next moment crucified Him. Jerusalem went out to meet Him to proclaim Him the king, and then Jerusalem went out to watch Him, and urge along, as He was crucified. It is a stunning shift, a pivotal moment, an extraordinary juxtaposition. It shows how little we humans can be certain of fame, that fickle friend. Even more, it shows how little we humans can be certain that our adulation of God is not tainted by the thought *as long as I get what I want out of it.*

There seems no doubt that Jesus' triumphal entry was driven by hopes that He would come as a conquering hero. That was why Jesus was very careful to make sure that, in the midst of this massive crowd, He sent the right signal. He symbolized His Servant-King nature and destiny by deliberately riding on a donkey. A war-horse might have made sense, a chariot perhaps, but a donkey? No one rode into a city on a donkey if he wanted to fight; it would be ridiculous. So as the crowd shouted the triumphant Davidic shouts that evidenced their hope for a king like David who would throw out those pesky Romans, and while there was in the air this false understanding of the Messianic hope, the misunderstanding was not dominant or, at least, not the only matter.

No, this is positive boasting, because while the crowd was confused or caught up in the moment, they were still saying things about Jesus that were true, and saying them in an exultant, celebratory, and positive-boasting way. 'Hosanna! Blessed is he who comes in the name of the Lord! Blessed is the king of Israel!' (John 12:13) These exultant shouts rang in the ears of Jesus, were about Jesus, and truly acclaimed Jesus as the King.

Summary

In each of the four Gospel accounts of the life of Jesus, then, there are instances of what we have called positive boasting. There are moments when either Jesus Himself is exultant, or His disciples are, or Jesus commends that kind of positive boasting under certain circumstances and for certain things. John recorded two instances: the triumphal entry and the attitude of John the Baptist to Jesus Himself. In neither case is the word 'boasting' used, but in both cases the idea of positive boasting – an exultant, audacious, confident, joyful, celebratory, positive proclamation – is present indeed.

Luke recorded this self-same positive boasting in a different context. In this case, Jesus' disciples returned from their mission full of joy that they had succeeded extraordinarily (even super-ordinarily or supernaturally). But Jesus told them that as great as that experience was, it was even better to have that kind of true positive boasting regarding their relationship to God and their eternal destiny, that their names were written in heaven. That would last beyond a temporary success of spiritual ministry; their names were written in heaven, meaning that they were fixed there, and they had a basis for lasting, eternal rejoicing, boasting, celebration, and exultation.

Matthew recorded Jesus' teaching about this eternal joy in the context of suffering. At the end of the Beatitudes, he recorded how Jesus taught that when His followers suffered for His sake, they were to leap for joy – positive boasting in extreme – because not only were they then being assured of their fixed status 'in heaven', but they also were assured that their reward would be great in heaven. Positive boasting then is related to the eternal, certain relationship that Jesus' followers can have with God, and is increased by the prospect of a particular, special reward, even great reward, within the context of that relationship.

Mark recorded two other instances of this positive boasting. The first took place at Jesus' baptism where there was an exultant rejoicing in Jesus (the Son) on the part of God (the Father). We are given a view into how this kind of positive boasting, this exultation, is characteristic not only of the possibility of a disciple's relationship to God, but of God Himself in His own nature. God the Father rejoices (eternally, and this moment specifically) over God the Son. Once more, we see this nature of God's positive boasting in the Son at the Transfiguration. Again, we are given a view to God the Father's sheer delight in and acclamation of God the Son.

It seems clear, then, that while different terminologies and language choices carry various elements of meaning with them, in context, and at an idea-level in terms of what is being communicated, not only of how it is being communicated, there are in the Gospel records accounts of Jesus boasting. Also there are recorded accounts of Jesus both speaking against negative boasting, as well as speaking for (and representing in His own person as God the Son relating to God the Father) a delight in positive boasting.

WWJD? Boast?

Clearly, the word 'boast' in the English language is nearly always employed in a negative sense. It tends to mean something like brag – that is, telling others how great you are in a way that is either inflated beyond what is true or real or, even if true and real, that is indelicate or insensitive to the feelings of others. Boasting in the English language is at the opposite end of the spectrum to being humble; it is not only being proud, it is speaking and acting in a way that is proud about being proud. It is in your face, unwanted, and not commended by any culture of which I am familiar that uses the English language.

It is tempting, therefore, simply to say that the kind of positive boasting that Jesus (and Paul as well, as we have seen) used is not the same 'language' as what we mean by boasting, that it would be better to use a different word for this thing that they mean by positive boasting – a word like 'joy' or 'confidence' or 'joyful confidence'. There is certainly merit in that re-translation of the word into contemporary idiom that will be understood and grasped by contemporary readers. The trouble with it – as we seek to understand the biblical idea of positive boasting with clarity – is that 'joyful confidence' (or equivalent) does not include all the elements of positive boasting.

For instance, 'joyful confidence' does not necessarily include the element of acclamation – actual speaking and declaring what is so wonderfully true. Confidence can be internal, and often is; a sort of quiet confidence. Joy can light up a face, but does not necessarily require being expressed verbally. It can even be hidden. Boasting cannot be hidden. Plus, the idea of positive boasting has a shock value to it, a turning on the head the idea of boasting. It says not just that boasting is wrong, 'don't brag', but goes beyond that and says, 'The element of desire to boast that you have, is actually able to be channeled towards something truly good to boast about, and truly great in terms of how you boast.'

If you go to a football game and your team wins, for example, afterwards the fans will engage in a lot of boasting. They will proclaim the greatness of their team; they will sing; they will shout. Things may perhaps get out of hand, but still there is a basic idea here where the fans are not just joyfully confident (which could include little more than going home and getting a nice cup of tea and smiling to themselves before turning the lights out). They are singing in the streets; they are chanting their victory songs; they are saying how great their hero is who scored the winning goal, or kicked the winning penalty, or made the winning tackle.

This positive boasting cannot be diluted, especially when we see it in Jesus. It seems that under certain circumstances and about certain things, Jesus either encouraged or exemplified positive boasting. But it is more than simply a few proof texts or discrete passages that even in their context can rightly be understood to exemplify or encourage positive boasting. It is also about the general trajectory of who Jesus is and what Jesus did.

When we ask, 'What would Jesus do?' we normally have in mind not simply a few stories or particular events, but the general picture of who Jesus is and how He would behave in certain situations that we then face. Normally we think of boasting as the very last thing that 'Jesus would do' in our situations today. We think of Jesus as gentle, meek, and mild baby Jesus. And even if we can get beyond the Christmas Jesus of popular, secularized imagination, we then go to the suffering view of Jesus. We tend to view Jesus solely as someone who suffered, a bit of a martyr figure in a sense, someone who always turned the other cheek – just as He encouraged His followers to do – and therefore would not in any sense boast (positively or negatively).

However, there is another side to the general overview, big-picture sense of who Jesus is and what He did. Clearly, the Bible teaches the wonderful truth that Jesus surrendered His dignity or status in becoming man, that He humbled Himself to become obedient to death, even death on a cross (Phil. 2:1-11). There is not much in that thoroughly biblical view of Jesus that encourages us to think of Him as encapsulating positive boasting. Or is there? Is it not the case that the old hymn, *When I Survey the Wondrous Cross*, has it right: 'Forbid it, Lord, that I should boast/ Save in the death of Christ my God'? Or that Paul correctly interpreted Jesus for us when he said, 'May I never boast except in the cross of our Lord Jesus Christ' (Gal. 6:14)? Could it be then that the very *apparent* conflict between the typical picture of Jesus as suffering, humble Servant and this view of Jesus as exemplifying or encouraging positive boasting is no *real* conflict at all? That when we boast, as Jesus encouraged, what we are doing is glorying in the cross of Jesus, just as Jesus Himself gloried in that cross?

The second half of John's Gospel points us further down this same route. Sometimes the first half of John's Gospel is called 'the book of signs' because of the predominance of the seven signs in John's Gospel. The second half is called 'the book of glory' because of the predominance of that latter message there. It is interesting then, for our purposes and in this context, that that second half of the book, while focused on glory, is also focused on the cross. For John, it appears, to glory in glory was to glory in the cross – as it was for Jesus also to glory in the cross. Jesus Himself taught this message as the Gospel of John began to pivot towards the crucifixion. He predicted His death and made it clear that His death (humbling, terrible, and shameful as it was at one level) was also the very thing that glorifies God, and then the thing in which He glories.

The context for this pivot towards the glory – or the positive boasting – in the cross, comes in John as non-Jews began to look for Jesus. Jesus saw this as a fulfillment of the gospel promise of the Old Testament Scriptures that the Word of God would go to all nations. And so Jesus said, 'The hour has come for the Son of Man to be glorified' (John 12:23). But this 'hour of glory' was not purely or simply about more and more people, from even farther-flung nations and people-groups, worshiping Jesus. It was about the *means* for the accompaniment of that end. Here we see how that barbaric cross was the means of the glory of God and was the focus of Jesus' glorying, positive boasting.

Jesus carried on, 'Very truly I tell you,' – a solemn pronouncement – 'unless a kernel of wheat falls to the ground and dies, it remains only a single seed. But if it dies it produces many seeds' (John 12:23-24). A little later in the same conversation, Jesus soliloquized, '"Now my soul is troubled, and what shall I say? 'Father, save me from this hour'? No, it was for this very reason I came to this hour. Father, glorify your name!" Then a voice came from heaven, "I have glorified it, and will glorify it again"' (John 12:27-28).

So the narrative of the cross continues with this overarching theme: that actually it is this which most glorifies God, and it is this in which we are most to glorify. In case that theme is not apparent, John returned to it again in his record of the Gospel events, when he described how Peter was reinstated as a disciple and shepherd of Christ's sheep. It occurred at the end of the Gospel in John 21. Jesus predicted that Peter would die, so embodying the shape of the shepherd that Jesus pre-eminently exemplified, who gives his life for the sheep. (See John 10:11, 'I am the good shepherd. The good shepherd lays down his life for the sheep.') And John, in describing how Peter would die, remarked, 'Jesus said this to indicate the kind of death by which Peter would glorify God' (John 21:19).

It begins to be apparent then that – far from being something which leads towards empty negative boasting or arrogance – in Jesus' life, boasting, in the positive sense, was centred around glorying in the cross, and those who follow Him will also glory in the cross in their words, as well as in their lives.

But it is still hard to grasp, understand, or apply it to our lives because it seems so foreign – an ancient thing, a Middle Eastern, an Old Testament thing, an ancient Jewish thing; or in some way an idea that is very different from contemporary culture and society. We need to dig a little more beneath the surface and discover the background to Paul's use of boasting, and also to Jesus' use of the idea (if not the language) of positive boasting too.

If we ask the question, 'What would Jesus do?' and we come up with the answer that – in certain circumstances and situations, and rightly understood by the definitions and contexts that we have been exploring – Jesus would boast, understandably we are left with a bit of a shock. Could it be true? How do we understand this idea of positive, as well as negative, boasting?

A lot of such an understanding will come from exploring the background, the worldview, and the larger context of the idea. For that we will need to turn to the Old Testament of the Bible.

3.
BOASTING IN THE OLD TESTAMENT

The background for Paul's use of boasting in a positive sense is found only in a few key texts. The Greek translation of the Old Testament known as the Septuagint uses the word 'boasting' in this positive sense at the end of Hannah's hymn of praise to God in 1 Samuel 2:10. More explicitly obvious, in our English Bibles the same quotation is found in Jeremiah 9:23-24. In addition, two psalms (Ps. 34 and Ps. 48) use the word 'boasting' in this positive sense. More frequently, however, the word is used in a negative sense – of arrogance, hubris, pride, and the like.

But whether positive or negative, there is considerable ballast, support, and interpretative weight from the Old Testament to help shape and form what is in the New Testament – both Paul in his explicit use of the term 'boast', and Jesus with His denouncement of negative boasting and characterization of positive boasting. Words, ideas, concepts, and thought patterns in the New Testament were given distinct shape and context by the audience or church to which they were being spoken. They were shaped by the thought-pattern of the individual speaking or writing, as well as by the extra-biblical background to that word.

But more prominently, given that the New Testament writers were self-consciously aware of their role of fulfilling the Old Testament Scriptures – and as the Nicene Creed puts it, Jesus' mission was 'according to the Scriptures' – the background of the Old Testament usage of any key term is important to understanding how it is used in the New Testament. This is especially the case when the term appears contrary to our expectations; that is, it is especially important that we dig into the Scriptures of the Old Testament to find the original root context of some of the usages of the word in that worldview, in order to be able to translate its meaning for the New Testament world, and from there for our own world.

Negative use of boasting in the Old Testament

Examples abound of the negative use of boasting in the Old Testament. There are many instances where God – through His prophets, through His word, through the judgments that He brings on individuals and peoples – declares that arrogance, hubris, boasting in a 'negative' sense is highly displeasing to Him. But while there are many examples of the use of the word 'boasting' in a negative sense, each of the examples is not simple canon fodder to a general meaning of the word 'boasting' as arrogance; instead, they shape a good understanding of what is wrong about boasting, how to avoid it, and what to do about it if we sense it creeping into our lives or the life of the community of which we are a part.

Judges

For instance, there is the story of Gideon who was told to fight for the Lord. He was called dramatically to do so, and after some considerable hesitation, he eventually and faithfully set on his way to do just that – to take on the enemy and defeat them in the name of the Lord. He gathered an army. Then here came the surprise: God told him that he had too many men with him! Few things could have been more shocking for Gideon, facing a massed army against him, than that the band of people he had with him was too big. He was probably hoping for more people, not less! But God was clear that Gideon has too many. And the reason why he has too many has to do with negative boasting. God said, 'You have too many men. I cannot deliver Midian into their hands, or Israel would boast against me, "My own strength has saved me"' (Judg. 7:2).

What was it that was concerning the Lord? His concern was that if the army stayed the same size as it currently was, then the people might be tempted to think it was their own strength that had defeated the Midianites. God knew that He Himself would be the One who would give the Midianites into the Israelites' hands and win the victory for them. But if they had a large army, they might be tempted to think that they did it in their own strength – and so end up 'boasting against' Him.

This is not the same as 'boasting in Him'! This kind of negative boasting would be, in effect, saying to God that they did not need Him and they could do it just fine without Him. The whole lesson that God was teaching His people was dependence on Him, and therefore their need for Him, and therefore the importance of following Him. So for them to win a victory without it being crystal clear to everyone – to themselves, to the Midianites, to their friends and family, to history, and to anyone else who would ever read about the story in the future – that it was God, not them, well, it would defeat the purpose of the battle. Israel needed to learn that it was God, not them or their 'own strength,' who blessed them. This lesson would make them faithful to God in word, deed, prayer, and devotion. It was critically important that they not be given reason to 'boast against him,' and therefore the numbers of the army had to be reduced.

It was quite a lesson for Gideon and the people, who must have been terrified to see all those people leaving the group! And – at least for a while, before the downward spiral of Judges continued – it showed them that they must be faithful to God, for it was God who gave them the victory. This kind of negative boasting, then, is not simply pride or arrogance. It is putting yourself above God, thinking that you do not need God, and therefore actually proclaiming, acclaiming, boasting, exulting against God (rather than in God). The song would not be to God; the song would be to the nation or to the individual, to 'I did it my way,' or 'we did it when we relied upon each other'. The song would be to the community, not to God; to Gideon, not to God; to the power of Israel, not to the power of God. This kind of negative boasting is then effectively making gods of ourselves.

1 Kings

Later in the history of Israel, Ahab the king was faced with an attack from Syria. The king of Syria, Ben-Hadad, gathered a fearsome army against Israel, including thirty-two kings with him. They marched against Samaria, and sent messengers to Ahab basically challenging him to war. Eventually, these challenges resulted in Ahab refusing to capitulate, on the advice of his elders and the people, and war was about to commence. Ben-Hadad sent a final message to Ahab telling him that he was going to destroy them: 'May the gods deal with me, be it ever so severely, if enough dust remains in Samaria to give each of my men a handful' (1 Kings 20:10). He was going to grind them into the dust. He was talking up his victory, vaunting himself over them, and trying to intimidate them by the certainty of their victory, their confidence, as well as the sheer size of the army arraigned against Ahab. But, 'The king of Israel answered, "Tell him: 'One who puts on his armour should not boast like one who takes it off'"' (1 Kings 20:11).

This use of 'boast' is clearly negative in one sense, because Ahab was saying that King Ben-Hadad was proud and arrogant, that he had unwarranted over-confidence in his abilities. He should not be boasting before the battle; he should not be so confident that he would win; he should not be counting his chickens before they hatched. However, there is a glimmer (if only a faint one) of a potential positive use of boasting as more legitimate celebration, because Ben-Hadad was not to boast as someone who takes off his armour, implying that boasting on the other side of victory is more legitimate. To celebrate then is understandable, natural perhaps. To celebrate beforehand is arrogant, foolish, boasting in a negative sense.

Eventually, Ben-Hadad was defeated, not once, but twice, each time on the prediction of prophets of God speaking to Ahab. Ahab, however, did not finish the job and left Ben-Hadad alone at the end of the battle and let him go back to his country, having made a deal with him which would financially profit Ahab. Another prophet came and rebuked Ahab for this commercialization of God's judgment for Ahab's own benefit – a commercial greed which became more famous in the notorious instance of Naboth's vineyard, where Ahab's wife Jezebel responded to Ahab's sick desire for Naboth's property by arranging a cunning piece of royal murder so that Ahab could have the vineyard.

So Ahab was far from a pristine character, but in these early stages of his 'career', he acted in accordance with God's wishes, at least partly, by executing judgment on those who arraigned themselves against God and God's people. And one evidence of that coming judgment, Ahab correctly discerned, was this negative boasting. Ben-Hadad, drunk and partying, was so certain of his military superiority that he did not take the opposition seriously, least of all the opposition's God. Ben-Hadad boasted over them and over God. He was not only attacking God's people, he was doing so in a way that displayed his extraordinary arrogance and celebratory glorying in the wrong things – in himself and in the thirty-two kings under his alliance against Israel.

2 Chronicles

This kind of boasting, evidence of coming destruction because it showed in extreme form a heart that was set against

God and His ways, was seen later in the life of Amaziah king of Judah. Israel, split into two, had a northern and a southern kingdom, and Amaziah was king of the southern kingdom, with Jerusalem as its capital. Amaziah fought against the Edomites and won a stunning victory after he had listened to God's counsel through a prophet. He had hired an additional force from Israel to supplement his army, but God told him to dismiss those troops. He did so, won the victory, but the Israelities raided the cities of Judah on their way home.

After Amaziah's victory, he started, bizarrely, to worship the gods of the Edomites, those gods whose vanity he had just established by defeating the people who worshiped them. God sent a prophet to warn Amaziah, but the king refused to listen, and the die was cast. Amaziah was becoming more and more confident, over-confident, in his own abilities, and his next step was to seek battle with Israel. This he did and was roundly defeated. Before the actual battle, Joash, the king of Israel, warned Amaziah, saying that his victories had given him a false sense of his own superiority, 'You say, "See, I have struck down Edom," and your heart has lifted you up in boastfulness' (2 Chron. 25:19, ESV).

This is obviously an example of negative boasting, as Amaziah moved from a victory (given to him by God) to refusing to listen to the God who gave him the victory, to worshiping the gods of the people he had just defeated, to seeking battle with a larger army who (at least ostensibly) worshiped the same God as he did. All because 'your heart has lifted you up in boastfulness'.

Something about boasting or the act of boasting has an effect upon someone's actions, demeanour, even destiny. To boast in the wrong thing – in Amaziah's case, in himself and his own power – is not just a chance to look foolish and silly. It is not simply celebrating a victory in a sports game before it happens, and then wishing you had kept your mouth shut when it turns out that your team loses. This kind of negative boasting leads to a pattern of living, a way of looking at events, that creates choices that lead to a fate that every individual would avoid if they could. There is a blindness, a hardness, a stubbornness in the face of reality, that sets in.

Amaziah's heart – his thinking, his feeling, and his decision-making – was lifted up. It was exulting. It was high and celebratory. He felt good about who he was and what he had done. Also, he was pretty sure that, given this victory of his, he could just keep on going and defeat those who were next in his campaign of self-appointed greatness. After all, he did not need those mercenaries from Israel, did he? So why should he fear the Israelites, whom God had said he was not with (at least in that previous battle).

'Strike while the iron is hot.' 'Keep going while the wind is in your sails!' They would have heard of his victory; the rumours, gossip and stories would have been of his impressive military prowess, so all the psychological momentum was with him. What could possibly stop him from winning the next battle as he had won the previous one? In all this, what we are calling negative boasting – his 'heart has lifted him up in boastfulness' – he made the wrong choice. It was a sign of God's coming judgment upon him.

So this kind of negative boasting is not just foolish or wrongheaded: it is a sign of something deeply wrong in the heart of an individual and in the relationship of that individual to God. No one who really has a high view of God can have such a high view of themselves. No one who has really reflected on where his victories have come from could, in a moment, start worshiping other gods – or, in a moment, ignore the advice of that God who had just given the previous victory.

So Amaziah was evidencing his own heart's split; his confused, divided relationship to God. As the chronicler summarized at the start of the Amaziah story, 'He did what was right in the eyes of the LORD, but not wholeheartedly.'

The boasting of that heart showed to all those with eyes to see and ears to hear that Amaziah's heart was not wholly devoted to the Lord.

Psalms

The Book of Psalms has an almost universally negative use of boasting (though there are two instances of positive boasting, as we shall see).

Psalm 5

Psalm 5:5 (ESV) says, 'The boastful shall not stand before your eyes; you hate all evildoers.' David was 'groaning' before the Lord (verse 1, ESV) because of his 'enemies' (verse 8) who were gossiping, slandering, or spreading infamy: 'There is no truth in their mouth; their inmost self is destruction; their throat is an open grave; they flatter with their tongue' (verse 9, ESV). He asked God to 'let them fall by their own counsels' because they had 'rebelled' against God (verse 10, ESV). Instead, he wanted the righteous to be blessed and 'all who take refuge in you rejoice' (verse 11, ESV).

In this context, the 'boastful' are clearly those who were boasting in a negative sense, and in particular they were associated in this psalm with 'evildoers' and evil speakers. Those who boasted were using their lips arrogantly to cause trouble, to cover up their evil intentions and deeds, and were doing so with the kind of wrongly-seated confidence that comes from being dismissive of the sovereign God. They thought that no one would notice or care, that God did not see, and they went about their rebellion against God with the kind of brazenness that was rightly described as boastful. Boasting, then, for David in this psalm was a verbal and attitudinal approach to God and to the king that arrogantly rebelled against God while hiding behind flattering words and deceptive talk. It was a flagrant revolt against God.

Psalm 10

Psalm 10 makes this description even plainer. 'He [the wicked man] boasts about the cravings of his heart; he blesses the greedy and reviles the LORD. In his pride the wicked man does not seek him; in all his thoughts there is no room for God' (Ps. 10:3-4). The one who boasts, then, speaks and acts wickedly because at root, in the foundation of his thinking, he assumes that not only does God not notice, but that God does not exist.

The psalmist here makes a connection between our ultimate faith structure – whether we believe in God or not – and whether we think we can get away with selfish or evil deeds because we think no one is watching. In particular, in this psalm, the boastful person used the arrogance that came from his assumption that there was no God looking over him to prey upon the weak. 'He lies in wait near the villages; from ambush he murders the innocent' (verse 8). Again, 'His victims are crushed, they collapse' (verse 10). Why? 'He says to himself, "God will never notice; he covers his face and never sees"' (verse 11). Because the one who boasts believes that God either does not exist or does not care, either that there is no God or that if there is a God He does not intervene, therefore this boastful person acts over the weak and vulnerable like a bird of prey devouring them for his or her own gain.

The psalmist is saying that the existence of God, the faith structure that proclaims that God is and there is no other, is the greatest guarantee in the world that the weak will be protected. Who is there who can rein in the power of the super-rich tyrant? Answer: God. And so the psalmist said, 'Arise, LORD; Lift up your hand, O God. Do not forget the helpless' (verse 12). God is the One who can right the wrongs of the weak and break the power of the evil, mighty man. This right kind of boasting (though the word itself is not used in that positive sense in this psalm) came because of who the psalmist knew that God was. 'The LORD is king for ever and ever; the nations will perish from his land. You, LORD, hear the desire of the afflicted; you encourage them, and you listen to their cry, defending the fatherless and the oppressed, so that mere earthly mortals will never again strike terror' (verses 16-18).

The man who boasted then, in this psalm, was the man who either did not believe in God or thought that God could not or would not prevent him from doing whatever he liked. This boastful man then used his power to oppress the weak, to benefit from them for his own good, to trample upon them. His words and deeds were boasting because they were in the face of God and against God, and he thought that there would never be an accounting.

How wrong the boastful are! Because of who God is, 'mere earthly mortals will never again strike terror'. Even evil robber barons, dictators, and mafia bosses have a boss, whether they acknowledge Him or not. And He will repay, and will protect the weak and the fatherless.

Psalm 12
Psalm 12 emphasizes more the actual speaking of the boastful. This theme, present in previous psalms, but more clearly emphasized in Psalm 12, builds until the end when it sounds a mournful note: 'On every side the wicked prowl, as vileness is exalted among the children of man' (verse 8, ESV). But though this psalm ends in a kind of desolate, plaintive cry, it is all within the context of David's confidence in God's power and goodness.

The previous verse said, 'You, O LORD, will keep them; you will guard us from this generation forever' (verse 7, ESV). The boastful claims of the wicked, who are 'this generation' – this type of person who boasts – will not threaten ultimately God's people, for God Himself will protect His people from the boastful. This psalm is a prayer and a confident assurance that God will so protect. 'Save, O LORD, for the godly one is gone; for the faithful have vanished from among the children of man. Everyone utters lies to his neighbor; with flattering lips and a double heart they speak' (verses 1-2, ESV). It is these lying words and flattering lips from which David was asking God to save him.

This is what it means to be boastful (in a negative sense): to use your tongue to manipulate other people, and to do so with brazen arrogance, irrespective of breaking trust with what was possibly spoken in confidence, or the maliciousness of the intention from the heart. David prayed, 'May the LORD cut off all flattering lips, the tongue that makes great boasts, those who say, "With our tongue we will prevail, our lips are with us; who is master over us?"' (verses 3-4, ESV) Once again, the boastful person, being boastful in a negative sense, was not only saying boastful things about himself. The boastful person was using his words to gain control over other people, the vulnerable and the naïve. He was so confident in his words that he thought he could use them to hide evil and to accomplish what he wanted. This confidence came from a basic rejection of God as his master (or any other human lord, like David, as his human king as well): 'Who is master over us?' And God's compassion and initiative about this situation *arise* because He discerned that it was these vulnerable poor who were being exploited. '"Because the poor are plundered, because the needy groan, I will now arise," says the LORD; "I will place him in the safety for which he longs"' (verse 5, ESV).

Contrast, then, God's Word with these flattering, manipulative, arrogant, poisonous, dangerous, exploitive, and boastful words: 'The words of the LORD are pure words, like silver refined in a furnace on the ground, purified seven times' (verse 6, ESV). God's Word – and in particular His promise to rescue the 'poor', the humble dependent upon Him in their awareness of their own need – is so pure it is like especially purified gold, removed of all its dross, over and over again seven times pure. Boastful words, by contrast – boastful in a negative sense – will not then finally prevail over this pure gold of God's Word. There is no victory from evil-speak.

Psalm 38
Psalm 38 also has a description of boasting in a negative sense, but this boasting is in quite a different context and carries, therefore, a significantly different flavour to it. This is a penitential psalm, at least in the sense (as popularly conceived) that David was confessing his sins and asking God to save him from his sins. He was very aware of what he had done wrong, was deeply sorry for it, and longed for God's salvation. He asked that God not rebuke or discipline him: 'O LORD, rebuke me not in your anger, nor discipline me in your wrath!' (verse 1, ESV) He was asking that God would have mercy on him and not be hard against him for the sins that David knew that he had committed. David was deeply aware of what he had done wrong: he used powerful pictures to describe his sense of the wrongness of his sins. The conviction of God was like 'arrows' sinking into him. As a warrior who had no doubt seen arrows cut into flesh, this was a powerful way of describing the reality of conviction of sin.

Also, God's 'hand' had come down on him – a heavy hand, a hand perhaps of discipline? (verse 2). He felt his 'bones' had no 'health (verse 3). His iniquities had gone over his head; that is, they were like a 'heavy burden' weighing him down, pushing him down, they were in fact 'too heavy' for him (verse 4). The wounds from those arrows 'stink and fester'; gangrene and sickness were growing from the sin and its consequences (verse 5). He went about 'mourning' all day long (verse 6). There was 'no soundness' in his flesh; his physical body was sick because of the conviction of his sin (verse 7). He was 'feeble and crushed' (verse 8). His very heart was out of beat, racing, pounding: 'my heart throbs' (verse 10). He could not see right, his eyes seemed dim; his conviction and sense of shame over what he had done were making his physical eyesight ineffective: 'the light of my eyes – it also has gone from me' (verse 10, ESV).

But what was worse was that this was leaving him open to the attacks, taunts and recriminations of his enemies. They sensed weakness, and they were going in for the kill. 'Those who seek my life lay their snares' (verse 12, ESV). Because of David's sense of moral failure, he was unable to exercise significant moral leadership against his enemies: 'I have become like a man who does not hear, and in whose mouth are no rebukes' (verse 14, ESV). Finally, he cried out that despite all of this, his deepest longings were for God Himself: 'But for you, O LORD, do I wait; it is you, O Lord my God, who will answer' (verse 15, ESV).

Why was he so confident that God would answer? What gave him the assurance that, despite his sins, despite the weakness of his physical body, despite the vulnerability of his political situation, God would answer and rescue him? It was because of boasting: most particularly because of David's attitude to the negative boasting of his enemies. 'For I said, "Only let them not rejoice over me, who boast against me when my foot slips!"' (verse 16, ESV). David's heart was 'only' that his enemies would not use their tongues – their evil, flattering, recriminatory, attacking speech – to vaunt themselves over him and therefore God who anointed him. It was David's attitude toward his enemies' claim to be on the right side, to vaunt themselves over him, which showed David that his heart was truly in the right place, and that he could be sure that God would not let such flattering lips, such negative boasting, prevail.

Boasting, then, in this psalm is the kind of activity that people rejoice in when they see others fail. They try to make the most of someone else's failure for their own good and the other person's further failure. It is disgusting; it disgusted David. Such boasting is against God's will. David was sure, then, that God would step in and rescue him from such attacks.

Psalm 49

Psalm 49 is a call to 'both low and high, rich and poor' (Psalm 49:1-2, ESV) to understand the truth about riches, success, pomp, human fame, and glory. The psalmist concluded, 'Man in his pomp yet without understanding is like the beasts that perish' (verse 20, ESV). This is because however rich or successful you become, even if whole countries are named after you ('though they called lands by their own names,' verse 11, ESV), no one can ransom the grave. And to have all this success, glory, fame, and money without having 'understanding' – meaning understanding about God and His ways – is the ultimate idiocy. 'Like sheep they are appointed for Sheol; death shall be their shepherd, and the upright shall rule over them in the morning. Their form shall be consumed in Sheol, with no place to dwell' (verse 14, ESV). Instead, those who trust in God can be confident that 'God will ransom my soul from the power of Sheol, for he will receive me' (verse 15, ESV).

So the psalmist compared what appeared to be the best life with what actually was the best life. He compared riches, glory, and fame – without God – with life with God, and realized that the wise person does not put his trust in riches. 'Man in his pomp yet without understanding is like the beasts that perish,' he concluded in verse 20. To be wealthy, successful, and yet not know God is to be no better than a brute beast, like a cow, a dog or a donkey. You live, you die, and then there is 'Sheol'. Only for those who 'understand', who know and trust God, is there a different, truly glorious, reality.

In the middle of this psalm, there is a question, a question that the psalmist (in this case 'the Sons of Korah' according to the ascription) asked of himself. 'Why should I fear in times of trouble, when the iniquity of those who cheat me surrounds me, those who trust in their wealth and boast of the abundance of their riches?' (verses 5-6, ESV). Here the boasting is plainly negative: the people were boasting of how rich they were, and in this case, these boasting people were causing the psalmist trouble, and cheating him; they were his enemies. They were conspiring against him in some way, and the activity that characterized them was one of boastful arrogance because of the 'abundance of their riches'. In this case, the boasting appeared to be specifically located in money or riches. It was about wealth or resources, lands and titles, and gold and silver.

Plainly, an individual who is well-heeled and also seriously rich has (in human terms) many resources that can protect him from the 'slings and arrows of outrageous fortune'. When such an individual is arraigned against you, he can use those resources not only to protect himself but also to attack you. In modern terms, he can hire the best lawyer, find the best private detectives, pay for the best advertising, bring on board the most skilled staff. There is ample reason to fear if a multi-billionaire decides that he has beef with you. If you find that such a person is cheating you, then it would in most people's minds be clear that the safest option would be to run and hide, and find something else to do and somewhere else to do it – a long way away from the mega-rich individual who has decided that he wants this particular corner of the market. Cut a deal, get away, back down. If you cannot beat them, join them. And there would be ample reason to fear, too.

But the psalmist did not fear – or at least he asked himself a question which suggested that he might fear, but was gathering strength to look on life differently. Basically, he looked at life from God's perspective. The boasting of the arrogant, boastful, foolish rich man, while scary at one level, when looked at from the point of view of God Himself, becomes just plain silly. 'Truly no man can ransom another, or give to God the price of his life' (verse 7, ESV). No matter how much money you have, you cannot use it to pay off God or give enough money so that you never have to die and face God and His judgment. 'For the ransom of their life is costly and can never suffice, that he should live on forever and never see the pit' (verses 8-9, ESV).

With this perspective – that of life seen from God's point of view – the psalmist gathered various reasons and arguments for himself, to end up realizing that actually the person who was in trouble was the rich man who had no understanding of God. He was like a beast going down to slaughter, not the psalmist who had far fewer resources and was being cheated by the rich man.

Money without understanding of God is living like an animal that will die. The boasting of such a person – negative boasting – is not only impolite, improper, or indelicate, it is an outward evidence of just how ridiculous the situation is. He is like a person falling off a cliff to the ground beneath holding onto a briefcase of money, shouting boastfully to everyone who watches, 'Look how much money I've got! I got it from him; I cheated him and I won,' as he falls to his doom. The negative boasting here was part of what could cause the psalmist to fear, but observing it in the context of who God is, from God's perspective, moved him past boasting to another truly real attitude towards life and money, and to what real success is in life and death.

What is doubly ironic is not only that these boasts, from God's perspective, were truly foolish, but that, despite all the evidence, other people still approved of these boasts. This is a common human experience. A person who boasts of his greatness and then dies – his greatness disappearing and dissipating with that death – still nonetheless has followers who approve of not only the way he lived, but the kind of boasts he made while he was alive. The psalmist put it like this, 'This is the path of those who have foolish confidence; yet after them people approve of their boasts' (verse 13, ESV). Despite all the evidence – despite the unanswerable reality of death that hangs over the head of those who have no hope but for this life – after such individuals have died, people write books lauding them, tell stories praising them, and fail to learn from the truth about their life and death.

Boasting then is a perennial condition, a way of shielding ourselves psychologically from the ticking time-bomb of the grave's imminent reality. The individual boasts of his lands and the cities named after him. Those who watch that 'success' boast of it and celebrate in it, at a distance one step removed, soaking up the edges of the limelight, not realizing (or wanting to realize) that it all ends so obviously in defeat. And so, the psalmist tells us, 'Be not afraid when a man becomes rich, when the glory of his house increases. For when he dies he will carry nothing away; his glory will not go down after him' (verses 16-17, ESV). Do not be intimidated by this kind of negative boasting.

Psalm 52

Psalm 52 focuses more on the actual speaking side of negative boasting. The context that the ascription gives the psalm is of the famous occasion when David was betrayed by Doeg (1 Sam. 21 – 22). David, on the run, had gone to Ahimelech the high priest. David claimed that he and his men were on a mission from Saul, and they ate the special shewbread because they were hungry. David also was given the sword of Goliath, the same sword that David had won all those years ago when he began his 'career' as a servant of God in his glorious battle against Goliath. Now David took that sword, having fed himself and his men on the shewbread, and left.

But Saul found out about David's whereabouts from Doeg, one of Saul's staff, who told Saul about David and what had happened. In a fury, Saul had the high priest Ahimelech killed. The soldiers refused to kill the priest, and so Saul turned to Doeg who killed Ahimelech and the entire company with him. Then Saul attacked the city of Nob, which was the city of the priests, and killed all the families of the priests – men, women, and children. Only Abiathar escaped, and he fled for safety to David.

So when David, in Psalm 52, spoke of the 'boast of evil' of one (verse 1), this evil of which he spoke was tangibly real and revolting. Nonetheless, David in the psalm did not speak much of the bloodshed, and only alluded to the 'evil'. The focus instead was on the tongue: the malicious words that can cause such damage to so many people. 'Your tongue plots destruction, like a sharp razor, you worker of deceit' (verse 2, ESV). Again, this speaking came out of an evil heart, 'You love evil more than good, and lying more than speaking what is right' (verse 3, ESV). David pulled no punches in recalling and recording the plain evil of what had happened – all because a word was spoken with malicious intent to cause harm, and that word was followed up with action that caused yet more harm in its wake.

It would appear that the victory was to the evil workers, those who were on the side of Doeg and Saul. It would have been passingly easy to assume that God was nowhere to be found, that God had turned His back on David – for even those who unwittingly helped him, entirely innocent of any part in any so-called plot against King Saul, were taken out and killed and their families and friends with them. Surely God was against David. Or, surely God did not care and evil would be flagrantly boasted of and pursued, and God was either not powerful enough to do anything about it or not loving enough to care. When a whole small city was wiped out in total destruction, with only one man escaping, the conclusion that those who supported David were on the losing side would not have been a hard conclusion to come to.

But David managed to move beyond such all-too-apparent failure and vicious violence, to give it but a passing glance, and to stare at the Almighty. 'But God', he writes, 'will break you down forever' (verse 5, ESV). Their victory was total but brief; God's victory would be truly total as well as eternal. 'He will snatch and tear you from your tent; he will uproot you from the land of the living' (verse 5, ESV).

Such language of vengeance is distinctly uncomfortable for those of us who read it in the comfort of our own centrally-heated homes. But for someone who had just seen such devastation – caused, he must have felt, at least in part by his own actions – it represented the true feelings of the one so devastated. Who would speak up for the downtrodden? Who would speak up for the suckling babe impaled on a spear; the teenager whose eyes were just beginning to open to life's possibilities; the grandfather who had served God well, but was now brutally cast into a pit along with the dogs? David would speak up for them, and God would act in justice on their behalf. This was his conviction: evil boasting would not outlast God's justice.

In fact, 'The righteous shall see and fear, and shall laugh at him, saying, "See the man who would not make God his refuge, but trusted in the abundance of his riches and sought refuge in his own destruction!"' (verses 6-7, ESV). The person who thought he would have safety by causing such destructive devastation, that person (it was now Doeg or Saul of which he spoke) would be laughable. He would be a figure of fun; he would be on the receiving end of taunts.

There are few things that a bully fears more than being laughed at. The evil workers would get their Charlie Chaplin moment: it was Chaplin who memorably painted Hitler as a figure of fun in *The Great Dictator*. Kill all you want: one day you will not only be defeated, but the righteous will be vindicated eternally and you will not; you will also be a figure of ridicule. It is not only wrongheaded to trust in riches and violence rather than in God and doing what is right, it is also stupid – stupid like the most absurd situation comedy, loudest joke, silliest song that you can think of.

Then David concluded beautifully with the contrasting fate of those who, like him, trusted in God. 'But I am like a green olive tree in the house of God. I trust in the steadfast love of God forever and ever. I will thank you forever, because you have done it. I will wait for your name, for it is good, in the presence of the godly' (verses 8-9, ESV). Because David trusted in the 'steadfast love of God' – His covenant love that was sure and certain – he had 'forever' on his horizon, 'forever and ever', an everlasting delight in God with God's people. He was like a green tree in the house of God, bearing fruit – supple, growing and fertile, giving shade from the heat of the noonday sun, and constantly nourished and nourishing. For he was in the 'presence of the godly'.

All this despite the 'boast of evil' that led to such evil, and which came from that 'mighty man' (verse 1). All this because David trusted (made his boast, in a positive sense) in the Lord God who is not only Almighty but eternally loving. A boast, in a negative sense, can do very great harm. But in God's power and compassion, those who trust in Him will not be overturned, despite the power of an evil boast.

Psalm 75
Psalm 75 is more descriptive in direction and tone, and less of a bombastic tirade against the evil, the boastful, and the arrogant. There is in this psalm a note of calm certainty, a certainty that centres on the description of God's declaration regarding the boastful in verses 4 and 5, ESV. 'I say to the boastful, "Do not boast," and to the wicked, "Do not lift up your horn; do not lift up your horn on high, or speak with haughty neck."' Once again, the negative boasting was associated with a particular kind of speaking, a haughtiness or a lifting up of the self (implicitly) against God and His ways. Here that haughtiness was dramatically personified in the physical attribution that often accompanies boasting. There was a puffing out of the chest in pride and here, specifically, a lifting up of the neck, stretching it out, forward and upward – saying with the body that the owner of the body was master of his fate and was in charge, and that his words are the words that matter.

Despite this descriptive tone in the heart of the psalm, there is nothing bashful about the psalm itself. It is confident and begins with assured thanksgiving. 'We give thanks to you, O God; we give thanks, for your name is near. We recount your wondrous deeds' (verse 1, ESV). The 'wondrous deeds' here are those actions of God which exalt the righteous but pull down the wicked. The psalmist declared that success or exaltation, or being 'lifted up', was not a matter of the happenstance of geography, or where one happened to have been born. It was all down to God's action and initiative. 'For not from the east or from the west and not from the wilderness comes lifting up, but it is God who executes judgment, putting down one and lifting up another' (verses 6-7, ESV).

This 'putting down' of one and 'lifting up' of another is not, though, random: it is personal and the personal action of God, not a matter of fate, or even our own human initiative; it is God's initiative. But still there is a declared rationale, purpose or set of expectations regarding such 'lifting up' and 'putting down', upon which we can bank our lives. 'But I will declare it forever; I will sing praises to the God of Jacob. All the horns of the wicked I will cut off, but the horns of the righteous shall be lifted up' (verses 9-10, ESV). Those then who are 'lifted up', according to God's revealed will, shall be those who are righteous. And those then who are 'cut off', will be the wicked. They may have 'horns'; that is, they may appear strong and mighty. But the true end of things, whether being lifted up or pushed down, will not be determined by human might or brilliance, human origins or location, neighbourhoods or countries ('from the east or from the west'). It will be determined by God, and God has revealed that His action will be on the basis of whether someone is righteous or wicked.

What constitutes righteousness and what constitutes wickedness is not here revealed, but it is defined by the character of God as revealed in the rest of the Bible: specifically in the context of the Old Testament in Moses' Law, and fulfilled ultimately in the context of the whole Bible in the person of Jesus Christ. Those who are lifted up will be those who follow Jesus – who model their lives upon and put their faith in Him – and imitate Christ. Such righteous ones will be lifted up by God.

As for the boastful, however – those who indulge in negative boasting, who have horns of strength about which they are so proud, and who speak with 'haughty neck' – they will not be lifted up. There is no amount of finery, clever or boastful words, or apparent human success which can overturn God's determination to exalt the righteous and to pull down the wicked.

Psalm 94

Psalm 94 has no such inner calm. It was a rage against those who are attacking God's people. It was a cry to God to hear what was being said, to see what was being done, and to take action against the wicked. The psalmist knew that truly God does hear: 'Understand, O dullest of the people! Fools, when will you be wise? He who planted the ear, does he not hear? He who formed the eye, does he not see?' (verses 8-9, ESV). Surely this God who planned the faculties of seeing and hearing can see and hear what is going on, so why should horrible things be happening to God's people? In this instance it has something to do with discipline. 'Blessed is the man whom you discipline, O LORD, and whom you teach out of your law, to give him rest from days of trouble, until a pit is dug for the wicked' (verses 12-13, ESV). God was using these events against His people as a way of refining them, and indeed planning to give them rest, and in the end the pit would be dug for those who were attacking God's people.

But who were these attackers of God's people? They were 'proud' (verse 2). They were 'wicked' (Ps. 94:3). They 'pour out their arrogant words' and were 'evildoers'; what is more, such actions were ones in which they boast (verse 4). They were so confident in their own victory, so assured of their own untouchable status – that no one would catch them, control them, bring them to heel or defeat them –

that they made no attempt to hide what they were doing. No, they trumpeted it, they were proud about it internally, but also they were pridefully talking about it externally. They poured out these 'arrogant words'. This was not an occasional comment here or there; it was a flood of arrogant speech. In this, then, they boasted.

In the face of this unembarrassed, overly confident, apparently victorious evil, the psalmist declared that he had almost fallen. But 'when I thought, "My foot slips," your steadfast love, O LORD, held me up' (verse 18, ESV). The love of God kept him in the face of these arrogant, boastful, and wicked men who were out to destroy God's people. God Himself was his 'stronghold' and his 'refuge' (verse 22). He was safe and secure, and those who attacked God's people, God 'will bring back on them their iniquity' (verse 23, ESV). In an extraordinary irony, the attacks and evil aimed against God's people would be turned to fall on those who were planning them and indeed boasting about them.

Psalm 97

Psalm 97, finally, has a negative boast that is specifically related to idol worship. 'All worshipers of images are put to shame, who make their boast in worthless idols; worship him, all you gods!' (verse 7, ESV).

This psalm makes it plain, then, that at root, the issue of boasting is an issue of the orientation of either correct or false worship. In whom do we boast? That is the question which frames whether boasting is negative or positive. But though it is related to worship – a matter of idolatry on the one hand or authentic worship of the true God on the other – there is a one-to-one correlation between boasting and worship, whether negative or positive. Boasting is a particular kind of soul-orientation; it is a certain sort of adulation.

So Psalm 97 lifts up a view of God as high and exalted, majestic, tumultuous almost, fearsome and loud in every sense. It is a matter of what causes our rejoicing: 'The LORD reigns, let the earth rejoice; let the many coastlands be glad!' (verse 1, ESV). Because the Lord reigns, it is then a cause of rejoicing for those who rightly discern the goodness and majesty of God. In whom (or in what) do we rejoice? That is the question that frames whether we are boasting negatively or positively.

It is not a mild-mannered, bashful kind of rejoicing and boasting either: 'Clouds and thick darkness are all around him; righteousness and justice are the foundation of his throne. Fire goes before him and burns up his adversaries all around' (verses 2-3, ESV). In a brief glance, God is shown to be scary – as scary as a storm flashing lightning – as well as solid as the foundations of mountains. This is a solid, yet fiery and stormy rejoicing! 'His lightnings light up the world; the earth sees and trembles' (verse 4, ESV).

What is it that makes us scared, that causes us to tremble? That's the question that lies behind negative or positive boasting. Are we most scared by the judgment of our peers, the fear of appearing foolish, unfashionable or unintelligent? Or are we most scared of the flashing, brilliant justice of the Almighty? That kind of question will reveal in whom (or in what) we are boasting and rejoicing.

This glory is not hidden: 'The heavens proclaim his righteousness, and all the peoples see his glory' (verse 6, ESV). For those with eyes to see, nature itself reveals God, and there will be people who see this glory from every single nation and tribe. The church, God's people, Zion, rejoices boldly: 'Zion hears and is glad, and the daughters of Judah rejoice, because of your judgments, O LORD' (verse 8, ESV). God's people discern this true reality all around them, the reality of the scary, beautiful, joyful majesty of the great God over all [false] gods (verse 9).

The psalmist ended by calling on God's people to act in a certain way as a result of these bold truths that he had proclaimed. He wanted God's people to 'hate evil' (verse 10). If God is like this, if He is this powerful, and this in favour of justice, then we are well-advised to avoid and shun evil. In particular, when such evil appears attractive and whispers in our ear that 'if you cannot beat them, join them', the psalmist reminded God's people that God 'preserves the lives of his saints; he delivers them from the hand of the wicked' (verse 10, ESV). No true evil, no final calamitous evil, that pushes past death to eternity will ever mark the destiny of God's people. There are fates worse that physical death, and God's people are preserved from those worst fates forever.

What is more, they have an unending source of brilliant, bright joy (boasting in a positive sense!). 'Light is sown for the righteous, and joy for the upright in the heart' (verse 11, ESV). Not every individual among God's people is always overflowing with joy, but the way to find joy is to pursue God and His right path with all our heart. Therefore, 'Rejoice in the LORD, O you righteous, and give thanks to his holy name!' (verse 12, ESV). In the midst of this loud rejoicing, there lie the 'worshipers of images' who are 'put to shame' because they 'make their boast in worthless idols' (verse 7). The psalmist shows us that we are to boast in something, or someone, and in whom we boast will determine our joy and our destiny.

Proverbs

The Book of Proverbs has a less expansive description of boasting, more practical in tone, but equally definitive for what is negative boasting (and by contrast what is positive boasting).

Proverbs 20:14 depicts that aphorism well-known to anyone who has tried to haggle in a marketplace. '"Bad, bad," says the buyer, but when he goes away, then he boasts' (ESV). The first rule of getting a good deal in a marketplace where you are allowed to haggle for the price is not to expose how interested you are in the product you wish to buy. You should show little, if any, interest, and when asked whether you want to buy, describe the product as something hardly worth your time and attention, and note that there are better versions elsewhere. You should not give the seller any hope that you think well of the product at all. And when it comes to the actual bartering, you should start low, far lower than you can possibly hope to get the product for, then only move up inches by complaining. Eventually you hope to end up with a price that you know is far less than the product is worth. You should keep muttering about what an expensive over-the-top price you are paying for the product, all the while you are completing the transaction, muttering 'bad, bad'. But then when you are out of sight and out of earshot of the seller, you can turn to your companion and with a big smile say, 'Wow, that was a great deal!' and boast of what you have, and for what an amazing deal you got it. Is this positive or negative boasting? Positive for the buyer, negative for the seller!

The point of the proverb is to describe, in a brief axiom, the kind of activity that would give wisdom to someone attempting to buy (or indeed to sell) anything to anyone. There is a tendency to undervalue the product you are buying, as well as to overvalue the product you are selling. As is typical with so many Proverbs, the writer was not making a moral judgment; he was merely describing what is. For our purposes, this proverb shows that boasting extends beyond the merely religious to the practical and business world. In other words, we have to boast in something, be proud about something, in all our contexts and human interactions. The question is: in what do we boast?

Proverbs 25:14 is similarly a little ambivalent whether the boasting it describes is positive or negative, though the impression is that it is mainly negative because certainly in the instance described it is negative. The proverb put it like this: 'Like clouds and wind without rain is one who boasts of gifts never given'. The image of a cloud forming, the sky darkening, the wind gathering strength, but yet no rain ever arriving – in an area of the world where rain is a much-cherished commodity – suggests promise without delivery. It leads to disappointment. This man is like that; he 'boasts' of a gift that he never actually manages to give to the person who is looking for the gift.

Whether any and all boasting regarding giving a gift is wrong, or whether only boasting of a gift and not giving it is wrong, is not clear. It leans towards suggesting that boasting of giving gifts itself is wrong, as if it is saying that the kind of person who talks big about giving gifts is quite often the kind of person who actually doesn't end up giving them. If you are *really* going to give someone a gift, then you will let the gift do the talking. You will not need to speak big about the gift if the gift itself is going to be big and impressive. If, however, what you are after is the effect of having given a gift, without actually needing to pay the expense of giving it, then it is quite likely that you will not be satisfied only with mentioning it; you will want to boast about it.

Certainly, if you are not planning on giving the gift, but want the other person to think you are giving the gift, then you will need to boast about the gift. There is, it seems, something about this boasting which by its nature is likely to promise more than it can deliver. It is a human way of puffing out the chest or standing tall to look impressive, to intimidate, or to get further up the pecking order of human society. The Proverb then is observing this tendency in order to warn the wise man against being taken in by it. People who talk big about what they can do quite likely are not actually able to do it because their talk, the impressiveness of the effect, is what they are after, and if they are good at making it sound impressive, then they may have already achieved their end goal – impressing you, not giving you a gift!

Proverbs 27:1 is more straightforward. 'Do not boast about tomorrow, for you do not know what a day may bring' (ESV). We are being told here that overconfidence about the future is foolish because no one can safely be certain of the future. This itself is a wise consideration given how often people attempt to draw trend lines from the present to the future, or indulge in futuristic kinds of predictions about what will happen to the economy or this industry or that business given the present tendencies. The proverb is telling us that such certainties about the future are pointless. We cannot know what even tomorrow will bring, let alone next year or a decade hence.

The Bible is not against planning. Joseph was one famous example of a wise man who stored in the good years to be prepared for the bad years. But the Bible is against acting as if the future were a foregone conclusion. This uncertainty about the future is what makes sport such a tantalizing feast. The best team often wins, but not always. The final whistle at the end of the game is the only point at which you can truly be certain of the result (when the result is in the past, not in the future).

But this proverb is not only saying that we cannot be certain about the future; it is also saying specifically, 'Do not boast about tomorrow.' It has in mind the person who has moved from the wise uncertainty about the future, to the more foolish confidence about the future, to the downright idiotic boasting about tomorrow. This is the kind of sports star who is so confident of his performance that he lets his trash-talking ahead of the game define his view of the future, and then may well fall down in flames as he crashes and burns during the actual game itself.

Boasting about tomorrow is not only foolish because we do not know what tomorrow will bring; it is exposing that foolishness to ridicule when your boasting proves to be foolish. You cannot know the future, you cannot know what will happen tomorrow, so don't boast about it. This proverb does not say specifically that all boasting is negative, but it does, in particular, tell us that boasting, overconfidence, public shouts of victory before the victory has happened, is a mistake of a serious kind because it risks showing your confidence to be groundless in the actual event that takes place tomorrow – tomorrow which lives in a land beyond human prediction.

Isaiah

No prophet used the language of boasting in his denunciations (at least ones in a positive sense, as we shall see) more than the prophet Isaiah. Isaiah prophesied when Judah was first relatively safe under the protectorship of Assyria, and later threatened partly due to its ill-advised temporary alliance with Egypt. Assyria was then roundly defeated under King Hezekiah, whose remaining years were in peace, before Manasseh king of Judah. Isaiah was a prophet during the reigns of King Uzziah (perhaps beginning shortly before he died), Jotham, Ahaz, and Hezekiah. Isaiah's writings are justly famous, the Book of Isaiah often thought to be the greatest prophetic book in the Old Testament.

Isaiah 10:12 prophesied this coming doom for the king of Assyria. He thought his ascent to greatness was his own doing, rather than under the lordship of the Lord of heaven and earth, and his arrogance was his own undoing. God 'will punish the speech of the arrogant heart of the king of Assyria and the boastful look in his eyes' (Isa. 10:12, ESV). Interestingly, the 'boastful' aspect that was being denounced was not actually speech. In this instance it was about a 'look'. There was a haughty, boastful aspect to the king of Assyria, which revealed itself in his lordly visage, and in particular in the way that his eyes were disdainful of others and lifted up himself in his own mind. Whether the king was known for his particular way of looking, or whether this was merely poetic language that described the special sort of arrogance and prideful way of being boastful that was peculiar to this king, is immaterial. The point here is that this kind of arrogance and boasting is an offence to God.

What is this kind of boasting? It is to think that success is your own doing. The king of Assyria thought that his victories were due to his canniness, his power or his strength, when in reality they were all part of God's long deliberate plan for His people. God would discipline His people and use Assyria for that end, but the king was not to think that thereby his activities were his own doing in any ultimate or real sense. He should not write the book on how to be great and attribute it to his own special technique; instead he should simply say it was God's doing. He was arrogant, he was boastful, and it was obvious to anyone who ever saw him that this was what he thought of himself. God will not put up with it and will show the king who is truly boss, who is truly the King – God Himself.

This change of perspective is made clear in a shock of rhetoric with a startling reverse metaphor: 'Shall the axe boast over him who hews with it, or the saw magnify itself against him who wields it? As if a rod should wield him who lifts it, or as if a staff should lift him who is not wood!' (Isa. 10:15, ESV). For all his apparent success, the king of Assyria was nothing more than an axe, a rod or a staff in the hands of God. How deliciously ridiculous it is, then, for this 'rod' to boast against the one who lifted it and used it!

The change of perspective in this verse also reveals the hidden inner dynamic of the word 'boast', in this context at least. To boast here means to magnify against. The king of Assyria was magnifying himself against God. He was, in effect, saying that he was God and that God was not! Negative boasting then is not merely pride, arrogance, or hubris; it is an overt, public, confident claim that the one boasting is really the one in charge of the events and destinies of his life. To boast in this regard means then to claim to be God. It is not merely idolatry, it is 'theocide'; it is an attempt to kill off God and take what is only rightly God's to be yours. Pride, hubris, and arrogance then is implicitly the beginning of such boasting: it is in essence a claim to be master of your own fate. And boasting takes that seed and grows it to be a tree of shouty, declarative, and arrogant boasting against God, magnifying itself over and above the one true God.

Later Isaiah gave an oracle against Moab, the people who historically lived to the East of the Jordan, who the Bible tells us were descended from an incestuous union of Lot with his daughters (Gen. 19:37-38). Their relations with Israel were sometimes more peaceful than others. David's ancestors on Ruth's side came from Moab, and he left his parents in the safekeeping of the king of Moab at one point (1 Sam. 22:3-4). Later, though, they were defeated by David and made to bring tribute to him (2 Sam. 8:2).

Isaiah's oracle about Moab in Isaiah 15 and 16 probably surveyed and had in view several different crises that faced Moab. Because Moab was viewed as a cousin nation, despite the disreputable nature of their origin, Moab in the midst of their crises went to Zion, and to David's king, the king to come in David's line, to ask for help. They were in severe distress, and they went to the king to ask for asylum, shelter for their refugees, and protection. They had offers of tribute to bring to the king as a gift to sweeten their request and make it more likely to be acceptable. However, the price of their admission to the protection of David's king was acceptance of David's king as their king – a price they could not and would not pay. In this context Isaiah lamented that their prideful refusal to face facts and humble themselves under the king would lead to their downfall. 'We have heard of the pride of Moab – how proud he is! – of his arrogance, his pride, and his insolence; in his idle boasting he is not right' (Isa. 16:6, ESV).

Boasting here was in the sense of being unwilling to accept reality. Their boast was a prideful confidence that they could do it their own way, and while they acknowledged their desperate need of Zion's help, they were unwilling to submit to Zion's king as the necessary price for such help.

Boasting here, then, is the outward sign of a heart unable and unwilling to submit to God's anointed. They would not do what was required to be rescued, even though they recognized the need of rescue! 'Therefore let Moab wail for Moab' (Isa. 16:7, ESV). The heart of the problem for Moab was the problem of their heart: prideful refusal to submit to God and to God's ways and to God's anointed. Judgment and destruction were the inevitable result. Beware of this kind of negative boasting! Instead, we are to humble ourselves under God and under His anointed in order to receive His protection and rescue.

Isaiah 20 also describes negative boasting, now in the context of Egypt and Cush (the Ethiopian dynasty that was in power). Isaiah enacted an oracle against Egypt, going about 'stripped' (as NIV) or 'naked' (Isa. 20:2, ESV) in order to indicate the wretched state of the refugees that would come. Ashdod, encouraged by Egypt, had rebelled against Assyria. Egypt was encouraging others, susceptible Jerusalem enamoured by Egypt as well, to rise up and rebel against Assyria. But as was typical in the eventuality, Egypt reneged on its promises, and Ashdod and allies were led as exiles and disastrously defeated by the mighty king of Assyria and his number two commander, the 'commander in chief' (Isa. 20:1, ESV). And so, 'Then they shall be dismayed and ashamed because of Cush their hope and of Egypt their boast' (Isa. 20:5, ESV). Their shame was the failure of their attempted rebellion, and the failure of their fallacious alliance, but it was made worse by their over-commitment to it, their 'hope' and their 'boast.' The 'boast' was the outward expression of their certainty that their alliance with Egypt was the right geo-political movement, when in reality the whole thing was useless and pointless and Egypt was as unreliable as usual at this time. And such 'boasting' in the wrong thing would lead to the misery of refugees, exiles, and captives. Be careful, then, in what and in whom you boast!

There is, then, a lot of negative boasting in the Old Testament! Each situation and circumstance gives colour to the meaning of the boasting in view, and is not readily summarized, nor is it possible to give justice to the idea behind them all merely by resorting to a dictionary series of definitions.

What are connecting themes for this negative boasting? First, it seems clear that humans are more than likely (perhaps inevitably?) going to boast in something. There is a need to have a focal point for our energies, pride and sense of belonging, and to celebrate something or someone. The boasting is not always therefore negative because boasting itself is negative, but because this kind of boasting is negative: boasting in the wrong thing or the wrong person. Much of the boasting is not critiqued because of the way of boasting itself; the arrogance is surely testified as being wrong in itself. But there is another element, which is simply that the confidence is in the wrong place, and therefore it is wrong because it is wrongly placed.

Second, behind this kind of negative boasting there seems often to be a basic heart orientation away from God. It is a 'theocide', a confident, overt proclamation or boast that the persons boasting are in charge of their destiny, not God. It is blatant and takes the human rebellion against God to a practical and emotional extreme; it is doing something about that rebellion against God, and magnifying against God.

Third, because of this extremity, this kind of boasting appears to be particularly offensive to God. Cultures or individuals that are now engaging in negative boasting appear to be living too close to the express judgment of God. They are – to use a story from the Old Testament that is not explicitly linked to boasting, but nonetheless illustrates it – building a Tower of Babel. And God will notice and scatter. There is only God, and idolizing self will not long go unnoticed by the God of heaven and earth.

Positive use of boasting in the Old Testament

There are only two clear-cut instances of positive boasting in the Old Testament. This itself is worth pausing to consider. Given that there is a broader and more proportionate use of positive boasting in the New Testament, and that Paul's use of positive boasting is one apparent characteristic of his writing tone, why this disparity in the Old Testament? Is there an aspect in which the New Testament is being fulfilled with a far greater affectional confidence, because of the fulfillment in Christ, that makes it easier, better, and more common for believers to be able to boast in a positive sense, because of the Lord and what He has done?

As we will see, there are other stories in the Old Testament (beyond the mere surface level, obvious dictionary-defined use of 'boasting' as a word) that have positive boasting as their backdrop, so the disparity between the Old and New Testaments may not be quite as stark as it at first seems. However, the distinction is still obvious: while the New Testament glories in a more overt, much more common positive boasting (both in number and by comparison), for the Old Testament believer, overt examples of that kind of positive boasting, exultation, confidence are rare.

They do exist, though. The positive boasting – as an overt word 'boast', which in context implies something positive – is found first in Psalm 34. This psalm, according to its ascription, was written by David, when he managed to maneuver a rescue from Abimelech. The story that the ascription claims was at the backdrop to Psalm 34 is found in 1 Samuel 21. There, though, the king that is mentioned is called Achish. This is one of the old saws of Old Testament interpretation: is the ascription to Psalm 34 accurate? The easiest answer probably comes from Rashi, the Rabbinic medieval commentator, and other medieval exegetes, that 'Abimelech' was a name for a hereditary king (like 'Pharaoh' or 'Caesar' or the 'Tsar') rather than the actual personal name of the king, which was Achish.

At any rate, David feigned madness before this king. He was frightened that his reputation for being a dangerous warrior would mean that the king of Gath would kill him now that he had the chance – and so David pretended to be insane, and the king let him leave untouched and unharmed. This ruse was clever and quite extraordinary from the point of view David's later glory. David 'made marks on the doors of the gate and let his spittle run down his beard' (1 Sam. 21:13, ESV). His pawing at the gates, scratching at them like a wild beast, and drooling must have appeared to be in the most revolting and insane way.

Given this background, Psalm 34, then, rather remarkably advises straightforward honesty: 'Come, O children, listen to me; I will teach you the fear of the LORD. What man is there who desires life and loves many days, that he may see good? Keep your tongue from evil and your lips from speaking deceit. Turn away from evil and do good; seek peace and pursue it' (Ps. 34:11-14, ESV). Evidently, the contrast between David feigning madness and David saying that we are to keep our lips from 'speaking deceit' did not strike the canonical editors, nor David himself. Is it that David did not actually 'speak' deceit, but only deceived by his actions? Such hairsplitting seems unwarranted to the passion of the text in favour of simplicity and directness. Yet, at the same time the psalm is clear about the desperate situation in which David found himself. 'This poor man cried, and the LORD heard him and saved him out of all his troubles' (Ps. 34:6, ESV).

David was not the perfect man (that Christ was and is), and at times he, like some of the other biblical heroes, was forced to choose between the lesser of two evils – whereas Christ was always able to find a way out, and not do or speak evil or deceive in anyway. David's real psalm of praise is to the answer that God gave to his prayer. 'When the righteous cry for help, the LORD hears and delivers them out of all their troubles' (Ps. 34:17, ESV). His situation was terrible, but God looks on those who are broken: 'The LORD is near to the brokenhearted and saves the crushed in spirit' (Ps. 34:18, ESV). This does not mean that those who are following God, and therefore are among 'the righteous', are immune from difficulties. No, what it means is that those difficulties are not the final word: 'Many are the afflictions of the righteous, but the LORD delivers him out of them all' (Ps. 34:19, ESV).

In the midst of this psalm of praise for God's deliverance come these famous words: 'My soul makes its boast in the LORD; let the humble hear and be glad. Oh, magnify the LORD with me, and let us exalt his name together!' (Ps. 34:2-3, ESV). These two verses hold a world of theology and practical wisdom, passion, and commitment in their brief expanse. Notice that the boasting is so different from pride, hubris, and arrogance that it is in fact the 'humble' who will hear and rejoice.

How could this be? How could it be that the boasting man gives cause for the humble to rejoice? It is because of the goal of his boasting and the person in whom he boasts. This man's boasting is not in himself or his country, his attainments or his church, or his business or his family. This man's boasting is in God. As such, the humble, those who are all too aware that they do not have much about which to boast, can be glad. They too can boast in the Lord!

The ultimate, best, and only truly worthy end of boasting is in the Lord Himself. Any other focus of boasting is foolish and pointless. When you stand before a vicious king who has nothing but bloodshed in his eyes when he first sees your (his enemy's) face, and you pray and cry out for hope, and you find that God rescues you – well, then, you realize that the end of all life is to trust and boast in God. And the humble – those who have little else about which to boast, and who are less tempted to boast in the wrong things because they have less of those other things to be drawn after – can rejoice that God is the best, and only true end of boasting.

Notice also that this positive boasting is the verbal equivalent to 'magnify' and 'exalt'. To magnify is to make look great. It is to take something that others might not notice, because it seems to them to be too small, and magnify it, making it bigger and greater. It is to put something under the microscope and magnify it so that its true beauty and glory can be seen, when previously it was invisible to the naked eye.

So with God, we magnify Him, not to make Him bigger than He really is, and not because He needs our help to show He is big and good, but because when we see how good He really is, we want others to grasp His glory too. We do that by proclaiming, by carefully examining, and by increasing the magnifying perspective on God. We take His attributes, His love and justice, for instance, and we describe them in ways that others can begin to grasp how great God is. We take His actions, the exodus and the cross for instance, and we describe them in ways that others can begin to grasp how great is this God. We magnify Him, we make Him to be a little tiny bit closer to the true aperture through which we can glimpse His light, His volume, and His massive glory. We increase the lens until we begin to see Him a little bit closer to who He really is.

We also exalt Him. To exalt is to lift up. Sometimes things are so low down that we miss them. They are on the floor or beneath our sight. We are on a pedestal, on a platform, and the things that are down below we don't observe or think are significant. Sometimes it is things or people that are below us in the social pecking order, and we think of them as beneath us because of the way they talk or act. To exalt something is to lift it up so people can see it for its true value. A child may be playing a sport in a lower league, and if someone spots his potential and brings him up to the higher leagues, then he exalts that sports player so that people begin to take notice.

Similarly with God, though again He needs none of our exaltation, there are many who view God as beneath them. They think of Him as something for the 'great unwashed', the lower classes, as the opium of the people, a projection of wish fulfillment for the uneducated. And we exalt God: we show His actions in history and in Scripture are worthy of the attention of the greatest; how they are rational and reasonable, and far beyond our human rationality and common sense. We show that God is not the lowest common denominator of the lowest group in society, or to be left behind once society advances and becomes modernized, but is higher and better, and elevated above all, and therefore worthy of worship.

So this boasting in a positive sense is about a confident, deliberate, passionate, reasonable exaltation and magnification of who God is. It lifts Him up, as it were; it increases His aperture, as it were; it is a conscious verbal and practical attempt to show God as being the great God of all: higher, bigger and better than anything and anyone else. The soul – all that is in the human, his thinking and feeling, all locked into this spiritual dimension – boasts in the Lord. It lifts Him up and shows Him to be big and great, massive and glorious, and high and exalted. This is, Psalm 34 tells us, to boast in the Lord, so that we with the psalmist boast in God together. It has an evangelistic, communal, discipleship purpose: 'Let us exalt his name together!' (Ps. 34:3, ESV).

But the most famous Old Testament passage related to positive boasting is Jeremiah 9:23-24. It is worth quoting in full:

> This is what the LORD says: 'Let not the wise boast of their wisdom or the strong boast of their strength or the rich boast of their riches, but let the one who boasts boast about this: that they have the understanding to know me, that I am the LORD, who exercises kindness, justice and righteousness on earth, for in these I delight,' declares the LORD.

For good reason these words are well-known, for they not only poetically and beautifully counterbalance negative boasting with positive boasting, they also in summation describe the aim and goal of positive boasting. They are a call to avoid a certain kind of boasting, and instead to rejoice in another kind of boasting. They also identify the aspects of this positive boasting that we are to be focused upon – namely, understanding and knowing God personally and directly, being confident of, assured of, and intimately acquainted with God Himself.

Not only do these words poetically, with skill, describe positive boasting (as opposed to negative boasting), and not only do they focus on the particular goal and endpoint of this positive boasting (knowing God Himself), they also commend this positive boasting winsomely. Why boast in the Lord? Because of who God is! He exercises kindness, justice, and righteousness. And He does not do these things because He must, or out of a certain burden, or in a way that is not entirely commensurate with His true character. No, God actually *delights* in justice, kindness, and righteousness. Boast in God because He does these wonderful things, and because He is in Himself this sort of wonderful God who delights to do such wonderful things.

So these words are rightly famous, but they also give direction to our understanding of positive (and negative) boasting by the way they fall into place in the context of the Book of Jeremiah itself. Jeremiah was issuing a lengthy lament over Israel. They had forsaken God's law, and they had abandoned obedience to God: they had broken His covenant. Therefore, Jeremiah was preaching that the only possible outcome was discipline and judgment. Be warned! He preached a sort of parabolic dirge over Jerusalem in verses 17-21 of chapter 9. The women who were particularly skilled at mourning, the professional mourners, were to be brought forward and to begin to mourn over Jerusalem. It would be as if all the funeral directors in a city gathered together and formed a procession through their city with placards indicating that the city was effectively now dead! This is not exactly an upbeat message! In fact, it is a calculated shock treatment.

Then, suddenly, Jeremiah switched in verses 23-24. Why this abrupt change? Was there any logic between his lengthy denouncement and then these famous words about delighting in God and boasting in Him? Yes, there was, if we notice the key introductory statement about 'the wise'. Often as a people and a group move away from God, they hear apparently wise teaching and prudent words that suggest they should compromise with the surrounding culture, bow before the pagan deities, and be practical in their religion. *Don't go to extremes! Don't be difficult or controversial! Stick to going with the flow, for this is wisdom.* Not so, says Jeremiah. It is wise to boast in the Lord. So-called wisdom looks for who is the strongest and seeks to align with that. Or it looks for where the money is and seeks to align with those resources. This worldly human wisdom thinks that, above all, it is practical (wise) to align with strength and money: *If you can't beat them, join them. When all is said and done, more will be said than done, and so let's get practical and go where the money is and go where the power is.*

But hold on, said Jeremiah; such wisdom was forgetting a rather important, key variable. That is, God Himself. It is not actually wise to align with money and power, not when such money and power are godless. No, indeed, it is far, far wiser to align with the God of the whole universe. To know Him, that is wisdom – to realize His powerful, resourceful nature. And not only is He God; He is a God of mercy and kindness, justice and righteousness. He will do what is right, and He will do it in a way that is kind.

What could be better? Why would we boast in anything else other than God Himself? Because those who boast in other things don't really know God. They haven't really taken the time to consider who He is. They may say they believe in God, but if their wisdom is to go with the money and the power, even when that money and power is contrary to God's covenant, then it shows that at a basic level they have not understood who God is. They have not grasped that God is, and there is no other. Any amount of human money (be it billions and billions) or any amount of human power (be it military prowess and massive modern armies) is of nothing compared to the God who made it all, controls it, and will do as He wills. When presented with the choice between aligning with human power and money, or with God, it is much wiser to align with God. This is wise!

So to boast in the Lord, says Jeremiah, is the wise path. He wanted God's people to understand this, to grasp this, and to boast in God. To trust in Him, yes; to worship Him, yes. Then in the most practical of ways, to make choices and select options that most clearly reflect what it means to know God. To avoid an adulterous affair, because however attractive the moment of titillation may be, there will be a judgment to come, and to boast in God is wiser than to boast in sex. To avoid cheating a business partner, because however large may be the rewards, there will be judgment, and to boast in God is wiser than to boast in money. To avoid trampling under foot an enemy or hated rival out of bitter jealousy, because however much the moment of apparent victory may be pleasing, it will soon pass, and there is a judgment to come. Instead, to boast in the Lord, to do what is right, and to do it rightly, to imitate God's character in our dealings with other people, for God is God and there is no other. And so to boast in God and to follow Him is the shrewdest, wisest, and most practical path of all the options.

Boasting in the Lord, then, in the context of Jeremiah, is not merely a matter of what happens when Christians gather together at church and sing songs to God. That surely is boasting in the Lord, but what Jeremiah is saying is that it is more practical, and a matter of day-to-day work and home life choices, than that. It affects our politics. Will we cheat to get our way, or do we do what is right, trusting that God is God, and that He sees and He will bring about what is best? It is the fundamental decision at the root of all business dealings, political campaigns, and parenting matters.

Will we serve our children for their good, trusting that God will take our efforts and turn them into something useful and good for our children, as well as for our own good? Or do we live through our children the life that we always wanted to live, or ignore them as unnecessary appendages so we can get on with our careers? Are we servants, trusting and boasting in God, leading with kindness, righteousness and justice? Or are we dictators, piling up connections with the wealthy and powerful, whatever their associations and morality may be? Do we accede to the easy wisdom that the enemy of my enemy is my friend, ignoring that God is God and what is right is what He desires? Or do we imitate His way out of the true wisdom that realizes that God will judge, that to obey God and His ways is the highest wisdom that there could be (even at a practical daily level)? Boast in the Lord, Jeremiah says![1]

With this survey of the explicit references to boasting in the Old Testament, we may make the following preliminary conclusions. First, there are plenty of references to negative boasting. This, in the main, is the reference point to boasting in the Old Testament. Boasting is typically used in a negative way to indicate brashness or foolish arrogance. In particular, this negative boasting has an element of worship gone awry. The endpoint of a person's life, goals, and ambitions is not to have money, fame or adulation from other human beings. To boast in such achievements is nonsensical, empty-headed, and vain: it will be shown for what it is, so much tomfoolery.

---

1   The LXX (the ancient Greek version of the Old Testament) expands 1 Samuel 2:10 to include a similar citation as found in Jeremiah.

There is no point in boasting in riches, for they will not last. There is no point in boasting in fame, for fame is fickle. All that kind of boasting is negative, not just because it is not pious or counter to the kind of basic feel-good Sunday School lessons we would expect. It is negative because in the cold light of day, it makes no sense. Money is a fickle friend, nice at the time, useful no doubt, but in the end it will not last, and can be rapidly taken away from you; today's cool toys are tomorrow's slag heap.

Good looks and beauty are equally pointless. They too fade quickly, but they also can distract you from the deeper meaning of life. Man looks on the outside, but God looks on the heart. To boast in your good looks is not merely a passing experience, undone by the inevitable ravages of time; it leads to a diminished life, a soul poverty. There is more to life than looking good, and even those who look good can find greater merit and joy in a deeper and better matter about which to boast.

On and on the list could go (and in the Old Testament the list is quite extended): negative boasting is bad for you and dishonours God. It is foolish, fickle, and fallacious. It does not do what it says it will do, and leaves those who delight in boasting in such passing fads marooned, stranded on a piece of rock, shipwrecked, and unable to stay afloat through the real matters of life and death.

Positive boasting, on the other hand, is wise and sensible; it lasts, and is rightly ordered worship. It recognizes God for who He really is: not only 'the boss' (the Lord of heaven and earth), but the ultimate endpoint of all that is worth worshiping. To boast in God is to begin to undo the lie of the Garden of Eden. God is good, and to follow Him is good, and to do what He says is a matter about which it is worthy to boast. It is to find the end of our desires, dreams and decision points, all in the One who is worthy of all our praise and adulation.

It is more, though, than simply adulation in a worship-service kind of way. To boast in God is not simply to sing songs about boasting in God. To boast in God is to orient our lives, in the most practical of ways, around His agenda and His desire. It is, to use Jesus' language, to seek first the kingdom of God and His righteousness, knowing that all these other things will be added to us as well (Matt. 6:33). It is not that God is against money, fame or beauty; it is that these are fruits, potentially, along with other fruits.

The real point is to focus boldly, confidently, and audaciously on God. Out of that come His blessings. To boast in other things is like going to a restaurant which has the best food possible, the highest grade culinary delights you can imagine, sitting down at a table, and refusing to order any food at all. Why? Because you so like the décor. And the waiters do their jobs so well. And the music being played in the background is so delightful. All these other things are merely 'mood music'; they are setting the tone for the real dish, which is to eat the amazing food. Money, fame, success – all these and other matters like entertainment are really only part of the mood music for the real dish in the restaurant, which is God Himself.

To boast in God, the Old Testament would say, is to not only acknowledge that, but it is to celebrate that, embrace that, and boldly proclaim that. It is going into that restaurant and looking at all these other people not eating, but enjoying the music; not eating, but analyzing the wallpaper; and shouting aloud, 'I'm going to eat! I'll have the dish of the day, please!' Then eating that dish with evident delight, telling all the other restaurant-goers just how good the food is, delighting in it, proclaiming it, boasting about it.

Such is the Old Testament trajectory and theme of boasting (both negative and positive). But is there no other way in the Old Testament Scriptures, beyond this amassing of texts about boasting, to show what true boasting is, what false boasting is, how to have true boasting, and how to avoid false boasting? I think there is, less obviously, and requiring more than simply going through a dictionary and analyzing the references to boasting. There is a story (one among others) which beautifully pulls out this theme of boasting in the Old Testament. It is not the only story there that does this, but it is the most surprising, and is rarely seen from this perspective of boasting. It is the story of Jonah, a man who almost did not (despite his professional status) know what it was to boast in God; and may have discovered (some think did not) what it was to boast in God by the end. We turn now to that much-loved children's story, and yet far more than an infantile narrative: the rambunctious sea tale of Jonah.

4.
ANCIENT STORIES OF BOASTING

Jonah

The Book of Jonah is not the first place you would think of going to discover a story about boasting. It is certainly ancient, that is for sure, but whether it is about boasting or not remains to be seen. The word 'boast' is not literally found in the book, after all, and by that token alone, we would think that the idea of going to the Book of Jonah to discover a story about boasting appears to be miscued. But while Jonah does not use the word 'boasting', either in its original or in any of its commonly translated forms, the narrative as a whole is peremptorily about boasting.

Throughout the whole story comes a message not so much about boasting, but which illuminates the theme of boasting that is plainly discoverable elsewhere in the Old and New Testaments. The story reverberates with many themes – salvation, of course, not only for Israel, but for all nations. What was it that prevented Jonah from seeing this necessity of taking salvation to Nineveh? What was it that prevented Nineveh from seeking salvation, or at least losing its notorious reputation for wickedness? What was it that caused the Lord to send His prophet to reach out to these rebellious people that He had made? All along we find a theme related to boasting at a *motivational* and *principled* level, countermanding, discerning, distinguishing, and directing the key actors in this wonderful drama known to history as the Book of Jonah.

In particular, each of the key actors in the drama had a message about boasting. There was Jonah himself, whose boast was not so much in the Lord, but in Israel, in himself, in his profession or calling as a prophet, and in his tendency to resist the particularities of that calling, in this case of going to Nineveh. Then there were the Ninevites themselves to whom this message of salvation came, and for whom responding to it appeared wonderfully easy. Why? Why did they so readily respond to Jonah's message from God? What had caused them to be so ready to hear of this salvation and so receptive to Jonah's preaching? In its midst we find that bifocal notion of boasting.

Then there was God whose boast was in Himself, in His salvation for the least of these, even to the ends of the earth, even to those who did not accept His message and identity as the Lord – yet. But they would by the end of the story, and would, in a great celebration, boast in God and His salvation. Discovering this theme of boasting, related to each of these three main characters of the story, and referencing those other characters – the great fish and the sailors – helps us unravel that old saw in this story.

What exactly was the nature of Jonah's repentance? Was it real, fake, part-real and part-fake? Examining it as at least a part of an illustration of this theme of boasting, helps with cutting that Gordian knot.

Jonah has often been caricatured as being a ridiculous figure, an unworthy prophet, unable to stand up among the great and the good of the Old Testament. A sort of buffoon, whose frightening story is good for children, but whose character cannot be in any way said to emulate the ideals of the prophets of the Old Testament. There are certainly elements of the story of Jonah that warrant such a conclusion. His initial unwillingness to obey a clear word from the Lord is pretty undermining to the credibility of a prophet of the Word of God. Then his capitulation to God's command through the agency of a fish – well, that is the sort of thing that delights children throughout the world and down through the ages. Then his, at least, discriminating repentance. Not to mention his final complaint at the end of the story.

But while it is understandable to view Jonah as something of an also-ran in terms of Old Testament prophets, if not actually a figure of fun for children, the reality is far different. His name occurs one other time in the Old Testament in 2 Kings 14:24-26. In that instance, he was honoured as someone through whom the Word of the Lord came, and by which Word God did indeed do as he had promised. The commentary on this Old Testament prophet in 2 Kings nowhere suggests that he was sub-par, even though clearly he was not as famous a prophet as Elijah, and did not have the massive glorious words of his recorded, as did the prophets Isaiah or Jeremiah (for instance). That said, recognizing the relevant infrequency of material about him in the Old Testament, his story is perhaps one of the most famous in all the Bible. And that fame was recognized by none other than Jesus.

Jesus referred to Jonah as an archetypal witness of His truth. Twice in Matthew's Gospel (Matt. 12:38-41, 16:4, 17) and once in Luke's Gospel (Luke 11:29-32), Jonah was brought in to show the Pharisees how wrong they were to ignore and attempt to discredit the preaching of Jesus. Jesus was teaching them that if the Ninevites, famous for their ungodliness, repented at the preaching of Jonah – a preacher who even then, as much as now, was infamous for his initial refusal to preach – how much more should they repent at the preaching of Jesus. He is greater than Jonah – much, much greater.

This comparison of Jesus with Jonah did not in itself elevate Jonah to a more exalted status, but it did show that Jesus approved of his preaching and that He believed that the Ninevites clearly repented at that preaching. What is more, however, Jesus spoke of the 'sign of Jonah'. What was that sign? Clearly, it had something to do with Jonah being in the belly of the great fish for three days and nights. Similarly, Jesus was saying, He would die and then on the third day rise again, and this sign of Jonah was the sign that would be presented to all, and was a sufficient and satisfactory miracle upon which to base their faith.

Jesus, then, associated Jonah's preaching with His own (by way of contrast) and Jonah's experience in the belly of the great fish with His own coming experience of death (by way of comparison). There was a greater miracle to come, and that miracle of Jonah set him up to preach, and at that preaching the Ninevites repented, so Jesus' listeners were to repent at His preaching, He who would die and on the third day rise again. Jesus, then, indicated quite clearly that Jonah was to be taken seriously, and that his work pointed to Jesus' work.

The story itself is similarly weighty, as well as funny (which is not to gainsay the clear elements of humour which are interwoven too). There was evident danger as the raging waters and the terrified sailors made a backdrop to the narrative that anyone who has experienced deep sea calamity could not but find disturbing. What is more, for the Israelite mind, the sea itself was associated with danger, which is why the Book of Revelation says that one of the signs of the new heaven and the new earth is that there will be 'no longer any sea' (Rev. 21:1). This place of turbulence, risk, and hidden dangers is gone in John's vision of the future reign of Christ in culmination. But here in Jonah, the sea, the raging ocean, played a frightening role in the description of Jonah's rebellion, return, and subsequent proclamation of repentance.

The humour of the story is there for all with eyes to see. What could be more intrinsically funny than a prophet of God's Word refusing to speak God's Word? It is a story of the near slapstick kind, like a story about a dentist with crooked teeth, or a doctor who does not practice medicine, or a taxi driver who refuses to drive taxis. There is an essential incongruence, the nature of humour at its most basic, which pervades not just parts of the story, but the story as a whole. Imagine if there were a story about how a medical doctor refused to practice medicine, ran away from the practice of medicine altogether to become a seafaring seadog, and was then eventually, through ridiculous (though also deeply scary) circumstances, returned to his practice of medicine. Can you imagine a Dr. Seuss version?

Except like all good humour (as well as tragedy), there is a point to the joke; it is not really just slapstick, any more than the one-liner which puts down a political opponent is really about being funny. In this case, the humour was not a power game to make an opponent look small, but a word tactic to open the reader (as well as the original dramatist, Jonah himself) to the truth of what was *really* going on. In particular, Jonah, as a story, has three overarching aspects to it that, through humour and seriousness, light and dark, illuminate by means of boasting in the truth about God's love for all nations: *the sailors, the sea,* and *the silence.*

The Sailors

Jonah was intended to be the one who boasts in the Lord, whose confidence was in God and His Word, and who was certain that what God wanted was best and good for him as God's prophet, and also pre-eminently glorifying to God and for the good of His own people. While this confidence was intended to be the case, Jonah was deaf to what God was saying – or at least he put his fingers in his ears and whistled a tune so that he could not hear. He ran in the opposite direction of where he was asked to go and took a ticket to the furthest possible place in the opposite direction to his calling.

The sailors, on the other hand, were pagans. They had no recognizable likelihood of hearing from God or representing God. They did not have a solid doctrinal worldview; they did not have the biblical statutes or laws or principles to guide them. They were flying blind and going to sea with a prophet of God unknowingly. And yet, when the sea rose up in rage, under the sovereign hand of God, it was they who began to think that something odd was going on. They must have seen many a sea storm before – experienced sailors, at least some of them, if not all of them – and a storm itself would not have caused them to decide that there must be a supernatural wrath against one of their companions. They had braved journeys when the seas raged against them at other times, and yet (we may assume) it was not their normal custom to agree to send one of their fee-paying travelers to the bottom of the sea at the first sign of danger.

No, they sensed in the rage of the waters the personal animosity of the God of the sea and land, of heaven and earth, and determined in their own way to discover what the cause of the trouble was. They 'drew lots', a rough way to find out the solution to their problem – random, illogical, and surely not likely to bring them to the right answer to the question. And yet it did, God sovereignly overseeing this process to point the finger resolutely at Jonah. They reluctantly agreed to Jonah's request to throw him overboard.

Why did Jonah think that if he were killed that God would be satisfied? Surely Jonah had no premonition of his rescue? Why did Jonah believe that the God he worshiped was the kind of God who delighted in human sacrifice? Surely he knew better than that? Or, could Jonah – in some small way like Abraham with his son Isaac – have perversely recognized the need for sacrifice to attain forgiveness and decided to put himself to the sword?

Having done the worst, deciding to throw Jonah to the waves, what did the sailors do? They started now to boast in the Lord; that is, they began to pray. 'Then they cried out to the LORD' (Jonah 1:14). And not only did they pray to some generic version of God that they now in some small way recognized as being the powerful God before whom they needed to ask forgiveness, they also specifically prayed to Yahweh, the covenant God. The author of Jonah was careful to record the prayers of the sailors – how extraordinary! This reluctant prophet, on the point of sealing his own fate, with the waters raging beneath him, an evident failure in every respect, now had some of his most amazing converts! 'O LORD' (Jonah 1:14, ESV), they prayed, asking for forgiveness for their act, and in doing so at least starting on the journey of calling upon the LORD, Yahweh, the covenant God of Israel. These words, the last that Jonah heard before being cast into the depths, would have stuck with him to be sure – like hearing your murderers suddenly start praying the Lord's Prayer or calling upon the name of Jesus, when before they had worshiped pagan gods, at the moment before they throw you off a cliff!

Supremely strangely, it was the sailors, the pagan sailors, who were now calling upon the Lord, and boasting in Him, in their dependence upon Him and their recognition that their deeds would be judged by God's holiness and not their own. In no respect did the story indicate that the sailors had a fully formed faith or any kind of orthodox creed as representative of high doctrine in the Old Testament form. But the use of the word 'LORD' is surely evocative of some sort of strange, unearthly, unexpected recognition – at least in its most base form, if not more – that the God to whom they were now accountable for this deed, because the prophet worshiped this God, was the Lord. They called upon this covenant God, using the name of the covenant God, even if they were still outside of that covenant.

It would be like hearing terrified passengers, about to jettison an unworthy fellow passenger from a plane at a dangerous height, passengers who previously had no faith, now calling upon the Lord Jesus to forgive them. You would not think that those passengers had formed a fully mature faith! But you would wonder why they were calling on Jesus and what they now thought about Jesus and whether at some level they recognized that they were duty-bound to show their dues to this Jesus.

So the sailors became those who germinally, and in a rough and ready and even dangerous way, listened to Jonah, as a prophet of the Lord, and then prayed to that Lord to whom they were being so strangely introduced. Jonah, in this bizarre fashion, was finding new converts, even as he was being disciplined by the God to whom the new converts were turning, even as he was living out his own rebellion against that God to whom the converts were now praying!

It would be like an evangelist rebelling against God and refusing to obey His Word in some clear way commanded in Scripture (the fulfilment of these clear words from God now revealed in the Bible), yet in that instance still being used by God to bring others to know God! A televangelist caught in some sin still being used by God to bring others to know God! And these sailors – the fellow travelers with the evangelist, simply going about their business, not knowing that he was fleeing from God – were now caught up in the same situation into which the televangelist had put himself. And to distance themselves from that, they gave the televangelist back to God, and in the meantime bowed and pleaded with God for mercy over their own lives. Even God's discipline of His prophet led to the prophet's ministry being effective! Truly God interweaves all things for the good of those who love Him – even, in this case, being thrown into the depths of the raging waters and about to be swallowed by a great fish.

The Sea

The silent, at least verbally silent, companion to the story is frequently, if oddly, overlooked. The natural phenomenon of the storm is, of course, often appealed to as a backdrop to the falling of Jonah into that sea, the great fish, and Jonah coming up again on dry land. You could not read the Book of Jonah without recognizing that the sea is part of the story.

But most often, the role of the sea does not go beyond that passive backdrop that at one level it seems naturally to fit into.

However, the sea is not silent in terms of its not having a message. The sea, remember, for the Israelites was a scary place, a place of uncertainty, unease and danger, representing the maelstrom of the world, a maelstrom that would be removed in the new heaven and the new earth – where there would be no more sea. For the sea to play such a prominent role here in the story was to indicate that something has gone very badly wrong. Jonah could have been caught in a storm on dry land, but no, it is in the sea, this symbol of the direct opposite of God.

For Jonah to flee to the sea, moreover, that is not the same as a young man seeking to find his fortune in the sea in Western culture! As a prophet, for Jonah to flee to the sea was a symbolic renunciation of his closeness to God. He was fleeing to the opposite direction to which God called him, but obviously he must have known as a prophet that at one level it was impossible to flee from God's presence. How can you run from the One who made everything and is everywhere? Where can you hide from the One who sees everything and through everything, to everyone? But the sea – that was a way of hiding himself in the place that represented going against God's will. It was saying, 'I will not have any more to do with this calling.'

Jonah, the prophet, was not just going away from where God called him geographically; he was going away from God's calling cosmically, spiritually and vocationally. He was not just going to be somewhere different; he was going to do something different, and become something different. He was going to find himself, to go on a journey to discover who he really was and what he really wanted to do with his life. This was as a midlife crisis, or a half-midlife crisis, a running away from God in the sense of reconsidering his life's priorities and purposes, goals and ambitions. If not

God, then perhaps the sea? If not God, perhaps that which was the opposite of being a prophet – being a sailor, a trader, a rough-and-ready seadog, a person who would attempt to be everything that God had not made him to be.

But while you can take the prophet out of Israel, you cannot take Israel out of the prophet – and soon enough, in the extremity of the suffering caused by the sea, Jonah rediscovered his faith. No, he had felt, he would not be a prophet – forget that! God had asked him to do one too many crazy things! He would not go to this new people and have them complain about whether his messages were exactly this way or that way, especially as they had a reputation for being so dangerous. Uh-huh, no way. He was going to go somewhere different, become something different, do something different. He had had enough. This new 'calling' that God gave him to go to Nineveh was the final straw. Hadn't he done enough for God already? Off he went in the opposite direction, and the sea was the perfect place to hide himself from God.

What though did Jonah discover? Not only that it is impossible geographically to run from God, but that even the sea – even the representation of all that is against God, anti-God and culturally moribund, negative and angry – even there God is. 'From deep in the realm of the dead I called for help, and you listened to my cry . . . all your waves and breakers swept over me' (Jonah 2:2-3). Jonah found that the sea was not a place of the absence of God, but the presence of God, and that the sea was *His* sea, they were *His* waves and *His* breakers, and even in the depths of all that, God heard his prayer.

Could it then be said that the sea was boasting in God? Certainly, it obeyed where the prophet did not. God commanded a storm, and a storm there was. God commanded that it be silent, and silent it was. The prophet, this expert in God's Word, was far harder to bring to heel. And in the sea, the great fish was also far more obedient than the religious expert! The raging waters were raging because God told them to rage, and in their obedience they spoke of the powerful God who called them to their stormy protestation. It was the sea who caused Jonah to make his first confession of faith to the sailors, 'I am a Hebrew and I worship the LORD, the God of heaven, who made the sea and the dry land' (Jonah 1:9). The sea worshiped God, obeyed to become a storm, obeyed to become a calm, and generated from the lips of the prophet a good confession of faith in the powerful, almighty God.

The Silence

Boasting is an intricately and expressively loud activity, or so it would seem, and therefore quite contrary to actual silence. How can you boast in something or someone without talking about it or even shouting about it – singing, proclaiming, exclaiming? While the intricate connection between boasting and volume of articulation, however, seems obvious, it is actually less so than might at first seem.

In our human duplicity, there is often a difference between what people say is the basis of their confidence, the ultimate goal of their lives, and what is truly the endpoint of all their ambitions. A man may say that his ultimate goal is to serve other people, but when push comes to shove, it is fairly apparent that he is willing to trample other people under foot in pursuit of his real ambition – be it fame or money, or success of some kind or other. A woman may say that she lives for her family, but if an outsider observer was able to catalogue the way she spent every moment of every day, where her thoughts were placed in the secret recesses of her mind, then a different story might be told – a story about insecurity related to beauty, whether she is a good mother or not, or about her desires for proving herself to be capable in some way.

So, it is not always the case that what someone professes most loudly is actually the thing about which they boast.

In fact, it can be the case that some profess loudly about something in order to make it less obvious what they are really boasting about. As Shakespeare said, 'He protesteth too much,' meaning that someone speaks so loudly about something in order to hide that really the truth is diametrically opposed. At times people are defensive, overly so, when the verbal attacks of an opponent have hit a little too close to the truth.

In the Book of Jonah there was a lot of noise. There was the noise of the sea, as we have seen, and there was the noisy working atmospheres of the sailors as they went about their seafaring tasks. There was also the noise of the city, a 'great city' (Jonah 3:2), a 'very large city' (Jonah 3:3), which 'took three days to go through it' (Jonah 3:3). In this great city there would have been noise (and smell) of human corruption, entertainment and life – babies and businesses, marriage and death, and entertainment and religious fanfare.

There were also some clear verbal pointers to God's will and His purpose. The word of the Lord came to Jonah for the first time in Jonah 1:1, and then again – after his repentance, such as it was – in Jonah 3:1. Again, the Lord spoke to Jonah, this time not to give him a new message or 'word', but to answer his prayers and his unjust anger, asking a question of Jonah in return twice (Jonah 4:4, 9) before finishing the book with a statement of God's compassion and love (Jonah 3:10; 4:2).

God is revealed as a speaking God, a prayer-hearing and a saving God: a God who has a message and has messengers, whose messengers are at times all-too-human, and yet God still uses them to speak His Word to other humans. God is revealed as a sovereign God, who rules the sea and the fish of the sea, and who is no tribal deity merely for Israel, but loves and saves to the uttermost reaches of the planet, the gospel of the Old Testament going to all nations – even to that tumultuous, pagan, 'great city' called Nineveh. God is revealed to be a merciful God, noticing the repentance of the Ninevites and therefore having compassion on them. God's judgment ('Forty more days and Nineveh will be overthrown,' Jonah 3:4) was shown to be a warning of impending doom, a punishment about which He relented when He saw that the warning had had its effect on Nineveh.

God was shown not to be picky about the doctrinal precision of those who repented. The decree of the king to Nineveh and its people was notable in a number of ways. First and foremost was the absence of the covenant name for God, a covenant name for God that the sailors (those rambunctious, seafaring, labouring, least-likely-to-be-pious kind of people) had themselves, by contrast, readily adopted. 'Let everyone call urgently on God,' the decree says (Jonah 3:8) – not 'call upon the LORD.' Their faith was distinctly rudimentary at best, but God will accept that very basic, even incorrect or at least sub-optimal, faith for the grain-of-mustard-seed faith that it is.

So there was much speaking in Jonah. But there is also a silence. The silence that hangs over Jonah as a book is the unanswered question about Jonah the man. Did he truly repent? The book ends on not so much a cliffhanger as an unfinished conclusion. The final word came from God; it did not come from His messenger Jonah. Whether Jonah in the end truly understood that God is a compassionate God for all nations, including those pesky Ninevites, is a question that remains unanswered. We are simply not told whether Jonah accepted God's rebuke or not. Past record might indicate that for Jonah to do what God said, when what God said did not line up with what Jonah wanted, was far from easy. But even that is not certain: perhaps Jonah had learnt his lesson. Perhaps the silence at the end indicates that Jonah was at a loss for words, had no more excuses, and had completely and utterly bowed before God's Word and accepted it as the truth about things, without any more question or interaction.

There is also a silence about the quality of Jonah's repentance in his prayer of chapter 2. At first blush it seems clearly to be repentance. At least it is accepted as such by God, who after Jonah prayed commanded the fish to vomit Jonah onto dry land. It was accepted by God, even if some of the details of the prayer (its reference to the temple and to sacrifice; its slightly sanctimonious tone; and most of all its evident half-heartedness when shown by the ongoing dialogue Jonah had with God after the Ninevites had repented) trouble theologians.

Perhaps like all prayers and like all repentance, it was far from perfect. If repentances were perfect, there would be little need for repentance. If we could say something perfect, do something perfectly, live perfectly, we would be able to repent perfectly. But we cannot, and we do not. At least God accepted this prayer, and the fish responded to His command for release, and it led to Jonah fulfilling his commission from God to preach to Nineveh – even if at the end Jonah was no more perfect in his attitude to his preaching than he was to his repentance. Unlike most preachers today, Jonah complained that the people listened to what he said, rather than that they didn't listen to what he said!

What kind of man was this? What kind of prophet? What are we to learn from Jonah as a man, as a prophet? So much silence hangs over the Book of Jonah. Are we to learn that prophets too are men and fail, and yet God still uses them? Are we to learn that God will reach the nations even through our half-hearted commitment to missions? Are we to learn that God is not a racial God, that He is committed to all peoples, and we too, the New Testament Church, are also to be committed to all nations as well? Are we to learn that imperfect repentance is okay, or that a repentance that does not result in a truly changed life is no repentance at all? Silence, silence, silence. There is a brooding silence that hangs over Jonah, dissatisfying for some, though it has given countless theologians and doctoral students much fuel for discussion!

What of this silence? Like an echo in a room after a voice dies down, it has its own question. The unanswered question at the end of the Book of Jonah, and the prayer recorded without obvious narrative commentary about its fidelity as a prayer,[1] and the lack of judgment about Jonah as a prophet – for all his failures, as well as successes – begs a question of its own. A silence into which a question looms towards us. What about us? Will we follow God where He leads us? Will we listen to the Bible, and not only listen to it, but obey it and do it? Will we be able to trust God in the depths of our sea of disaster or calamity? Will we complain in ministry when the ministry does not go the way we want it, and someone else – some other individual, or even people whose theology is definitely inaccurate and imperfect – is still accepted by God, and their repentance recorded as exemplary?

After all the noise of Jonah, there is a silence, a silence that begs the question: in what is our boast? The skilled narrator of Jonah has constructed a story that not only appeals to children down through the ages, not only is a warning to preachers to practice what they preach, not only is a message to the church to be a missionary as well as missional church, but asks a question more directly of each one of us. Are we boasting in God, or are we boasting in our ministry, our effectiveness as a minister, our church, our family, or our racial group? When push comes to shove, when God asks us by His Word to do something which runs against the grain of our preferences, and may not fit with our identity, do we still do that thing He asks, or do we run in the other direction, and only ever do it reluctantly, and then belly-ache to God afterwards when we have done it?

---

1   Jonah 2:1-9; though some would say verse 10 is God's comment on Jonah's prayer!

The silence asks the question. Let the silence be silent: in whom do you boast?

Esther

The story of Esther is famous for, among other things, being the only book in the Bible that does not include the name of God. This – apart from being remarkable on its own in a book that is found in the Bible (which surely if it is about anything, is about God) – is indicative in some shape or form of the purpose of the *Book of Esther*. Most commonly, *Esther* is said to be a book that is about God's hidden purpose, His sovereign arranging of the details of our lives, even in the midst of calamity. You might not be able to see God visibly at work; you might not even be able to determine at the time what God is doing; you might not even be likely to give honour to God during the experience that He is at work – but despite all this, the *Book of Esther* tells us that God is at work. The very hiddenness of the name of God, in other words, serves to magnify that name or (to put it in the terms we are using) boast in that name.

If you go into a kitchen, you expect to find certain items: a stove or cooker, for instance, a sink, some cutlery, some utensils for cooking. Imagine, if instead, you went into a kitchen, and while there was a place to do cooking, there were no utensils, no plates, and no sink – and instead of all that, there was a giant sofa and a bed. You would feel a little confused. Why was there a place to do cooking, a great big whacking stove, right next door to a bed? Was this a bedroom or a kitchen? Or was it some combination of the two, some new-fangled bed-kitch-room? The very absence of what you expect serves to emphasize what is missing.

In a similar sort of way, *Esther*, by a literary technique of absence, does not actually hide the name of God. Instead, that name of God is highlighted dramatically, emphasized powerfully, and brought into focus in an unusual technique of boasting in God's name. More than simply emphasizing the name of God, though, by this technique of absence, of hiddenness, the narrative of *Esther* serves to answer a question related to the presence of God when God does not seem present.

In many pious circles, the presence of God and the feeling of the presence of God are constantly connected. When I sense God's presence in worship, when I feel God speaking to me, when I am aware of the presence of the Almighty in some personal sensibility, then I can be sure that God is with me. Of course, I know that theologically God is always present. But I am aware of His especial empowering presence when I sense that presence, when I feel that presence.

But *Esther* comes against that in a bold move by telling a story that is so replete with coincidences that none of them can truly be by accident – not for the person with a biblical or Christian worldview. These events could not have happened except for the sovereign hand of God. And yet, by leaving out the name of God, *Esther* provocatively asks: could it be that God is most at work when He feels most absent? Could it be that those who are least aware of God's presence could actually be most intensely in the story of God's present sovereign activity?

The name of God is not the only thing absent from *Esther*. There is also absent much of the normal expectations of piety. Prayer is there, to be sure, and powerfully inserted into the story. But unlike Daniel, where prayer and piety play such a prominent role, in *Esther* the prayer comes in at the end in desperation, rather than (at least in the story) as an overflow of the prayer life of a pious man or woman. We do not know about the prayer life of Esther or her relatives and family, and we must resist the urge to judge based upon the little information that we are given. But from the story that is in front of us, piety is not self-evidently a strong part of the story itself. Which brings up another provocative question: if God is for us, then can the poverty of our prayer lives be against us?

There is deceit and cunning in the *Book of Esther*, too, and a general savvy, worldly-wise kind of approach. It is not commended, but there is a human wit that is present and upon which Esther and her family lived in this very difficult time. Again, if God is for us, does that mean that our human brains need to leave us? Evidently not, for in *Esther* the human ability to scheme, in the best sense, is apparent and not overtly criticized by the narrator.

That said, there is one overriding commendable virtue in Esther: bravery. She was courageous, brave, and strong in the face of extreme risk and danger. She did what was right, conscious that in doing so she might not just lose her job or her reputation, but her very life. She had no guarantees, no certainties; she did not know how the story would end. And yet she acted with the courage of her convictions on behalf of her people.

It is this combination of surprise (by the absence of the name of God and the relative infrequency of traditional piety) and human scheming, good and very bad, plus the extraordinary bravery of what we are expected to believe was a young and very beautiful woman, that all adds up to a compelling narrative. But it is more than a story that entertains in its own way and purely for the sake of entertainment alone. The hiddenness of God, in this extreme situation, leads the story to be a bold boast in the name of God by the very absence of that name overtly, where you would expect to find the name so obviously.

The Tomb of the Unknown Soldier speaks more loudly of the bravery of a generation that fought for freedom than do even the massed ranks of graves with names on them. The fact that the sacrifice was so great that there are many who never found a grave makes the boast in their sacrifice yet more compelling and tragically thrilling. So with *Esther*, the book without a name of God that boasts in the name of God. And it does so in three ways especially: the *commitment*, the *courage*, and the *crisis*.

The Commitment

Commitment is one theme that runs throughout the *Book of Esther*. The 'young woman ... had a lovely figure and was beautiful' (Esther 2:7), and yet even more impressive was her ability to commit to the right things at the right time. The narrator passed lightly over how disturbing it must have been for Esther to have been taken from Mordecai (her older cousin who was her father figure), emphasizing instead how pleasing she was to Hegai, the eunuch in charge of the king's harem, and how much she won his favour.

Evidently, her charms were far more than merely physical, as was also revealed by her commitment to playing the game as Mordecai had advised and commanded her, and her willingness to submit to wisdom from this older man who was looking out for her. 'Esther had not revealed her nationality and family background, because Mordecai had forbidden her to do so' (Esther 2:10). Esther stuck to following the advice of those who had taken care of her; she trusted Mordecai and committed to do what he asked her to do. She began to flourish in this extremely complicated and compromising situation into which she, a pious, orthodox Jew, found herself unexpectedly.

She then submitted to the process of beautification, a process that perhaps at one level must have felt a little like being fattened for the slaughter, being made to look beautiful for a man she did not know, who may or may not like her, and whose will and whim would decide her destiny. But she threw herself into the process; she lived in it and was committed to it. Her willingness to commit to follow sound advice was not limited to Mordecai, but also extended to her new ally Hegai, the eunuch in charge of the king's harem. He gave her advice as to exactly what she should ask to take with her from the harem to the king's palace and into the king's presence. Presumably Hegai knew what pleased the king more than anyone else, and it is also likely that Hegai could have given advice that would have been counter-productive to Esther. But because she had already won Hegai's favour, his advice was sound advice. Esther had committed to that relationship, and made the most of it, and had become someone in whom Hegai had affection, and to whom he was well-disposed. Esther took that advice, bringing with her only those things that Hegai suggested she bring before the king. With her beauty and charm, clothed and set apart with the accoutrements that Hegai knew were most likely to please the king, Esther was picked as the royal favourite. Before too long, she became the queen.

Throughout all these complicated, interwoven relationships, opportunities, and dangers, Esther showed herself as someone who knew how to commit and what was worth her commitment. She was wise, but not only in a dispassionate, distant, or academic way. She was committed; she threw herself into the new life that had been picked for her. She charmed the man in charge of the harem when it would surely have been so easy to be sour, disdainful, and bitter. Esther listened carefully to the advice of her older cousin Mordecai, when it might well have been easy to think how little he knew about this oh-so-very female world in which she found herself. She even listened to the advice of her chief jailer, the eunuch in charge of all the harem, and so was well-positioned to win the favour of the king, which she duly did.

In all of this (as for the whole *Book of Esther*), the name of God is not mentioned, but the wisdom that comes from God is on display. Nowhere here does Esther overtly boast in the Lord, and she was certainly not overt about her relationship to God. In fact, she was deliberately secretive about being a part of the people of God at all! Yet, as the *Book of Esther* so carefully records, her wise canniness in this situation displayed a boasting in the God who is in charge of all things (even harems), and whose wisdom is higher than our wisdom. Whether or not Esther herself at this moment was displaying a mature belief in God, whether or not she was at this point characteristic of a godly disposition and attitude in a pious or spiritually-minded sense, the story about Esther shows that God is to be boasted in, even in the most potentially abusive of situations.

Could God rescue a sex-slave? The *Book of Esther* says yes. Could God use the life of a sex-slave for the redemption of His people? The *Book of Esther* says yes. Could God be at work through the charm and discerning commitment of a person who had been sold into slavery into a harem of a Middle Eastern dictator? The *Book of Esther* says yes. This is a God in whom it is worthy to boast even in these highly discriminating, disturbing, morally gray, and dubious areas of life and the rancidness of human experience.

The *Book of Esther* says that 'religion' is not just about 'church'. It is about politics, sex, marriage, dynasties, betrayal, the wisdom to gain friends in high places, and the wisdom to obey the wisdom of those older than you who have seen more of life than you. The commitment of Esther to God's way (even when God is not evidently present and God's name is not even used, so strange does God seem to this story) and the commitment of Esther to the counsel of God's people (even when Mordecai in so doing gave her advice to hide her allegiance to God's people) reveal a God that the *Book of Esther* is to become famous in its boasting.

In all this, we are never to forget, the *Book of Esther* ended with a note of joyful, boastful celebration (Esther 9:22), a conclusion that was commemorated in Judaism in the festival of Purim. The silence about the name of God because of the commitment, ultimately underneath all because of God's sovereignty, led to a place of feasting and commemoration and all-too-apparent joyful boasting and celebration in God's deliverance.

149

The Courage

Esther's extraordinary courage was summarized in the famous line from the story of Esther in chapter 4, verse 16: 'If I perish, I perish.' Esther was told by Mordecai that she must make an appeal for the saving of her people. Having told her before to stay quiet about her national (and religious) identity – an identity that she had so scrupulously hidden that the Book of *Esther*, up to this point, is also completely quiet about that identity, and remains quiet about the name of God throughout, as if mirroring in its narrative the care that Esther took to be 'in the world but not of the world' – now, though, Mordecai strongly urged a change of tactic. God's people were under threat. It was 'for such a time as this' (Esther 4:14) that Esther had risen to this position so close to the royal throne that she might intercede for her own people. In case this moral appeal to Esther alone was not enough, Mordecai (wisely, again) made it clear that Esther herself would not be immune to the decree that had gone out to kill the Jews (Esther 3:13).

Esther was caught between a rock and a hard place, though, for while she could appeal to the king, the law at the time dictated that no one could go into the king's presence uninvited. The king must give explicit permission and first call someone into his presence. For Esther to wander in of her own accord, under her own steam, by her own initiative, was tantamount to a potential death sentence. The penalty for encroaching upon the king's presence without permission first from the king was death – unless the king condescended to extend his gold sceptre and so remit the sentence and allow her into his presence.

With this courage was commensurate canniness; with the commitment the courage was also balanced by a similar wisdom. Esther, even though admitted into the king's presence, right there and then did not come out with her request. How urgent it must have seemed! How extraordinary must have been the providence that she had been allowed to see the king and would not suffer the penalty for temerity in seeking his presence unbidden. Surely now was the time to lay out all her concerns, while his favour was on her and while he was in a good mood? Strike while the iron is hot, Esther! Do it now!

But, instead (oh, so wisely) her request once asked in this moment of high drama was not the request that Mordecai had commissioned to ask. Instead, her request was for another opportunity – a lengthier, less pressurized, more intimate, less business-like opportunity – to be with the king. In a sense her request was to ask for more requests, like the person who conjures up a magic genie and is told that he has one wish, and he replies that his wish is for an infinity of wishes. Esther's request was for a more expanded opportunity to make the request.

It was even bold in the kind of setting she suggested. She took the king out of his domain, the realm of business and politics, surrounded by his lackeys and the trappings of his power, and brought him into her domain. She cooked for him. Perhaps she was a good cook! At any rate, at this private banquet, she was now in the corridors of her own power, waiting on the king in different surroundings, with time and leisure to speak, and with the tastes of her own delights provided for the king to sweeten him up, so that her message might be a less bitter pill to swallow. How canny, wise, but also how courageous! She was going all in.

This was not just a quick request, something that she was asking in the heat of the moment that the king might dismiss as something not that serious and which then she would be less risky in asking. No, by setting up the context for her request in this way, she was making it very clear that this was a big deal and it really mattered. She was therefore in a sense risking even more this time by making it clear to the king that this thing she wanted truly mattered.

There was even more to it than the personal courage to invite the king to her own private banquet. There was the courage in overturning a pattern that had led to her predecessor's demise. Queen Vashti had refused to come to the king's banquet and so embarrassed the king in front of his courtiers and other leaders. But Queen Esther was now inviting the king to her own banquet. It was a clear message that not only was she different from her predecessor, she was different in the very way and in the very matter which had caused the king so much angst. And yet courageously, she took the bull by the horns and made this difference crystal clear to him and to all his courtiers by asking him to a banquet. This banquet was to be a private affair, just the king and Haman, the enemy of the Jews, but the request was public, in front of the court, and so the overturning of the previous pattern – if the banquet was successful – was clear. It would also be clear if it failed. This was the king whose wives messed up parties! They could not get banquets right! Esther could not afford to fail at this banquet. Everything had to be just right, and so she was courageously risking everything.

And yet, the courage continued. Some read it as her prevaricating, not sure whether she dare ask. That is certainly possible, and who would blame her? But it is also possible that Esther was deliberately ramping up the pressure. The banquet at which Queen Vashti had failed to appear had been her demise. Clearly, lengthy banquets raised the mood of the king to a high-handed kind of disposition. She wanted a quick and urgent decision from him. She did not want a lengthy drawn-out bureaucratic process. So, the Queen asked the king and Haman to come back again for yet another banquet.

Meanwhile, in a move divinely orchestrated, Mordecai was honoured before the country and city at the expense of Haman (Esther 6), and it becomes clear, even to Haman's friends and family, that fate and fortune had turned and Haman's doom was at hand. Then, in chapter 7, Esther, with the king and Haman once again in her boudoir – at her table, at this banquet prepared by her hand which had been less than precipitous for her predecessor – she now launched into her speech. It was not only carefully constructed as a speech, it was not only diplomatically masterful; it was passionate. It read like the last desperate throw of the dice. 'Grant me my life,' she said, 'and spare my people' (Esther 7:3). She insisted on making the whole request personal. Diplomatically, she said that if the problem were only that she and her people would be sold into slavery, she would not have bothered the king with such a thing (Esther 7:4). But it was her own life, and the life of her people, that were at stake.

This speech was not only carefully worded; it was an extraordinary risk. She at this moment made it crystal clear that her own life was now being gambled. She could have told the king there were some people she cared about who she heard were under threat and asked for his help. She could have kept her own identity a secret, and so, if the king had refused her request, spared her life. But Esther did not take the safe option. She most courageously risked everything, even her own life, to play the final hand of the game. 'Spare me!' And the king did – and Haman's doom soon followed.

Such courage weaves throughout the story of Esther. It is the kind of courage that can only come with a personal belief in the sovereign hand of God – that God has put on our plate certain things, and it is our job to eat them; that He has set the table, and it is our job to dine; that He has arranged the portion, and it is our job to delight in it; that He has made the enemy that opposes us, and therefore we will win against that enemy. Without that kind of conviction, the kind of courage that Esther displayed is simply not possible. It relies upon God, and reading about it, noticing the courage, boasts in the God who generates such remarkable human conviction and courage.

No wonder at the end of *Esther* they celebrated so loudly what God had done for them! No wonder the *Book of*

Esther is named after Esther herself! This is a God who can inspire humans, male and female, to the most courageous, honourable risks for the sake of God's people. Such a God is a God that is worthy of honour and in whom it is right to boast.

The Crisis

While there is one obvious crisis in the *Book of Esther* – the moment when the Jews are legislated to death – there are many other sub-crises that build and envelope this one to create a dynamic tension throughout the story. But they do more than create tension; they lay the groundwork for the relief that explodes in joyful boasting and celebration of God at the end.

The first crisis is at the end of chapter 2 when Mordecai uncovered a plot to kill the king. Given that this was the king who had just recently stolen his prized cousin, co-opted her into the king's harem, forcibly taken her as his consort and wife – and for whom the last wife was no honourable predecessor that was predictive of the likely outcome – given all this, it is not inevitable that Mordecai was disappointed at the idea of someone trying to kill the king. You wonder whether Mordecai at moments had similar feelings towards the royal personage – a king who delighted in taking the most beautiful girls he could find, enjoying all of them, discarding most of them, and only employing one of them as his special partner.

This king was no latter-day constitutional monarch whose discrepancies extended to a bit of salacious dalliance on the side. This was an Ancient Eastern dictator whose power knew no limit, and who had already shown himself quite capable of regicide – killing a queen. The story does not tell what other atrocities this king had given approval to. But if the Ahasuerus (his name in Hebrew) of the *Book of Esther* does equate to Xerxes 1 ('the Great'), we know from elsewhere in history that we are not talking about a whiter-than-white, purer-than-pure figure.

Soon after he ascended peacefully to the throne, he crushed revolts in Egypt and Babylon – a single sentence description that does not give much detailed red colour to the bloodshed involved. Xerxes is famous for his botched invasion of Greece, another bloody war which Herodotus said included two million soldiers on Xerxes' side. In particular, and especially concerning no doubt to Mordecai and to Esther, Xerxes had a preponderance to intrigues and mistresses, and disaster reared its ugly head around his beautiful harem. Some of the stories are too awful to repeat in this book, but mutilation and betrayal, even among family members, were present.

How then would Mordecai not have perhaps been tempted to rejoice at this news about a plot against Xerxes? It surely could not have been a rare occurrence for the king (dubbing himself 'King of the Nations,' that is, of the world) to have been the victim of attempts to wrest power from his dead hands. And if the man in charge of such power was so awful a man, despite his famed building projects, those plots against his death would not only have been from the lunatic fringe, but also from those closer to real power. Xerxes was, in fact, in the end murdered by one of his own bodyguard.

But with this crisis, Mordecai not only took the high road; he viewed the providence of God at work, even in Esther's sex slavery to Xerxes, and decided to make the most of a bad job and curry favour with the king. It was this single decision that in the end was the crisis point from which all else rolled. It was because of this that the king favoured Mordecai, at Haman's expense; it was this which laid the path to Haman's destruction; and it was this that allowed for the rescue of God's people – a crisis, and a decision in that crisis, from one man to protect a bloody tyrant.

Life, to be sure, is not as straightforward for the godly as some pious books would have us believe. We are to be as innocent as doves, and yet as canny as serpents. Boasting in God is not always straightforward, especially in times of crisis, and it can require canny reading of God's providence, especially when serving in the courts of a pagan king.

The next crisis was Haman's plot to kill the Jews. Mordecai's response to this crisis is more predictable. Almost inevitably, he was opposed to the plot! But what is less predictable was the manner by which he chose to oppose that plot. His one way in to the court was through Esther, and so naturally he approached her. Naturally enough, she objected. To come before the king and complain about a decision he had made, especially one endorsed by the king's own right-hand man, the most powerful person in the Empire after the king, well, that was tantamount to suicide!

So while approaching Esther about this plot was predictable, what was less so was the tactic that Mordecai took with Esther. He told her, in no uncertain terms, that if she ducked this responsibility, she could run, but she could not hide. Disaster would overtake her too. It would become known to her ancestors. And is there a hint that Mordecai would, as the keeper of her secret identity, make sure that it was known? Was he suggesting to her that he would no longer keep her identity secret if she did not approach the king directly now?

Mordecai was like some master spy-handler in a spy novel, whose agent behind enemy lines is being given a highly dangerous and potentially fatal task. To motivate the agent to do his duty, the master spy-handler gives the agent no other option. He will die one way or another because the agent's identity will become known; his handler will ensure it does become known.

Certainly, there was risk in approaching the king. But there was absolute certainty of death the other way! Esther was given far more than a little nudge. She was pushed in the back and shoved over the cliff. She really had no choice – though I suppose she could have denied her ethnic background, or hoped that, at this point, the king would change his mind, or revert the law if it became known that his currently favoured queen was a Jew too.

To sweeten the implicit threat, Mordecai then provided an honourable motivation too. No one wants to do the right thing for the wrong reasons. They want to do the right thing for the right reasons, even if the wrong reasons provide a backdrop of motivation at the same time. An expert amateur psychologist, Mordecai gave Esther good theology, once more hiding the name of God, in the most famous verse in the *Book of Esther*: 'And who knows but that you have come to your royal position for such a time as this?' (Esther 4:14). There is a hand of providence behind all these human dealings, as hard as the writing of that hand in the sand of human lives is to read accurately. And it could be, could it not, Esther, that your moment of greatness is before you at the same time as your moment of greatest danger? This second crisis, the great crisis in the book, then, reveals the hand of God – invisible to the human eye – behind all, a providence that gives emotive rationale for the later boasting in God at the end of the *Book of Esther* too.

Hannah

Hannah's prayer in 1 Samuel 2 is well-known. It is beautiful and powerful, both in praise of the God who delights in redeeming the weak and broken and, more specifically, in His delight to do this through the means of His 'anointed' – immediately through David, later through the Christ (the anointed).

However, Hannah's hymn of praise to the Anointed One was not only about these specific doctrinal matters; it also had a tone of exultation and boasting. She began, 'My hearts exults in the LORD; my horn is exalted in the LORD' (1 Sam. 2:1, ESV). This tone of exultation, of boasting, continued through her song of worship to God.

Most notably, the LXX, the Greek translation of the Old Testament, actually included in this hymn the same message about boasting that is found in the Hebrew (and our English translations) of Jeremiah 9:23-24 (ESV): 'Let not the wise man boast in his wisdom, let not the mighty man boast in his might, let not the rich boast in his riches, but let him who boasts boast in this, that he understands and knows me, that I am the LORD who practices steadfast love, justice, and righteousness in the earth.' Whether this was original (and most scholars evidently believe not) or a comment upon the text by a later scribe that became inadvertently included in the text at some point, makes no difference to the fact that at least it functions as one ancient commentary on the meaning of the story of Hannah, as Hannah saw it. It was a story about boasting.

Hannah's adversary was fertile; she was not. Her adversary would tease her and provoke her because of her infertility. And so Hannah, 'deeply distressed,' prayed to the LORD (1 Sam. 1:10, ESV). The priest Eli noticed her praying and, in a telling comment about the current spirituality of the day, mistook her fervent prayer for the fervour of drunkenness. It evidently had been a long time since Eli had seen someone pray with passion. Perhaps it had been a long time since he had prayed with passion.

Hannah's dependence upon God and her determination to rely upon Him was a foreign thing to Eli by this time. He misinterpreted her prayer as the muttering and crying of someone who had drunk too much alcohol. When he was corrected by Hannah, however, he at least understood enough of her situation to have compassion on her and bless her in the name of the Lord, sending her in peace and asking God to give her what she had asked.

Samuel was born and was dedicated to the Lord as Hannah had promised. And in a marvellous, extraordinary song of devotion, this mother's heart broke with joy for the way that the Lord had answered her prayer. She had been granted justice against her adversary. She had been given reason to exult in the Lord when previously she was weeping in prayer. Her fortunes had turned around, and somehow (prophetically) she understood the significance of this moment and this child, so supernaturally born. He would be involved in God's plan to put things right way up again. So she called upon the strength of the Lord at the beginning and end of her song, and she pointed to the power of God's anointed.

In the middle of her song was her heartfelt, exalted boasting in God. Hannah's story shows us that boasting in God can be as a result of something as simple as an answer to prayer about a sick child and as profound as the coming of Christ Himself. At one level, it all centres on Jesus (everything does, as all Sunday School children the world over realize). But at another level, our access to this centring upon Jesus can be as deeply personal as an infertility problem, a sick child, a woman teasing another woman, a vow to God fulfilled, or a priest or Christian leader who is slow to spot genuine prayer.

Hannah's story calls on us to pray; to depend on God in prayer, as well. It calls on us to boast in God; to exult in Him. In doing so, through the midst of our pain, we land in the exultation of the Anointed One Himself.

These three ancient stories of boasting – Jonah, Esther and Hannah – each in their own way add colour and poetry to the more prosaic analysis of when the Old Testament uses the word 'boasting', and in what context. Jonah is silent about boasting. And in its silence, by contrast, it calls on us to do what Jonah did not do: to obey where Jonah did not obey, and to boast in God's salvation in the way that Jonah did not boast in his salvation (but complained instead).

Esther, likewise, does not use the word 'boasting', but the story of Esther ends in a famous great feast of boasting in God's salvation – the feast of Purim. Also, the story of Esther, devoid of the specific name of God, shows how boasting in

God is not merely a 'religious' thing, but something that can take place in the world of work, politics, and even the sex trade. Esther was sex-trafficked, given an impossible situation in which to flourish, and yet through a mixture of bravery and canniness, triumphed, believing that she was put in such a place for such a time as was before her. And so she and all God's people boasted in the Lord.

Hannah's prayer is most obviously about boasting, and the Greek translation made this connection plain with its comments upon the text – and yet in some ways it is most challenging. Could we, driven to such a low place, so desperate, call upon God with that desperation and so be led to such a great height from which we can boast in God, exult in the Lord, too?

These stories sing and dance, weave patterns in our minds, and leave an atmosphere in our hearts of the sea and the Middle Eastern intrigues of a harem and of a childless woman, all to call us to be people who boast in the Lord (not in riches, power, or wisdom).

5.
THE PSYCHOLOGY OF
BOASTING

The act of boasting is usually thought of as something that is self-driven, almost by definition wilful, determined, out-there, and therefore probably having little, if any, more subtle inner motivations or ramifications. To boast means to be supremely confident in your achievements, we often think. Even if the boasting is of a positive kind, it still requires a kind of coherent, consistent confidence that does not suggest that much time needs to be spent 'looking under the hood' or figuring out what is really going on in some semi-Freudian or therapist sort of way.

What's more, the conversation we have been having about boasting does not suggest immediate connection points to psychology per se. We have been having a theological conversation, a conversation about what the Bible says about boasting and how that might apply then to the Christian life, but we have not been asking ourselves psychological questions in any strict or precise fashion. We have not thought of the emotional components of boasting or the triggers of a certain kind of boasting, what might motivate negative boasting, and what might alternatively encourage positive boasting. None of this has been occurring within a conversation that is primarily about mental states (however so defined).

To start then to ask about the psychology of boasting might appear to be asking a question that is quite different from the one we have thus far been trying to solve in this book. We are now either delving into pop-psychology; beginning to take a higher route of more sophisticated examination of neurological matters or truly appropriate psychological investigations; or now adopting a more pastoral counselling approach (even if this has nothing to do in this regard with strict counselling, therapist, or sitting-on-the-couch questions). Why would we now start to delve into quite a different realm? Why not stick to either the more theoretical, theological questions regarding what the Bible says about boasting or, if we are trying in this chapter to apply boasting in a more practical way, do that application with regard to the instructions about behaviour that do not cross over into the language of psychology? The reason why it is necessary, though, to ask this question about the psychology of boasting is that boasting by definition has something to do with an assertion related to the self. When we are talking about positive boasting, that assertion related to the self is also by definition a self-denial – in the paradox of grace and taking up your cross and following Jesus. To die to self means to find yourself; to boast about Christ means to put yourself under His rule and submit to His lordship, and to do so by boasting about it is to do so with audacity, bravery, confidence, and self-assertion in the denial of the self. It is taking up your cross and following Jesus, and the active taking up of your cross is a killing of the self in order to find the self.

There is no boasting at all because of grace – it is excluded, to use Paul's language – and yet because of grace, now we do boast in Christ, and for what Christ has done in us and through us. We self-assert that ourselves are self-submitted to the One who is worthy of all praise – not the self, but the King of all kings and Lord of all lords. Because this boasting, even of the positive side, by definition relates to some form of confidence, audacity, and joyful assertion, it is therefore related to our inner state, our psychology (to use that terminology), our affections, our heart, our psyche, our soul.

Far then from being an odd sudden jump to a different topic, to talk about boasting in relation to psychology is a necessary part of the discussion for us not only to understand boasting (in both its positive and negative forms), but also to be able to think of boasting in more practical ways as well. How does the act of boasting shift our consciousness? When someone boasts in a negative way, does it say something different about their inner state than when someone boasts in a positive way? What is the function of boasting in terms of helping or hurting the inner soul, mind, heart, psyche, psychology of a human being? Does boasting become some way to deal with blockages in the inner life, taking down strongholds with the sure Word of Christ, if it is a boasting that is positive? Conversely, does boasting, when it is negative, shore up those self-same boundaries and make them stronger and harder to break down and more perilous for the inner life? Does boasting either harden the heart further or soften the heart that was hardened?

The more I have thought about it, read about it, studied it, talked to others about it, considered it, the more it seems to me that boasting has a somewhat special (if not unique) role, not only in representing inner states of the mind or heart, but also in reinforcing them, affecting them, changing them for good or ill. There is something about the act of boasting, whether positive or negative, that impacts the inner space – when for the positive, it has the potential for doing great good, and when for the negative, the converse potential, too. In particular, boasting affects the way our inner state is orientated emotionally, neurologically, and logically.

Of those three claims (emotionally, neurologically, and logically) the most outrageous and contentious is the middle one. That this matter of boasting could actually affect the inner workings of the firing of the physical neurons might seem at first blush to be an astonishing claim, and yet digging a little deeper, its impact in that realm is nearly self-evident and of great consequence. Because the neurological claim is least likely to be acceptable to the average reader, I will begin with the impact of boasting (positive and negative) upon the neurological realm before then tackling the emotions and finally the logical or rational or ratiocination sphere.

The Neurological

Given the advances in MRI scanning, it is now possible to watch the brain 'light up' as it processes thoughts, ideas, emotions, concepts, reasons, and emotions. This has meant some adjustments to the models that we have in discussion regarding the basic functional spheres of operation of the brain with relation to thinking and emoting. I have written about this elsewhere,[1] and Antonio Damasio in his book *Descartes' Error* gives insight into one take on the latest thinking in this regard.[2] Bestselling books like *Blink* or *The Art of Choosing* also suggest that our conception of how our emotions and our thinking work together – or don't work together – are shifting today into a more integrated and less separated model of the interactions at a neurological level. That is, some of our best thinking is fuelled by our most passionate feeling, and some of our most-ordered passion is put together by our best thinking.

The way this interrelates with the idea of boasting, whether of a positive or negative kind, may not be immediately obvious. But what we are talking about here, when we are talking about boasting, is a mental state that is at the very least passionate. We are caught up, driven, determined, and audaciously pushing forward some passion, dream, or desire. This is not emotional in the sense of being

---

1   Josh Moody and Robin Weekes, *Burning Hearts: Preaching to the Affections* (Fearn, Ross-shire: Christian Focus, 2015).

2   Antonio Damasio, *Descartes' Error: Emotion, Reason, and the Human Brain* (Penguin Books, 2005). *See* also, the *Handbook of Affective Sciences* (Davidson, Scherer, & Hill, 2003).

out of control, unpredictable or a 'basket case'. This is emotion as in passion, as in core drive for something, and for someone. In the case of boasting, furthermore, it is not only a core drive; it is taking that core drive to the next level, and making it crystal clear not just to ourselves, but to the people around us, what we believe, why we believe it, and why it is so important that others catch the same vision and desire that we have. This affects our emotional state, and our emotional state is affected by this.

In other words, we need to do away with the idea of the brain solely as a thinking machine. The brain is a thinking machine, but it is far more than the most complicated biologically-based computing device ever discovered. We are not simply dealing with an organism that has immense computing power – though it does have this. We are dealing with something that has constant, ongoing mental operations, normally not visible to our own conception of what we are thinking about, that regulates our heartbeat and our various body rhythms. The brain is involved with memory, the storing of memory, and its maintenance within our minds for as long as our minds are operational in the best state of our mental capacities.

Memory is a powerful force. By memory we are able to transcend space and time and inhabit a different world from where we are, to call up not just the thinking of the past, but the sound of the past, the feeling of the past, the taste of the past, the smell of the past. We time-travel whenever we remember something vividly; we can travel backwards in our minds. We can also travel forwards, even though our visions of the future are projections, not records in any sense (granted our memories have, in all likelihood, elements of personal projection to them as well, they are still records of what happened in some shape or form in normal circumstances).

This mental ability that we have with memory is far more than simply ratiocination or computing power. It is the ability mentally to move oneself to be somewhere else – sometimes to be someone else by the power of imagination. If memory is a time-traveller, imagination is a universe-hopper. We can imagine worlds and universes, kings and paupers. We have the ability to conjure pictures and shapes, sights and sounds (not so much image-making as audition-making).

Our brain is far more than merely a computer or a thinking machine. Even if a computer could be built to work with the same mental ratiocination as the best human brain – and some, no doubt, believe that such a computer has already been built – even if that kind of super-computer were indisputably possible and real, the computation would but only scratch the surface of the human brain. We have memory, we have imagination, we have the ability to form an identity, to have a sense of self, who we are, what we want, the great 'I' of the mystery of human consciousness.

Not only can we realize that we exist; we can reflect on why we exist, and on what the meaning of our life is. We can have late-night philosophical discussions about Kierkegaard or Nietzsche, and then be caught up in the exhilaration of our football team winning a game, imagining ourselves scoring the touchdown as we watch our hero scoring it.. We have this ability to leap mentally from one state to another, from one person to another, from one time to another. And through it all, there is this mysterious 'I', an 'I' about which we can reflect, talk, and consider.

On top of all this, more than imagination or memory, or identification with other people and hero figures, and even more than the mystery of human consciousness, there is the extraordinary tendency of all humans everywhere in every place to build societies that have within them the concept and practice of worship. Humans need to find a sense of transcendence, and if they cannot find it, they are driven to build it and create it.

I remember my visit to Moscow soon after the collapse of the great atheistic regime which was the former Soviet Union. In this country, where religious observance was, if not outright banned, at least repressed, and sometimes violently persecuted, there was in the centre of the most famous square – known then as Red Square, in front of the Kremlin – a mid-size, box-like shape. There was a line of people waiting to go inside. In this capsule was the shape of a man, encased in glass, a famous small beard and pert chin, balding hairline, lying flat on his back. Each night the corpse was treated and cared for by specially selected temple servants, and each day the devoted stood in line, travelling from all over Russia, to see the face of the one who had declared that no supreme being existed and none should be worshiped.

Worship is a factor of human life whether we want to believe there is Someone to worship or not. We will worship in the same way that we will breathe. While there is life, there is not only breath, there is also worship. We worship sport, we worship Lenin, we worship ourselves, we worship sensual intimacy, we worship gastronomical delights, we worship fame and success. You can always tell what you worship by what you sacrifice to. What is it that you give your sleepless nights to? What is it that you sacrifice time with your children for? What is it that you give your money to? For what achievements are you willing to sacrifice friendships? Worship is inevitable, and our real objects of worship are revealed by the pain of the sacrifice that we are willing to bear for the sake of that which is worshiped.

Into all of this extraordinary mental activity, like a pebble in a pond, like a storm in a Mediterranean winter, like a tsunami in the Pacific, there is then one more factor which relates directly to the neurological effects of boasting. That factor is the will. To boast about something is to operate deliberately and decisively in favour of something and (probably) equally deliberately, and decisively, against something else. It is to assert by will on the basis of a decision, a living, large response to something that is true, or we wish were true, or we hope were true. It is not simply to decide in a cold, analytical way, but on the basis of picking an option out of a plethora of options, boasting then when that decision-making engages the emotional and wilful aspects of the neurology of our circuitry.

In recent years there has been much renewed research in the processes of the brain, using tools like functional MRIs that have given new insight into the complexity of the brain processes. Little has been finalized in any overarching theoretical model, and especially not when it comes down to the will based on a decision that has been made. While it is possible to identify areas of the brain that are primarily related to visual stimulation, for instance, when it comes to making a decision – because such a decision has to pull from many different aspects related to the options, reason, memory, experience, emotions – it has not proved possible to identify a specific area or even areas related to such decision-making.

In monkeys, there appear to be a primacy of three areas related to decision-making, but these areas are significantly far apart from each other, and it is not clear how each of them interrelates when it comes to decision-making (even in monkeys). When it comes to humans, the role of the brain in decision-making is far from clear and continues to be a new area of research and discussion, looking for working hypotheses without any overarching grand narrative or theory to pull the different pieces of data together.[3] In short, we could say that decision-making in the brain is so complicated that it shows just how complicated must be not only making a decision, but also then putting wheels or legs on that decision in such a way that it gathers momentum,

---

3   http://www.kavlifoundation.org/science-spotlights/neurosci-ence-of-decision-making#.VmGQZ4SMDq0

action is taken, and in the topic under our consideration, boastful action is taken or boastful words spoken.

Perhaps this is unsurprising. By its very nature a decision is not always the same because it relates to different matters, depending on the aspect of the decision under consideration at any one time. For instance, a decision about which school to send your child to is not really (mentally) similar to a decision about what to eat for dinner that evening. While both are decisions, the data that are required for that decision are significantly different in either case. The one requires weighing up the different schools in your area: your budget should you consider private education; the different environment that a private education might provide for your child, or the social network it might create; the kinds of expertise that your child has, and how to maximize them in any of the options under consideration; the needs your child has socially, and who else among his or her peers might be attending which school; etc. This is only superficially similar to a decision about which restaurant to eat at that evening, or whether to cook chili con carne or hamburgers. It is hardly surprising that tying down decision-making to a particular area of the brain is a bit like trying to get mud to stick to a wall. It is possible, but it depends on the viscosity of the mud and the stickability of the wall.

Add to this the additional factor of boasting – not just a decision, but a confident decision, an audacious decision, a decision that is trumpeted loud and clear for all to hear – and it is, if the research would ever be done, likely to be hard to gain any meaningful information at the neurological level about 'where' boasting takes place. But what might be garnered is the effect of that 'loud decision', or boasting, and its impact neurologically. What happens when someone who is under psychiatric investigation, is depressed and undergoing clinical trials, finds something not just to live for, but to die for? What happens when someone has a meaning for their life, and not just a meaning, but a boast –

something that so moves them that they tell everyone about it who will listen, even if they are not the kind of person who speaks particularly loudly about other things? What happens if they become an enthusiast for something, and that enthusiasm is evident to others and self-evident to themselves? How does that affect their mood, their rationality, their depression, their mental state?

It seems as if addiction is related to poor decision-making, which is connected to impaired reward choices and decision-making circuitry in the brain. If that is true, then what would happen if that decision-making circuitry discovered a reward far greater than anything that could previously have been conceived, and starts to live large with a thrill, a lilt and a shout? When we think in these terms, it becomes unsurprising that encounters with Jesus left the sick healed in every area of their minds and bodies, when Jesus willed, and when there was faith to receive His grace. The brain's imaging, circuitry, and functioning are affected at a neurological level by what it sees, hears, and, yes, decides. Then how would that brain be impacted by a decision that is huge, enjoyable, meaningful, rewarding, and boasting in a positive sense? Hugely.

This was what the psychologist Viktor Frankl discovered in the concentration camps during World War 2, and which he recorded in his famous *Man's Search for Meaning*. Without meaning, without something about which to boast, man gives up the will to live, especially in the harshest of environments. Further, that will to live comes down to a choice, perhaps more than a simple logical, analytical choice, but a willful determination, an engagement (if you will) of the boasting circuitry of the brain, and so life transcends the grimmest of realities. This boasting does something to us internally – its external proclamation of what gives us true lasting joy. It has a by-product internally, mentally, and that by-product is a meaning and a vigorous toughness that gives resilience to humanity in the face even of immensely-challenging, countervailing odds and circumstances.

In essence, what we are talking about is an extreme form of what mechanistic psychologists call 'the hard problem of consciousness'. It is apparent, from observable scientific data, that our brains 'light up' when certain physical activities take place. It is also apparent, from slightly disturbing tests done when humans were decapitated, that certain functions are instinctive and happen even without a brain immediately attached – physical response to pain, for instance. Neurons 'fire' and computational responses occur, such that the overriding scientific approach to the human being is that we are essentially neurological. That said, the idea that 'gray matter' – a squidgy-looking mass of inedible nervous tissue – however extraordinarily complex, with billions of neurons and chemical neurotransmitters, can actually produce consciousness, well, that to many seems incredible. There appears to be an insoluble – and irreducible to reductionistic notions of 'merely machine' – thing that feels and thinks, and is 'I'.

Well, given this 'hard problem' (or an indicator that a paradigm should be shifted or changed), we are left with an intense form of it when we come to boasting. Boasting is the ultimate assertion of something related to the self – whether in positive or negative forms. It is an act of will against which mere computational models have little if anything to say. It is not simply a recognition of this 'I' that is so hard to define; it is an observation of this 'I' on the move, asserting will and taking life by the lapels and demanding attention. It is not passive, responding to stimuli, but active, creating stimuli. By-the-by, it is unnecessary, in any non-reductionistic or mechanistic mode of human consciousness, to adopt a strict, old-fashioned, Cartesian dualistic 'ghost in the machine' approach. Nor is it necessary to attempt to reconcile two apparently irreconcilable models – the mechanistic and the dualistic.

Instead, what this consciousness and especially this boasting do is that they show us there is another model: a 'third way', if you will, which we might term 'three-dimensional'. When we look at a painting, say a Van Gogh, at one level we are correct to say it is nothing but paint. At another level, there is a huge difference between a Van Gogh and the colour of your own wall in your living room. There is a 'thing', – an artistic (creational) 'thing' – imputed to that paint in the case of the Van Gogh, which makes it essentially and fundamentally different from a can of paint or a painted wall. With humans, it is nearly infinitely more complex again – for the Van Gogh that is our consciousness is not simply beautiful or artistic; it is an 'I' too. It looks out from life and demands attention. Especially when it is boasting – whether in a positive or negative sense. It does not sit on a wall waiting passively for an observer; it is an observer.

This model of consciousness is three-dimensional in that: (1) it accepts the neurological nature of the brain, or the basic scientific model that is indisputable at a purely mechanistic level; (2) it does not accept that it is the entirety of the description, any more than saying that a Van Gogh is nothing but paint is the entirety of a Van Gogh; and (3) it goes further to look in wonder as that particular Van Gogh painting looks up and observes us. The ultimate in human (daringly, we could say scientific) hubris is not to observe that what we are observing is observing us. The consciousness that we dismiss looks out at us, and says, 'What about me?' It observes us as we observe it, and it will suddenly get down off the wall, refuse to be consigned to the eugenics of evolutionary disaster, grasp for attention (for revenge against its Frankenstein-like scientific torturers), and ask – no, insist – on being taking seriously. Each step in this three-dimensional approach is underlined – and made obvious and plain – when the human consciousness (the Van Gogh painting), moves from being the observed to being the observer: by way of an assertion – an audacious assertion – that the mind is there and is thinking and desiring, and has ambitions and aims, and exists for more than running neurological programmes.

The Emotions

When we move to the emotive, the affectional, the passions or emotions, we are also dealing with an 'I' that feels. It feels sad or joyful, happy or proud, jealous or bitter – sometimes all at once, or immediately one after the other. Our emotions are extremely hard to pin down, observe, and understand. If they are merely mechanistic, we might accord to them the lower kind of hormonal responses, but there is a consciousness to our feelings, our intuitions, that is observable as something which has an observer behind it, an 'I' as a part of it.

Recent research in functional MRIs has shown that the emotional realm is not as distinctly different from the rational, as has long been thought; that is, there seems to be special overlap between the thinking and the feeling areas of the brain. That itself, however, given the extraordinary complexity of the brain, does not necessarily conclude that emotions and reasoning overlap; there may be more than one reason why these processes occur in similar areas of the brain. The brain functions along parallel processing power, hence its extraordinary capability to do things, like recognize faces in less than a blink of the eye (a computing power that a two-year-old has, that is far in advance of the most complicated computer even today).

Thinkers then have long attempted to categorize emotions to understand them. Aristotle, in particular in his work on *Rhetoric*, had an approach to emotions which has shaped much of Western thinking ever since. Essentially, in that work on rhetoric designed to train a public speaker how to communicate by using the hearers' emotions, Aristotle adopted a fairly pragmatic approach. Emotions are not the higher reasoning faculties of the mind, but they are a real deciding factor, very often, in whether people accept the case that is being made; therefore the speaker must learn how to raise emotions (the right kind of emotions) to the right degree, when speaking. Aristotle defined his view of the various emotions and then taught the orator how to raise those emotions: to what degree, at what time, and with what kind of argument they best support.

The emotions that Aristotle discussed tended to be quite basic; that is, they referred to things like fear, jealousy, and anger. They were almost visceral, gut-like, hormonal, we might say. Aristotle appeared to be primarily talking about the kind of emotions that happened with the 'fight or flight' response in the human, when a particular hormone kicks in and we respond in certain kinds of ways. Aristotle appears to accept that, other than in the highly trained and carefully self-observant, these hormonal-emotional responses will most likely win the day over any particular argument. Therefore, the speaker must raise the emotions in order for his logical argument to gain sway. That is why Aristotle divides the key aspects of speaking into three: the logos (or the argument), the ethos (or the character of the speaker, which is to be indicated during the actual speech), and the pathos (or these hormonal-emotional responses).

To take an example, say someone unknown, without credited academic achievements, stands up and starts to make a cogent argument that time actually is not fixed, and the argument he makes is sound. That argument is unlikely to be viewed as compelling, at least not the first time it is heard, but the result would be very different if the speaker were Einstein – especially if the speaker were by then well-known, and especially if during the speech he indicated his credentials and attainments in various subtle ways too. If in addition to the logos and ethos, the speaker added an element of pathos – say he indicated that the hearers were particularly privileged to hear this groundbreaking work (raising ambition or jealousy), or that someone else was trying to stop this work that would deeply impact human flourishing from coming to light (raising anger) – then the case would likely to be not only accepted, but enthusiastically accepted.

What does this have to do with boasting? Well, boasting is not merely a logical response. There is an emotional energy to it, a passion, a desire, an audacious joy when it is positive boasting. But is this emotion – that is related even to positive boasting – like the kind of 'passion' of a hormonal-emotional kind, to which Aristotle was referring, or is it something different?

More recent theories of emotions include that of the historically situated, but less distant, great American theologian and philosopher, Jonathan Edwards. Edwards developed an approach to emotions that viewed them as more holistic (to use modern jargon) than the dichotomous view of emotions versus rationalization that was developing in his time and, until recently, was dominant in Western culture. But for Edwards, the 'heart', to use biblical language, was a node of emotion, reason, and will. These were certainly distinguishable aspects of our interaction with ourselves and with the world, but there was an inherent connectivity to them. What you had an 'affection' for, what you had a 'heart' for, was something that you had an emotional, rational, and willed response towards. Affections, then, for Edwards were not merely the kind of emotional life that Aristotle seemed to assume – that is the lower, more animal, more hormonal aspects of a person's being and thought life and mental processing.

Emotions also affect – to talk in terms of biology for a moment – the lobes of the brain, the 'higher' (if we may talk in those terms), more distinctly and differentiated human aspects of the personality. It was then quite permissible, and indeed essential for success, to target human emotions in preaching. Edwards believed that no great change in a person towards love for God or obedience of God was ever done without engaging the 'affections' – emotion, reason, as well as will. The affectional-passionate side of the human personality had to be engaged for any change to occur. He saw his aim as a preacher to raise the affections as high as possible as long as they were raised in accordance with truth – that is with the truth of the Bible in a more 'logos' kind of way.

Now this more Edwardsian (less Aristotelian) framework has huge implications for how we think of boasting. It appears then from our study of boasting in the Bible that boasting is related to the way a human takes what it perceives to be of value, of truth, and then projects that value and that truth large scale onto the world around. Whether that boasting is positive or negative depends upon whether the perception of that value or that truth is accurate or not, and whether the kind of projection of that truth is itself done in a way that is ethically compatible with the truth, even when it is genuinely true and surely of value.

But given that the projection of that truth is ethical, and given that the truth so perceived is actually of value and genuinely true, then it is apparent that boasting by its nature is a way of ramping up that affection. Boasting becomes a way of magnifying that affection, of engaging the will, and doing it in a non-bashful, slightly 'bling', 'out-there' kind of way. To 'boast in the Lord' is, if anything, not to be mousey-quiet about one's faith or commitments, but to take the great risk, the audacious step, of trumpeting those commitments to the world around. That requires emotional engagement, and the Edwardsian model seems to suggest that for that emotional engagement to be true, it needs to be a fair representation of the truth.

If truth is, we must add, also trumpeted and boasted in a way that is ethical and in accordance with the value that is being boasted about (he who boasts in the Lord must live a life in accordance with the love of his Lord), then the boasting becomes a way of taking that Edwardsian affectional response, and making it apparent to those around. It's like taking the idea of Edwards and hitting 'publish' on the nicely crafted website, putting it out there in cyberspace where everyone can see it – online, in actual local community, in church, in work – making that affectional response something that has to be engaged with, accounted for, by those around the person doing the boasting. It is pride (in the good sense of that word, meaning confident security and pleasure in something worthy and valuable), but it is also more than that – it is boasting, taking that value, engaging the affections (in an Edwardsian, and not merely Aristotelian, sense) and making them live large in front of everyone around, for their own assessment and benefit.

Once it is put like that, it becomes fairly clear that this kind of boasting could be too in-your-face, too out-there, and if not manipulative, at least potentially so. How do we guard against the negative ramifications of even well-intentioned (and perhaps also well-directed) boasting? For that we need to think through, not just the trajectory of very distant, Aristotelian, and slightly more recent, Edwardsian, aspects of the way that emotions engage with boasting, but also look at contemporaneous theories regarding the emotions.

The world did not stand still after Edwards, and certainly not after Aristotle, and we now live in a post-Kantian – and therefore in some sense, post-Edwardsian – place and worldview. For us, it is assumed that higher and reliable, verifiable reasoning has little, if anything, to do with the emotions. All this is as a result of complicated views of epistemology, formulated by Kant in various massive tomes – including *The Categorical Imperative* discourse, and his *Critique of Pure Reason* – which he put forward and which have very gradually seeped their way through the academic institutions, and into the common parlance of everyday sets of assumptions. There have been counter-movements, most famously the Romantic movement of the nineteenth century touted by great poets like Wordsworth and Coleridge, the existentialist movement with its non-Christian and more Christian forms (with Kierkegaard), but still today we live in an assumption that science (or knowledge) is what happens with a dispassionate approach to life, based upon empirical method. This appears to have very little to do with boasting, and undermines the project of seeing boasting as in any way of any value.

Critiques of this set of common assumptions today are not hard to find. Particularly cogent is the 'paradigm shift' theory of Thomas Kuhn, who influentially postulated that genuine scientific revolutions actually take place when enough new evidence has been gathered to shift the framework to a new theory. This does not so much undermine the post-Kantian set of assumptions, as it does relativize them within a wider spectrum of human engagement and indeed intuitive judgment. The post-modern movement and the relativistic movement all are reactions against the pure rationalization of life, where knowledge to be true knowledge must be dispassionate.

To understand the veracity of these reactive movements, and their relation to our project regarding boasting, as well as the continuing power of the dichotomy of the post-Kantian worldview, it is important to engage with current views regarding what emotions really are. Summarily, the dominant theoretical framework with relation to the emotions currently is an evolutionary one. It has been observed and verified by various experimental data that, for instance, facial expressions related to emotions are not culture-specific. There are certainly cultural variations. The way an American typically smiles is different, for instance, than the way an English person typically smiles. But there is overall general similarity between such facial expressions. It is even known that babies smile, pre-verbal, and what is more surprising, it is known that babies born blind smile. So that smiling is not something that is taught by social interaction, but something that has become hardwired into human, trans-cultural behaviour. What is smiling? Superficially, we would think that smiling is related to the human emotion of happiness or joy. But, it turns out, this is not quite accurate. In actual fact, smiling is far less about the emotional state of the person who is smiling than that person's desire to communicate that sense of happiness to someone else.

So studies have been done of American bowling; when a person gets a strike, knocking down all the pins, that is a happy moment. But while the person who has just scored a strike is looking away from his friends, the person does not smile. When he turns back to his friend, that is when he smiles – to communicate to them a sense of happiness. So the feeling of happiness is related to a facial expression, but it is the intention, apparently, of that facial expression to cause someone else to share in the happiness. That is the purpose of the smile.

There also seem to be at least two different types of smile. There is the genuine smile which involves not only turning the mouth up, but also the eyes as well. It is found that only about one in ten people can fake a smile from the eyes as well. The other smile, sometimes termed the Pan Am smile after the fake-looking smile of the flight attendants in the early days of the Pan Am Airways, smiles from the mouth, but not from the eyes. It is also attempting to communicate happiness, but it is not a happiness that is genuinely felt, more like a greeting smile at best.

It is not only related to smiling and happiness, which is the way these emotions are analyzed today in terms of evolutionary tendencies or communicating social cues. Studies have been done of what makes people afraid. It appears that what makes people afraid are things like spiders and snakes, or leaving home alone, and other naturally occurring phenomena. A study was done of children in Chicago asking them what made them afraid. You might think that the answer would be guns or getting run over by a car. In fact, these children, many of whom had never seen a spider or a snake beyond at best a visit to a zoo, listed spiders and snakes as their fears – not the far more likely dangers of cars, buses and guns. Theoreticians today, then, postulate an evolutionary rationale for this: what in our primeval past were real, daily dangers biased the future generational, genetic data towards those who acted in fear towards these dangers, and those residues still remain with us.

By contrast, contemporary theories also postulate that emotional life is necessary for proper human functioning. Unlike the stoic approach to emotions – the sort of *Star Trek* motif of the character Data, with his computer-generated robotic self without an emotion chip, or Spock, coming from a world without emotions – actually emotions are necessary and essential for healthy human life. We need motives, drives, and emotions to do things and make appropriate decisions. In the book *Descartes' Error*, Damasio analyzed one particular patient of his known as Eliot, who could not make any reasonable prioritization anymore because he had a biological impact to part of his brain through medical disease. He would sit at his desk at work and take hours figuring out what sort of categorization to use for filing, rather than actually doing any filing.

Similar is the great old historic example of Phineas Gage from the nineteenth century. A man who was working as a foreman in a blasting operation had a large, long metal bar blasted through his brain, going from under his eye out the top of his head, and landing yards away with blood and bits of brain on it. But he did not die, was only unconscious for a moment, stood up, and after being asked whether he was okay, was taken to the hospital, stopping on the way for a glass of beer. Phineas Gage contracted an infection and had to be hospitalized, but he recovered. What he lost were parts of his personality or character. He swore uncontrollably, had fits of rage, and had to take a job in the circus, travelling around the country with the metal bar that had gone through his brain, telling his story. Neither of these individuals lost their emotional capacities altogether, but their emotional range was significantly impaired, and this likewise impaired their normal functioning and their rational capacities as well.

Boasting, then, clearly has an emotional component to it. In the key text related to boasting, this is made apparent: 'Through him we have also obtained access by faith into this grace in which we stand, and we rejoice [or literally 'boast'] in hope of the glory of God' (Romans 5:2, ESV). Is this emotional element therefore irrational? Not at all, for the emotions are the drivers of our actions, whether rational or not. In this case, to boast in the Lord is most rational and also thereby, when rightly considered, becomes passionately joyful. But what could be the possible evolutionary framework for explaining this sort of emotion?

Freudian analysis would dumb down the religious sense everywhere to a sort of massive wish-fulfilment desire for a big father-figure type. But while Freud's general analysis of the unconscious seems undeniable, his more particular theories here, as elsewhere, are frequently rejected by researchers today. What, from a purely Darwinian evolutionary point of view, could be the purpose of this sort of emotion-fuelled rational boast in God and what God has done? What is the genetic advantage? There seems little, if any, from this kind of positive boasting as we have called it. The negative boasting, on the other hand, a sort of puffing out the chest, chest thumping, self-assertion is almost intrinsically primeval, if not related to behaviour observable in other primates in the wild. It is a way of trumpeting domination of a particular pack, tribe or social group and, with such domination, becomes at least the possibility of genetic reproduction and thereafter protection of your offspring.

What is happening when such boasting is turned towards God, however, is that the selfish gene is transcended by a spiritual other-worldly dynamic, a desire for that which is bigger than the self, bigger than genetic reproduction, bigger than the flesh, and far better. This kind of positive boasting is a way of affirming – more than affirming, shouting about, crying out – that the real purpose of life is far more than genes. Life's real purpose is something eternal, and Someone eternally beautiful and bountiful. Those who stay stuck in primate behaviour are analyzing one side of life and missing out on the three-dimensional possibilities of life to the full – now and forever. This positive boasting then affirms this trajectory and propels it, as well, by gathering our emotional drives and turning towards something far bigger and better than mere animal-like, worldly, flat, two-dimensional analysis, at best. It is more than, not less than; better than, not worse than; higher than, not lower than; transcendent, not merely reductionistic.

The Rational

A classic example of the complexity of thinking clearly under pressure is called 'the prisoner's dilemma'. In this example, two prisoners are caught and imprisoned by the police for a particular crime that they have committed. The thought experiment goes as follows. Say the police visit prisoner A and tell him that if he rats on his criminal partner, then he will be left off from the crime; what does prisoner A do? What is most rational for him to do? The police add that if he does not give up the goods and tell them everything that has occurred, and if the other prisoner (prisoner B) does tell the police, then prisoner A will go away for a very long time.

At a theoretical level it would be better for both of the prisoners if they kept to their pre-jail pact not to say anything to the police whatsoever. In that instance they both would be sentenced for a minor offence and only get some jail time at worst. However, in this prisoner's dilemma, if prisoner A says nothing and if prisoner B confesses to everything, then life will go very badly for prisoner A. In actual fact, then, while theoretically it would be better for both prisoners if they both stayed silent, at a coldly-rational bargaining level, it would be better for prisoner A to confess everything. If prisoner B also confesses, then they will both be let off. If prisoner B does not confess, then it will go badly for him. But if prisoner A does not confess, and if prisoner B does confess, then it will go badly for prisoner A. Therefore, at the level of this thought experiment, it is better for prisoner A to break their pre-jail pact and tell the police everything. The theoretical best-case scenario, that they both say nothing, only will work out if they can truly rely on each other in this situation where there is no further contact between them, and where the police are exerting pressure on them. Such a scenario, the classic thought experiment often known as the prisoner's dilemma, is frequently used to show the complexity of cognitive reasoning at a social level and in conjunction with others. Rational thought is less obviously clear-cut than it is sometimes assumed to be, when it comes to how to do what is best for the self in any particular situation.

In another example, two partners are asked to show each other one or other side of card saying either 'defect' or 'collaborate'. If both sides of the card that they show each other say 'collaborate' then both partners receive five dollars. If both sides say 'defect' then both partners receive one dollar. But if one side says 'defect' and the other 'collaborate', the partner with the side that says 'defect' receives 20 dollars. What is the best ('rational') approach to this situation?

Experimenters built computers, programmed with various response mechanisms, to play this game over a long time to figure out which was the best approach. It turned out that the computer program that did best was also one of the simplest. It was programmed first of all to say 'collaborate', and then afterwards to do exactly what the other partner had done in the previous round. It began with 'collaboration', but was not a pushover if it found that the other partner had 'defected', and then responded with 'forgiveness' by reverting to 'collaborate' if the other partner collaborated.

This game-theory approach to what is best in terms of reasonable actions in certain situations does not exhaust the theory of logic, and how to establish truth or true knowledge at a logical, rational level. It does show, however, that such a subject as boasting (which does not by its nature appear to have much to do with rational thought itself) can impact the rational behavior in ways that may not be entirely predictable at first glance. You would think, then, that it would be rational, in a selfish survival-of-the-fittest kind of way, to always be inclined to a more negative sort of boasting – to assert yourself, to trumpet your own agenda, to dominate, to live large, to get yourself out there, and generally to be an 'alpha male' or the equivalent 'queen bee' – an aggressive self-assertion through negative boasting. In actual fact, however, even at the most prosaic and practical, social and even animal level, this sort of behaviour is not beneficial long-term.

Scientists have studied how animals, even animals such as the vampire bat, of all creatures, have a tendency to act in what is known as mutually-beneficial altruism. That is, if one animal finds food, it will look to help the others in the pack (whether or not they are related physically to the first animal) to also find food. There are, observers have noted, 'cheaters' in these animal packs who receive such altruism, but do not themselves give it back. But what happens to these 'cheaters' is that over time, the rest of the group refuses to give them the benefits of the mutually-beneficial altruism.

Negative boasting, then, for all its perceived sort of individualistic benefits for the self, is actually, long-term, detrimental to others and also to the self. This is true even at a biological, animal level. How much more so for humans, and how much more when it comes to God and His rule over the whole earth. We are not, then, to think of a call away from negative boasting to positive boasting as a sort of boy scout, good guy, always-be-nice attempt to get people to do something which is actually intrinsically (in the 'real world') bad for them. Not at all: the call to put God first, and to boast about that God, is genuinely what glorifies Him and also what benefits God's people.

Why not, though, from a rational and humanistic, basic and almost animal point of view, behave instead in a quietly passive, receptive mode rather than in a pumped up, boasting-behaviour norm (even if that boasting is about God and not about self)? Another experiment, this time one called the 'ultimatum game', illustrates the situation here. Say there are two partners, and one partner has the ability to offer to the other partner money from a range of 1 to 10 dollars. Say there are another hundred or so people in the same room who all know that the range of possible offers is from 1 to 10 dollars, and are going to hear at the same time what everyone else gets. What do you offer the person? And how does the person ('rationally') respond to such an offer?

What turns out is that if someone is offered 1 dollar (rather than the alternative, nothing at all), while it is at one level completely rational to accept that offer and be grateful for it, that is rarely the case. Because the person being offered the money knows that they could have been offered more, and can even hear others being offered more, they are usually somewhat miffed to only have been given one dollar. The experiment goes further. As this game is repeated, it turns out that the person who acts in this way somewhat 'irrationally' – that is, they protest at only getting the one dollar, and do not merely accept it quietly – that person is more likely do better in the long run. There is, then, something to be said for speaking your mind, standing up, making a difference, not being a pushover.

However, understanding how much one is actually doing this, versus how much you think that you are boasting and making an impact on others around you, is notoriously difficult to ascertain. This is, in fact, a phenomenon known as 'the spotlight effect', whereby we tend to overestimate how much anyone actually notices what we are doing, what we are wearing, what we are saying. Because by definition we tend to be always, in some sense or other, at the centre of our own world, or at least looking out from that centre at the rest of the world, we are naturally likely to view ourselves as noticeable by others. We are noticeable by ourselves all the time, and so we tend to think that the clothes we wear, the style of music we listen to, whether we have spinach in our teeth, or a glob of shaving foam left from the morning shave still attached to our neck, are all immediately obvious and noticed by others. However, it appears that this is much less the case than we tend to think. We are much less in the spotlight than we tend to assume.

Boasting, whether negative or positive, is a way to counteract that tendency to think that what we have said or done is really being noticed by others. For the person doing negative boasting, the spotlight effect is counteracted in unhealthy ways, ways that are going to be detrimental to their long-term well-being. But for the person doing positive boasting, boasting in the Lord, this boasting is a way of putting forward the best ideas, the real truth, the greatest Person that ever was or will be – who is, and was, and ever shall be – putting Him into the centre of attention in a way that He deserves to be, and is truly best for all His creation. Because we tend to think that we are noticed or in the spotlight when often we are not, we need to compensate for this tendency by realizing that people are probably not talking about us, thinking about us, wondering about us, or even noticing what we are saying, even when it is atypical or different from the norm. To be instead conscious about finding ways to step into the spotlight, or to put

God in the spotlight when it is positive boasting, is a way of compensating for this common social-psychological tendency that influences how we rationalize our impact on the world. 'Faint heart never won fair lady,' and the one who attempts to be neutral with regard to boasting, perhaps out of a false sense of people around noticing what they are doing, is likely to miss out on the impact, whether for good or ill, that he or she could have in this passing world.

Boasting then, from a rational point of view, is not a psychological attempt to don another personality, certainly not in a sort of morbid, multiple-personality sense, nor is it an attempt to be someone that you are really not. It is not a regression to a less than ideal type of person, who is nefarious in his impact upon the surrounding world. It is a way of taking what is good – when the boasting is positive – and ensuring that that goodness is noticed so that it has an impact. The civil rights movement in mid-century America was, it may be said, from a certain point of view, one long exercise in positive boasting to gain an impact: consciously stepping out of the spotlight-effect, and genuinely having an impact, by the end with the march on Washington D.C. and the famous 'I have a dream speech' (that was desired and hoped for). It took guts and a certain audacity, a bravery and a conscious 'putting yourself out there': even the cause of that which is good and righteous, and worth fighting for.

The psychology of boasting, then, from a psychological point of view – looking at the impact and causes emotionally, rationally, and neurologically – is a healthy attempt by the self to have an impact in the society that is meritorious – as long as the boasting is of a positive kind. It is a tool to turn up the dial, to put something or someone in the centre of attention and make a difference. It is not deleterious of social norms, disadvantageous to psychological health, something that is only possible for certain personality types (however they are characterized, whether more choleric, or Type A, or whatever description is used). It is a way that the self, any human self, can grab the initiative, put the issue or the person into the centre of the dialogue, and sit up and be noticed. When positive, it is not only a healthy manifestation of a psychological norm now writ large, it is also good for the world around and for the glory of God.

6.
THE KEY TEXT: ROMANS 5:2

The key text for this paradigmatic shift in our understanding of boasting is found in Romans chapter 5. For many people, myself included, Romans is the greatest letter in the greatest book ever written. That is not to say that somehow Paul's letter to the Romans is more Scripture than any other part of the Bible, for all Scripture is God-breathed and is useful for teaching, rebuking, correcting, and training in righteousness (2 Tim. 3:16). Romans is no more God's Word than any other part of the Bible. Nor is it to say that Romans somehow contains doctrine or teaching that cannot also be found elsewhere in the Bible – that is the 'Roman secret' to the true meaning of Scripture, as if Scripture can only be properly understood when one has mastered Romans. It is true, to be sure, that Jesus commissioned His apostles for the establishing of the teaching of the church, and so the way that Jesus wants us to understand what it means to follow Him is by following the teaching of those He commissioned and the writings they authored or authorized. It is also true that Romans is pre-eminently doctrinal of all the teachings of Scripture. It is especially satisfying for an eager mind, a mind that enjoys reading, thinking and understanding, to find in the Bible a treatise that can not only satisfy the eagerness of that mind but stretch it and (at times) blow that mind away by the sheer expanse of the vision of the apostle Paul under the inspiration of God.

But Romans is not more special than other Scripture. It is simply the place where we find the outlining and teaching of the gospel as understood by Paul to be pre-eminently on display. It is no surprise, then, to find in Romans the right location to understand this matter of boasting. Especially, as we saw in Chapter 1, boasting was something that the apostle Paul was particularly inclined to discuss and teach about. If Paul was concerned with something, then we look to his writings to discover what he thought about it, and of all his writings we are most likely to discover his most developed thoughts about it in Romans. Not without exception: the church, for instance, is relatively absent as a doctrine in Romans, or at least ecclesiology by the specific name of the church, even though 'body life' is addressed clearly in Romans 12. But Romans is often a bellwether for what Paul says about many matters.

And with regard to boasting, it is no exception, for we find in Romans a key text about it. Other parts of Paul's writings teach on boasting more fully in terms of length or volume of words. But we are not to judge the significance of a teaching simply by the amount of paper or words used to describe it. Voluminous discussion does not necessarily equate to significant discussion, as anyone who has watched the rather bizarre parliamentary procedure of the filibuster knows. Someone can speak on and on, write on and on, but have less to say than the single well-chosen word – like an apple of gold in a setting of silver.

This particular apple of gold in a setting of silver in Paul's letter to the Romans is found in Romans 5:2. It reads quite innocuously at first glance:

'Through him we have also obtained access by faith into this grace in which we stand, and we rejoice in hope of the glory of God.' (ESV)

In many English translations, the word 'boast' is not even present, translating the word for boast here as 'rejoice' or equivalent. The word in Greek is the same word for boast as is typically translated 'boast' elsewhere: in Romans 3:27 (ESV), 'Then what becomes of our boasting? It is excluded.' Why is this word not translated 'boast', then, in Romans 5:2 as it is elsewhere translated 'boast'?

The reason for that is because of the complexity of the word 'boast' in the English language. In English, at least in non-religious English, it is very unusual, if not unheard of, to use the word 'boast' in a positive sense. It nearly always means something like arrogant self-expression or (in the American English vernacular) 'tooting your own horn': or (in the British English vernacular) 'blowing your own trumpet'. To boast, normally, if not exclusively, in English means to cross the line from self-confidence to arrogance. A boastful person is by definition not a humble person, not a godly person, and probably not someone you want to hang out with a whole lot. Without the benefit of the very extended conversation, or at least parts of the background, of what we have discussed in this book, to use the word 'boast' in an English translation might cause the less-well-informed English reader to think that to be a Christian is to be someone who is boastful in an arrogant, self-absorbed sort of way. This would be a complete misunderstanding of what Paul is saying.

So this is probably the reason why the word in Romans 5:2 is often not translated as 'boast'. It would lead to confusion in the minds of many readers. That said, however, the fact that Paul did use the word 'boast', albeit with a different semantic range to the word 'boast' in English, leads us to the discussion of what Paul meant by 'boast': at least in this particular place, and as it contributes to the wider discussion of what Paul meant by 'boast', and of what the word 'boast' means in the Bible. And, as I say, it seems to me that the word here, in this context, is especially important to grasping the significance of boasting in practice: and in conceptual terms too, for the richness of the Christian life, or for those seeking to follow Jesus.

To understand how this one verse – Romans 5:2 – functions in such a significant way, it is important to grasp the *flow or argument of Romans as a whole*, to understand the *flow or arguments of Romans 5:1-11*, and then see *how this verse shifts our understanding* of boasting to the one that we have been exploring in this book. Boasting becomes not only an expression of the wonder of being a Christian, a natural result of being in Christ, it also becomes an active positive tool for us to experience that reality more and more. This is the key insight, a paradigmatic shift, of Romans 5:2.

Romans as a whole

The summary message of Romans, hotly debated down through church history, is usually thought to reside in the key thesis statement at the beginning of the book. Ancient letters of this kind – formal, public renditions of the author's message to his auditors and others to whom the message would be read – followed a standard set form. Scholars have also debated to what extent Romans, and other letters (particularly the letter to the Galatians), follow this set form, whether precisely, somewhat, or not at all. But despite all this conversation, it is still normal to look at the particular thesis statement at the beginning, where the message of Romans would reside within this set form of ancient letter writing, and it does indeed appear to be in this case. Romans 1:16-17:

> For I am not ashamed of the gospel, for it is the power of God for salvation to everyone who believes, to the Jew first and also to the Greek. For in it the righteousness of God is revealed from faith for faith, as it is written, 'The righteous shall live by faith.' (ESV)

Again, there is much discussion about the meaning of these verses (in fact, there is little place in Romans where there is not much discussion!), but in my view these verses are indeed a thesis (if not the only thesis) statement for Romans and can be explained relatively simply. Paul was saying that his message in Romans was all about the gospel; this gospel is God's power for salvation. He was saying this comes by faith – emphatically so using the word 'faith' cognates four times (in the original) in these two verses. This salvation comes, he was saying, because of righteousness or justification (the same root word in the original), again emphasized by repetition in these verses. So in summary, we may say that Paul is writing to the Romans about a gospel that comes through faith in Jesus and that gives the believer God's righteousness.

However, this simple summary is far from the end of the matter when it comes to discerning the basic meaning of Romans. To begin with, there is another well-known way that Paul indicated the basic message of Romans. He started with an unusual phrase and ended the whole letter with the same unusual phrase. This kind of envelope to the letter was a standard way of indicating the basic message of the letter. He says, in Romans 1:5, that he was there to call the nations to the 'obedience of faith' (ESV). Then he ended the letter with the same message, that this gospel was so that there might be an 'obedience of faith' from all nations (Rom. 16:26). It is true that in some early manuscripts the last paragraph of Romans was placed a little earlier in the letter, so this makes it harder to absolutely argue for the prominence of the 'obedience of faith' as the only or main theme of Romans. But even so, it does give us a simple 'trick' to the message of Romans.

Paul was saying – against his detractors whom he indicated were also in his view (see Rom. 3:8) as he was writing this, his magnum opus – that salvation comes through not just (what we would term) 'easy-believism', but a radical 'obedience of faith'. This is not merely the obedience that comes from faith, but means the kind of faith that is in itself, and in principle, submitting to God and obeying His gospel. Paul is using this language to talk about what elsewhere in the Bible is termed regeneration, the gift of the Spirit, the new person who comes about as a result of the gift of God and His Spirit that is received through faith. This person submits to God's Word, believes in it, has the 'obedience of faith', and therefore is born again and lives a different life now as a disciple of Jesus.

So the message of Romans is a message of the gospel that comes through faith and that gives us right standing before God. This faith, though, is not merely easy-believism, but the obedience of faith, a complete change of orientation away from obeying our self to obeying God, a change only possible by God's Spirit who makes us born again.

There is one other indicator of Paul's main message, not so commonly noticed, but equally if not more important. This indicator describes not only what Paul was saying, but also the answer to that even more vexed question about Romans, namely *why* Paul was writing this letter. Despite the strangeness of the admittance, scholars and preachers down through the years have found it hard to identify what caused Paul to write this letter, or why he wrote it. Some have said it was merely written as a magnum opus. It is a masterpiece theological treatise, and there is no cause for its writing other than Paul's desire to put down in writing the kind of theology and preaching that he delivered in synagogues all over the Roman world at that time. Others have baulked at that view, and said Paul must have a reason for this great theological treatise to the Romans; otherwise, why not write to some other group at some other time?

More recently, some have said then that the main reason Paul wrote Romans was to solve a Jewish-Gentile problem in the church. It seems quite likely that Jewish believers, along with their compatriots, had been expelled from Rome. And it seems quite likely that they had only just returned. In their absence it is possible that tensions about the 'Jewishness' or 'Gentile-ness' of the Christian church had grown. Paul as an apostle to the Gentiles, but a Jewish believer himself, was uniquely placed to be able to address these concerns. So some have said that the letter is written to show both Gentiles and Jews how to get along together in the church of God. Others, however, have said that this is too 'horizontal' a meaning or rationale for Romans, which is so God-centred and focused on salvation. The message must in essence have a rationale beyond a mere peace-making exercise.

This other indicator, then, is introduced by Paul's great little phrase at the start of the letter: 'the gospel of God' (Rom. 1:1). Unlike the other introductory phrase in Romans 1:5 ('obedience of faith'), this little characteristic phrase was in the first phrasing of the letter. It was then picked up in Romans 15:16, where Paul explicitly used that same phrase to teach and to tell the Romans why he had written. For some reason, this specific description of Paul as to why he had written is under-studied (though certainly not entirely ignored) by people trying to work out why Paul wrote Romans! Paul himself explains, when he says:

> But on some points I have written to you very boldly by way of reminder, because of the grace given me by God to be a minister of Christ Jesus to the Gentiles in the priestly service of the gospel of God, so that the offering of the Gentiles may be acceptable, sanctified by the Holy Spirit (Rom. 15:15-16, ESV).

So, Paul himself said that he was writing for a particular purpose, as well as in a particular way. He was then giving the Romans *a bold reminder of the gospel of God for the sake of all nations*. In my view, Paul viewed the church at Rome – Rome, the centre of the world at the time – as a key opportunity for the gospel to go further and further to the Gentiles and to the nations. It seems quite likely that any potential tensions (never indicated explicitly in the letter, be it noted) would need to be solved among the Roman church itself if there were tensions between Jews and Gentiles. But this is not the focus of the letter.

The focus of the letter is on the mountains beyond, the nations that are influenced by Rome, and could then be influenced by the church at Rome. In this regard, then, those who (rather cynically) say that Paul's letter to the Romans is merely a fundraising letter are not very far off the mark. Certainly it is more than that. But Paul did say in Romans 15:24, 'I plan to do so [visit the Roman church] when I go to Spain. I hope to see you while passing through and to have you assist me on my journey there, after I have enjoyed your company for a while'. Paul was asking for funds for his missionary work. Romans was not *merely* a fundraising letter. But it *was* written with a purpose of making Rome the great centre of world mission. Paul gave them so much theology, weight and clarity around this gospel of God because if they were going to be this great mission-sending centre for the nations, they would need to have a very clear view of the gospel that they were proclaiming. In my view, the Book of Romans is in summary *a bold reminder of the gospel of God for the sake of all nations*.

It is critically important we keep this summary in mind when we consider the significance of the key text for boasting, Romans 5:2. For that verse fits snugly in the canopy of this overall message of Romans and cannot be accurately interpreted outside the context of this bold reminder of the gospel of God for the sake of all nations. There is a boldness that this boasting will give them too.

The context of Romans 5:1-11

To understand the context of Romans 5:1-11, it is necessary to understand the structure of Romans and therefore how this section fits in that structure, as well as the particular message of this section. Romans is structured around a number of interlocking patterns. One way of looking at the letter is to divide it into two: Romans 1 to 11 (the gospel) and then Romans 12 to the end of the book (implications of the gospel in practical living for the Christian).

That said, while that sort of massive bird's-eye view is useful, its simplicity hides other interlocking aspects of the structure which are equally significant. For instance, another way of looking at Romans is the following:

Romans 1 to the first half of chapter 3—the problem.

The second half of Romans 3—first exposition of the solution.

Romans 4—answering an initial question that the solution would raise in the biblically literate hearer: Was this way of salvation how the Old Testament people of God were saved too? Answer, yes, they were also justified by faith even then.

Romans 5:1-11—rejoicing in confidence or assurance at that solution: This message of assurance then carries on until the end of chapter 8, which is in many ways a mirror of the first half of Romans 1 to 11.

Romans 5-8—answering problems that this declaration of assurance would naturally raise: What about ongoing sin in the believer? What about the law?

Romans 9-11—addressing the question of the promises given by God in the Old Testament, specifically to the ethnic people of God: have they been abrogated? No, they are fulfilled in Christ, and all who believe in the promises believe in Christ, and the Gentiles are grafted into that vine, and one day many of the ethnic Jews will also be grafted into that vine, likewise by faith in Christ.

Romans 12 to the end—various practical implications for the Christian: A description of the body-life of the Christian in the body of Christ with the various gifts given; how to relate to each other; how to relate to a secular state; Paul's role as an apostle; his reason for writing all this to them; and concluding with Paul's expression of affection to many of the individuals in the church at Rome, and a final benediction, which also once again summarizes the gospel message of Romans.

The overall structure of Romans

Then you could look at the structure of Romans a bit like this:

Simple Overview of the Structure: Romans 1-12 (gospel); Romans 12-16 (gospel applied).

More Complete Overview of the Structure: Romans 1-3a (problem of sin); Romans 3b (solution to sin); Romans 4 (objection answered); Romans 5a (solution celebrated with assurance); Romans 5b (position gives grounding to assurance); Romans 6 (objection of ongoing sin in the believer answered); Romans 7 (objection of ongoing function of law answered); Romans 8 (celebration of assurance again); Romans 9-11 (what about God's people the Jews specifically?); Romans 12-16 (the gospel applied to practical Christian living of the church in a secular state like Rome).

Now with this overall structure in mind, it is relatively easy to see the part that Romans 5:1-11 more specifically plays in that structure. Romans 5:1-11 is the most extraordinarily, highly vaulted and exalted piece of celebration that you can find in Scripture. It is celebration of the Christian, the true believer in Jesus, of the absolute certain assurance that a Christian can have because of what Christ has done on the cross. It is beautiful, it is majestic, it is a highly emotive and affective piece of writing that is intended to lift the Christian to the heights of praise.

But it is also itself structured with particular care. It starts with a summary and reminder of the key message of Romans: righteousness by faith. Since this has happened (Rom. 5:1), since what Paul had argued thus far in Romans was true, since we are made righteous by faith, then the rest of this assurance will naturally and inevitably follow.

So the structure begins by summarizing the message of Romans at a doctrinal level with a simple phrase: 'Therefore, since we have been justified by faith ...' The rest of this section is then what is known as an 'inclusion' or an envelope structure. At the beginning Paul said that we have peace with God. And then at the end in verse 11, he returned to this idea of peace by using a different word for the same idea, reconciliation. So the whole passage is built on justification by faith (the message of Romans at a purely doctrinal level), and it is therefore consequently true that we have peace with God, are reconciled with God – emphasized by the position in the structure of this section at the beginning and end. This peace with God, it is then emphasized by the structure, is emphatically through Jesus Christ: 'through our Lord Jesus Christ' (Rom. 5:1) and 'through our Lord Jesus Christ' (Rom. 5:11). Because of all this (our key verse 2) we 'boast in the hope of the glory of God,' which is also emphasized by the mirror repetition at the end of the section that we 'boast in God' (Rom. 5:11). This boasting takes place even in sufferings (Rom. 5:3) and even as something that functions to rescue us from God's wrath (Rom. 5:9). Sufferings and wrath here function as mirror elements of things that are a result of the fall that we can either boast in God in the context of them (sufferings) or boast in God as we are rescued from it (wrath). At the heart of all this is love, emphasized by being repeated (at the tip of the spear of this structure) in the middle of the passage. 'Because God's love has been poured into our hearts through the Holy Spirit' (Rom. 5:5, ESV), and 'God shows his love for us in that while we were still sinners, Christ died for us' (Rom. 5:8, ESV).

So the context of Romans 5:1-11 shows us that this section is particularly focused on joyful celebration because of the certain assured state we have in Christ Jesus, that is fixed and immovable. It also shows us that this joyful, confident assurance is centred on the person of Jesus Christ and His love for us. It shows us this joyful confidence takes place even in sufferings and especially because we are rescued from God's judgment and wrath on the last day. We are entering, with Romans 5:1-11, into the loudest, brightest, most celebratory part of Scripture that you can find, perhaps with the exception of the end of Romans 8 (which itself in many ways is a mirror of this section anyway).

How verse 2 shifts our understanding of boasting

To explore how Romans 5:2 shifts our understanding of boasting, and what its implications are for our thinking and our daily living, it is important for us to first clearly grasp *what* this verse is saying, and then *why* we can be sure it is saying that, before we see how this verse applies to our thinking and living.

I believe this verse is saying: *Rejoice with brave courage because through Christ you are now established forever in a realm of grace and glory*. I define the way that Paul used the word 'boast' as an audacious and brave, confident and deliberate act of rejoicing. It is something active, not passive, and it is something that may appear even outlandish, audacious, and certainly a kind of rejoicing with brave courage.

Let me now explain why I think it means this. It means this, first, because of the context of this verse which we have outlined above already. By way of reminder, in Romans 1 to 4, Paul argued that we are all sinners, every single one of us, and how therefore we are under the wrath of God; and that, out of His great love, God in Christ atoned for our sins at the cross through His blood, so that if we believe in Him, we might stand right before God, freely forgiven and righteous with the righteousness of Christ. This was his message that he proved, demonstrated, and articulated in the first four chapters of Romans, and that he referred to at that start of chapter 5 in summary form simply by saying, 'Therefore, since we have been justified by faith.' This is past tense, the aorist, denoting completed action, and so Paul was saying it was something that had taken place. It was not an ongoing potential; it was done; it was over, finished, accomplished: we have been justified by faith.

The next section of Romans then runs from chapter 5 through to chapter 8, and the whole of this new section is emphasizing one thing: that this state of justification is fixed, certain, assured, definite, and unchanging. So chapters 5 to 8 are Paul's argument that, because of the doctrine of justification by faith, those who believe in Jesus are now assured of their relationship with God forever. Paul returned to this theme at the end of Romans 8, where he told them that nothing 'will be able to separate us from the love of God that is in Christ Jesus our Lord'.

Paul returned again and again to Jesus, and indicated that Chapters 5 to 8 was one whole new section by ending each part of this new section with the same phrase 'through Jesus Christ our Lord' or 'in Jesus Christ our Lord'.[1] Because of this justification, Paul was saying in Romans 5:1, immediately before this key verse 2, that we have peace *with* God. This is not the peace *of* God, an emotional or internal peace. It is also not a peace between people. This is peace *with* God, a reconciliation with God that is now fixed, certain and definite.

So we come now to Romans 5:2, where Paul told us that there is another part of this sure and certain, assured state that we who believe in Jesus have. 'Through him' – that is through Jesus Christ – 'we have also obtained access by

---

1   Romans 5:1, 11, 21; 6:23; 7:25; 8:39.

faith' (ESV), The phrase 'by faith' may or may not have been in the original manuscript. It is indicated in the footnote of some modern translations that it may or not have been there. Either way, it makes no difference because Paul had emphasized so often that this is all 'through faith'.[2]

So, in the context of this theme of the fixed, certain, and assured state of having been justified by faith, Paul now says, 'Through him' – that is Jesus Christ – 'we have also obtained access by faith.' Now this 'access' is a very important word. It is used only three times in the New Testament, here and in Ephesians 2:18 and 3:12. Each time it comes with what one renowned biblical scholar called 'a certain touch of formality'. So in Ephesians 2:18, 'For through him we both have access to the Father by one Spirit.' Then in Ephesians 3:12 (ESV), 'in whom we have boldness and access with confidence through our faith in him.'

This note of formality to the word 'access' has a particular picture behind it. The picture is of someone being introduced or presented at a court of a king or queen. It could also have the picture of gaining access to a religious temple, and it may have both pictures in it because sometimes in the ancient world the two, kingly and priestly, were combined. At any rate the picture is something like this. Someone is a beggar on a street. He is living out his existence begging for food outside a palace. The rich and wealthy, celebrities and royalty, drive by and have access into the king's court. Now to gain an audience with a king is not something you can do on your own; you have to be presented at court. You cannot just march in; you have to have someone introduce you in order for you to have access.

So this beggar is now given a whole new set of robes and clothes, and is washed and put in the best courtly attire. Someone who has the privilege of access to the king's court then leads him in and makes an introduction to the king.

---

2   Papers on the historical reliability of the Bible are available at www.godcenteredlife.org.

This person now has access through the other person, and is now in the court. He has gone in; he cannot fall out again. He is now entered into the courtly realm; he has gained access. He is part of that circle now; he has been introduced, presented at court.

All this comes out of this word that Paul uses here: 'access'. Note it is something that has taken place. This has been obtained by Jesus Christ; He has made the introduction. Having been justified by faith, we are therefore introduced and presented at the court of God Himself. We are now in the court; we have obtained access. That is the picture here.

Now what have we obtained access into? Paul said 'into this grace'. It is a somewhat rare use of the word 'grace', but here it means a 'realm of grace'. Paul was now using it as a sphere, a place, a realm. This court into which we have obtained access through Jesus Christ is all the place, the realm of grace. Paul here made the use of this word clear when later in this section of Romans 5 to 8 – which is all about the certain, definite, and assured relationship we have in Christ with God – he says that we are no longer 'under law'; we are now 'under grace' (Rom. 6:14). That is the same idea. We have this new realm, this new master, this new place, this new court, into which we have gained access, and it is the realm of grace. In other words, we are now, through Christ and faith in Him, in a place of boundless and bountiful blessing, opportunity, privilege and honour – a realm of grace.

It all seems a little bit too good to be true, and we will naturally wonder whether it is possible to exit this realm or fall out of favour of this king, and no longer have access to his court. So Paul next makes sure that we understand that that is not possible. This is the grace, he said, 'in which we now stand' (Rom. 5:2). In other words, he was emphasizing what we could have understood already, because we have been justified by faith as a finished act, but he was emphasizing this by picturing us as *standing* in this place. This word 'stand' has the sense of fixed, established, or permanent. We are standing. There is confidence in it; we are not groveling. One ancient commentator said that we are standing because we used to be flat on the floor. There is something of that to it. The beggar has new palatial garments on him, a nice new set of clothes, and he's at the court of the king, not hiding in the corner. He is not worried that he is about to be kicked out at any moment should he say a wrong word, forget his courtly manners, or do something wrong. No, he is standing – secure, definite and certain, fixed and established.

So that is where we are, through Christ, in this realm of grace into which we have been introduced – a realm of blessing, opportunity and constant access to God, a realm in which we do not grovel, but we stand confident and certain. As Hebrews puts it, we now approach the throne of grace with boldness (Heb. 4:16).

Therefore Paul then tells us that because of this new realm in which we are fixed, as those who believe in Jesus, 'we rejoice in hope of the glory of God' (ESV). Each of these words is so important to understand. They have thrilled me as I have studied them! I want you to see them so you can get a sense of that same thrill. 'We rejoice' is actually the same word translated earlier in Romans as 'boast'. Paul had said in Romans 3:27 that boasting was excluded, that is, boasting is not possible. Why? Because no one can keep the law, and we are only saved by faith. So we have nothing to boast about. Jesus saved us; we were not saved by our own efforts or any good that we do.

But now he says we do boast. He says that we have nothing to boast about in ourselves. But when we are in Christ, we do have something to boast about. We are now in the court! We are fixed standing, established in the realm of grace. Now we do boast!

So it doesn't mean bragging about what you have done; that is a kind of boasting that is excluded. The kind of boasting here means a rejoicing confidence. It has a sense of brave declaration, and audacity: a declaration that is not just determined, but that has joy throughout it. It is congratulating yourself: but now because of where you are through what Christ has done. It is exuberant, a rejoicing confidence, that sort of boasting, because of what God has done in Christ, and because of where we are now in Christ, in the courts of the king, in the realm of grace.

For some reason this whole idea has been under-taught in Christian circles for a long time. It means that people who are not yet Christians wonder why they should bother becoming a Christian because it all seems so down in the mouth. We walk around with our heads down when we should have our heads held up high. We exclude one kind of boasting, but there is a rejoicing confidence that we have which is exceedingly exuberant.

What are we rejoicing in? We are rejoicing in 'hope'. As always, that word in the Bible does not mean 'I hope so'; it means something that is certain about the future. The hope of God is what will definitely come about because of what God has done in Christ. Our future hope is not uncertain; it is certain, definite, and so to rejoice in hope is not to hope that things will turn out for the best. It is to know for sure that we have this eternal life of which we are now a part because we are in the realm of grace which will never end. This hope we rejoice in.

But more than that, we rejoice in the hope 'of the glory of God.' Again, this is not well understood, and the more I have thought about it, the more it has thrilled me too. It thrilled Paul. He had seen the glory of God when he was converted on the road to Damascus, the blinding light shining around. This glory is something that we as humans beings used to have. But because we rebelled, we lost it, as Paul explains in Romans 3:23, 'For all have sinned and fall short of the glory of God.' We used to have this glory in the garden, but because of Adam's rebellion, and because we all have rebelled, we lost this glory of God and have fallen short of it. But now in Christ we are going to have that glory again!

'And those whom he predestined he also called, and those whom he called he also justified, and those whom he justified he also glorified' (Rom. 8:30, ESV). This glory is something not only out there in God, but something that will happen to us. 'For I consider that the sufferings of this present time are not worth comparing with the glory that is to be revealed in us' (Rom. 8:18, ESV). This is something not only spiritual, but physical; it will happen to our bodies. We will be changed in a flash, in the twinkling of an eye (1 Cor. 15:52), and take on a glorious body. This is something that is going to happen. It is certain if we believe in Jesus: it is assured.

Paul makes a giant leap from justification to glorification in Romans 8, and here at the beginning of this whole Romans 5-8 section too: this is not as a result of an ongoing process of gradual sanctification. That is important, and we need to do that. But our glorification is now certain because of our justification. We will be glorified.

Once we see this, we can understand why Jesus told His disciples not to rejoice that the demons submitted to them. He had sent them out to do ministry, and they had been very successful and had a remarkable impact. But 'do not rejoice in this,' Jesus said. 'Rejoice that your names are written in heaven' (Luke 10:20, ESV). Why? Because of this glory.

This is not a vague spirit either, floating around in a cloud. This is being restored to the glory of God, physically, as well as spiritually, in our own bodies, having true beauty, reflecting Him with unveiled faces. This also is something certain, definite, and assured: this is something that is even beginning to take place now. A Christian, though very weak and with many sins and broken body, with a jar of clay, has inside jewels of glory being prepared forever. As Paul put it in 2 Corinthians 3:18, 'And we all, with unveiled face, beholding the glory of the Lord, are being transformed into the same image from one degree of glory to another' (ESV). So the great hymn says, we are 'changed from glory into glory, till in heaven we take our place'.

None of this has to do with personality or temperament; none of it has to do with what we have done. It is all 'through him', the Lord Jesus Christ, that 'we have obtained access'. We have been introduced to the court, and we are now fixed, 'we stand', we are established in the realm of grace, a place of boundless blessing and opportunity. We have access to this God; freely and boldly we may approach the throne of grace. We do not grovel, we do not apologize, we do not crawl around on our hands and knees. We stand, we are fixed, we are secure, we are in the realm of grace, and nothing can separate us from the love of God. We have access to all the bounty of heaven's glory.

We have, as Peter put it, 'all things that pertain to life and godliness' (2 Pet. 1:3, ESV) already there for us. We have this extraordinary opportunity as children of the King, heirs of the whole universe, in the King's court, and so we rejoice confidently. We look around and say 'Wow! Am I really here? Wow! This is amazing!' We say to ourselves that it is great that we are here. We rejoice confidently in hope, certain of the future, of the glory of God, that we will be glorified, physically as well as spiritually, and that as we behold Him, we are now being changed from glory to glory. So, *rejoice with brave courage because through Christ we are now established forever in a realm of grace and glory.*

So now let us apply this to our lives. If Paul was saying that because of what Christ has done, we are now entered into the courts of the realm of grace, that we are fixed there, standing there, and that therefore we rejoice in hope of the glory of God, this fixed future and the glory that will be ours, restored to the glory of God, a leap from justification to glorification that is certain, and that glory we are now being gradually changed into as we fix our eyes on His glory

– if that is the case, then why do we not rejoice, and how are we to rejoice?

There are two reasons why people do not rejoice. Some people think this kind of boasting, rejoicing confidently, is the wrong thing to do at any time. They think it sounds too much like bragging. They think we should be wary of any kind of confident rejoicing. They don't want to brag, so they are not sure that they can rejoice confidently. Other people think it's the wrong thing to do because it is a little bit risky. They don't want to rejoice confidently because they think if they do someone will shoot them down. They are wary of what Australians call 'the tall poppy syndrome'; that is, they want to keep their head down, stay below the parapet, don't get ahead of anyone else, in case they cause someone to feel jealous or notice them. They want to stay in the background and be unheard from and unseen. So they don't rejoice confidently, or boast, because they don't want someone making sure that they go back again into their shell and cut down the tall poppy.

Some people just think that boasting, even this sense of rejoicing confidently, is the wrong thing because it is just not proper. It is not appropriate; it is not what we do. It feels too forward, too out-there; it is uncomfortable for them to rejoice confidently. So some people don't rejoice confidently because they think any kind of boasting is the wrong thing.

Other people don't rejoice confidently, because actually they are happily boasting in the wrong thing already. It is a little bit like ashes in their mouths. Some boast in their own moral goodness. This was the big part of what Paul had been trying to help the people of the religious Old Testament law of his time to realize, that they were not to boast in what they did morally. Some though still boast in their own moral goodness. They live a good life, and they congratulate themselves about it, but it doesn't lead to this kind of rejoicing confidence, because no one actually lives a good enough life.

Some people actually boast in their own sin. They sin bravely, they try to exult in it, but sin is its own reward: while the devil offers pleasure, he does not create pleasure, and his pleasures are only pale imitations of the real thing. The cut flower in the vase dies; only the living flower of God's pleasure is a place where you can find real confident joy.

Some people don't have this rejoicing confidence because they are boasting in their own nation. This was very common among the Jews of Paul's day, and it is still common among most nations of the world. They are very pleased about their own nation, and they congratulate themselves that they are a citizen of that particular country, but it does not lead to real rejoicing confidence because no nation is perfect, and it always disappoints.

Some people don't have this rejoicing confidence because they boast in their own gifting or abilities, being so confident in themselves: but this does not lead to real, rejoicing confidence because however gifted you are, there is always someone more gifted, and so it leads to frustration, not true rejoicing confidence.

So those are the reasons why people don't have this rejoicing confidence. They either think any kind of boasting, joyful confidence is wrong, or they have boasting, joyful confidence, in the wrong thing.

How do we have this joyful confidence? Well, it comes down to realizing and believing, accepting and revelling in the truth of what Paul was saying: *rejoice with brave courage because through Christ you are now established forever in a realm of grace and glory.*

What does that mean? It means these four things.

One, it means we boast in Jesus. We rejoice confidently in Jesus; it is all through Him, not ourselves. It is in Him, and in Him we think to ourselves how amazing! We rejoice confidently because we are fixed, certain, in the realm of grace, in this place of opportunity and blessing, with certain hope, and the glory of God that is sure, into whose glory we are now being changed from glory to glory. So it means, we boast in Jesus.

Then, two, it means we boast in Jesus by moving from hesitant to confident praying. We boldly approach the throne of grace. How are we praying? Are we praying like impoverished beggars with no right to talk to God? Or are we praying like children of a heavenly Father, whose relationship with Him is fixed and certain, who stand in the realm of grace and have all the blessings of heaven in front of us? Do we pray freely to our Father in heaven, with confidence, or do we grovel? Do we pray like impoverished beggars before a distant deity or like children of the heavenly Father?

Three, we boast in Jesus by moving from worship as distant performance to worship as gospel participation. We worship now as those who have been introduced into the realm of grace, into this grace in which stand, rejoicing in the hope of the glory of God. We are a part of this, welcome to this, in this; we are in the realm of grace now, introduced by none other than Jesus Himself.

Four, we boast in Jesus by moving from heads-down religion to heads-up Christianity. We do not wander around with our heads down, under a cloud of uncertainty, not sure about what will happen to us, or whether God really loves us, or whether we are still in God's good books. No, we hold our heads up high as children of the heavenly King and so *rejoice with brave courage because through Christ you are now established forever in a realm of grace and glory*.

The Game-changer

With this in mind then – with the concept and the message that Romans 5:2 teaches us, that we can *rejoice with brave courage because through Christ you are now established forever in a realm of grace and glory* – we can begin to see what a game-changer, what an impact on our lives, this truth can have.

If it is really true that our standing before God is unaffected by our circumstances, then that will forever release us from being ruled by them. Can someone with cancer rejoice the same way as someone who has just won an Olympic gold medal in the 100 metres? If not, then our circumstances are ruling our 'rejoicing with brave courage'. If it is not true that our standing is the same, whether we are facing death by drowning or exaltation on a podium to the applaud of millions, then our circumstances are still the contributive cause to our rejoicing.

This rejoicing with brave courage, if truly based on nothing else but what God has done, then given that what God has done is what God has done, and is not changeable by our passing circumstances, then our status as being one worthy of rejoicing also does not change. If any circumstance whatsoever can change our status, then our status is not fixed irrespective of circumstances. If we can imagine a circumstance where it is no longer true that our status with God is fixed and immovable, then however extreme that circumstance may be, it must be true by definition that our status is not fixed and immovable, but is subject to change on the basis of some circumstance or other.

But if it is true that, whatever the circumstance, we remain the same status as before, then our ability to stand tall and to take courage, whatever the situation, is extraordinary. We cannot be moved; we shall not be moved. We are immovable, because our status before God is only based upon what God has done. It gives us deep foundation, a foundation of security in the face of adversity: it also gives us a foundation of security in the face of prosperity. We can treat both those imposters – riches and poverty – as alike immaterial, and know that our status is not changed by either.

Our status is not changed by the car we drive, or the house we live in, or the aptitude of our children, or the beauty of our wife, or the strength of our husband, or the quality or coolness of our friends. We are at peace with God.

Therefore, we have reason – whatever the circumstances – to rejoice with brave courage.

But this verse – Romans 5:2 – is teaching us more than that we simply can rejoice, or that we have reason to rejoice, or that we are fixed and immovable. This verse is giving us a tool to realize our status. The *rejoice with brave courage*, the boasting, is an active tool, an app that can be applied to this and any situation to bring out what is truly there. By a deliberate decision, by an active decision, we begin to rejoice with brave courage. We take the decision to do so. We say aloud to ourselves and to others, 'Isn't this amazing?'; 'Wow that I am a Christian!'; 'Isn't God extraordinary?'; 'Isn't His Grace amazing?' We begin to wonder with amazement at the truth of our status, first by an active discipline, boasting over what we know to be true, whether we feel it to be true or not. We rejoice until we rejoice, and it takes bravery to do so.

I remember a particular family who had just received extraordinarily bad news about their son. He was travelling in a developing country, and a life-threatening accident occurred. I went to visit them, and found them sitting in their living room singing songs together and praising God. They knew full well the seriousness of the news. They understood with clarity the gravity of the situation – highly educated elites that they were. And yet, even because of, and in the context of this suffering, they deliberately rejoiced. As they rejoiced, they started to gain victory over these circumstances; they were no longer tempted to be bound by them, but began to be able to discern God's purpose through them, and in those very devastating circumstances.

It is a way for us to go on the offensive. To take courage in both hands and say, 'You know, actually I'm glad; I'm glad this has happened because it gives another opportunity for God to show His power. And that's going to be great. I'm looking forward to seeing it. Actually, you know, I rejoice. Yep, right now, I rejoice with brave courage.' It takes chutzpah, audacity, if not quite cheek in the face of circumstances, certainly giving circumstances a deliberate, spiritually minded: 'Forget you, I'm not doing that, no way. I'm not going down into the pit with you. Uh-huh, I've got the truth that I am at peace with God. Nothing is going to move me; I've got gospel chutzpah. I'm going to rejoice with brave courage. I'm going to go to Mount Carmel and challenge the prophets of Baal, and you know what? I'm going to win because God already has won. I'm going on the offensive.'

Obviously, we are to act with wisdom too, but this book and this text are not about prudence, nor are they against prudence. They are about fuel. It is about the place where we find that inner courage, the strength that comes from within, to run and not grow weary, to walk and not grow faint. To pick ourselves up again and fight some more. To look the monster in the eyes and laugh! And to boast over that Goliath with that gospel chutzpah that God is on our side, and victory is coming.

No more can you be timid once you see this truth. No more can you think to yourself, 'Well, living that way is for some super-spiritual Christians, but not for me.' This is true for all who believe. All who believe are justified by faith, and are introduced into the court of the King and stand in His presence, fixed, immovable. There is no distinction, for all have sinned and fallen short of the glory of God, and all who believe are justified by faith in Christ and are now fixed, established, and assured of their status before God, and at peace with God and reconciled with Him. And therefore, we rejoice.

We do not back down. We do not quail at the changes in culture or the situation around us. We see God's hand in it all. With wisdom, prudence, and care, but also with rejoicing bravery, we take the battle to the Goliath before us. We rejoice with brave courage. And our lives are changed. The confidence seeps throughout the whole individual, and from that individual throughout the whole team with whom he is playing. We start to play an entirely different way, with more courage, confidence, and certainty, as if we have nothing to lose (for we do have nothing to lose), and as if we know we are going to win (because we know we are going to win). The whole game of life changes as we deliberately, actively boast in Christ. *Rejoice with brave courage because through Christ you are now established forever in a realm of grace and glory.*

7.
A BRIEF HISTORY OF BOASTING

Stephen Hawking's famous book, *A Brief History of Time*, played off the notion of time and its history being able to be recorded briefly (or otherwise). Likewise, boasting is not the kind of thing that you would immediately think of as being worthy of having a history. If someone boasts, you would think that they would want to hide it, not record it, and if it were recorded, it would not be something about which they would want to, well, boast. Given that history relies on eyewitness accounts and given that these accounts are by their nature something that someone would wish to record, there seems at first glance a circumstantial likelihood that a brief history of boasting would be indeed somewhat brief. If you boast, would you want to boast about boasting? Probably not. What you want others to boast about is not the fact that you are boasting, but the achievements about which you boast.

To look at it another way, then, a brief history of boasting could be excessively extended to include pretty much a history of almost anything – or at least almost all human achievements. People may not want to be known as boasters, but they do want to be known for the things about which they boast; otherwise, they would not be boasting about them. Looked at this way, every record of human achievement, from the individual curriculum vitae to the longest narrative of *The Great Kings and Queens of Ye Olde Faire England*, is a record in some sense or other of people boasting. After all, are not these records of achievements in themselves in some sense a boast? Albeit, granted, they are not a boast always of the person who has achieved the matters about which they are boasting (unless they are in the form of that most fictitious history, the autobiography). Still the matters concerned are achievements, if not always, at least often.

Yes, there are many debaucherous, salacious, and downright evil matters which history must record too. But because they are notable, they are (I am sad to say) often things about which those involved can take a perverse pride. The criminal returning to the scene of his crime does so not just out of a guilty conscience, I am told, but also out of a strange sense of accomplishment and pride in a job done (I could not say a 'job done well', but you get the point). In this sense, even a history of the greatest mistakes of the human race might in some sense be records of boasting, for in recording these greatest mistakes, we are by contrast also tipping our hat to the great successes of the human race – like a woman who knows she is beautiful delights to be surrounded by those she thinks are less beautiful, in order to set off her own beauty. Or like a wedding gown is designed to make the bride look beautiful, and often the dresses given to the bridesmaids are by contrast distinctly frumpy. A history of the making of bridesmaids' dresses would in some sense be a history of the intended boasting in the beauty of the excellence of brides' dresses.

We might, then, say that in some sense either there is no history (however brief) that can be given of boasting, for no one wants to be known for boasting – or we might also say that all history instead is a record of boasting, for the very fact that we are recording shows that there is something noteworthy about it, and that others want it to be known (or in the extreme, boasted about). Either approach is not particularly productive for giving even a cursory (or brief) history of boasting, so by that standard would be easy to dismiss.

But could it be that actually the task of having a history of boasting is pointless to begin with? No, the truth lies somewhere in between the two – that no history of boasting is possible, and all history is boasting. The truth is there is plenty of history, of myth and accounts of both the negative boasting described in the Bible and analyzed in previous chapters, as well as the positive boasting. There are stories that illustrate the mythic principle of Icarus flying too close to the sun. He boasts too high of his own achievements, attempts too much, is too proud in his own abilities, and comes crashing down. There is plenty of material in history of this kind of negative boasting. It could fill many volumes to describe all the instances in human history that evidence that 'pride comes before a fall', or that boasting in yourself or your own achievements is unpleasant to others and unhealthy for your own self.

By the same token, it is possible to find instances where a brave confidence in God in the face of all adversity, and based upon the solid ground of the gospel, takes an individual, a church, or a community forward, advances the kingdom significantly, and gives real and lasting joy. I will give one instance from history of the negative kind of boasting – for the pages could easily fill up with this kind of illustration, and, while worthy of taking note, they are not particularly encouraging to read of at length. And then I will give three instances of the more positive kind of boasting, a rejoicing confidence that led to significant gospel progress and kingdom advance.

A brief history of negative boasting

By negative boasting, we mean, let me remind us, that kind of boasting which is in the wrong thing and done in the wrong way. It is a tooting your own horn, blowing your own trumpet, kind of activity. It is not just pride or arrogance. It is being overtly proud about being proud, or loudly arrogant about being arrogant. It is a certain self-assured hubris that is taken to the next level of being so self-assured that that hubris is not only something about which the individual is no longer in any sense ashamed, but he boasts about all his achievements to others, often even about his hubris. He is a fool and foolish about being foolish, proud about being foolish, trumpetting his foolishness to everyone, with supreme self-confidence. This is what it means to be negatively boasting.

Perhaps the most powerful, albeit painful and controversial, recent example of negative boasting in relatively modern history is that of one Adolf Hitler. Hitler, it is widely recognized, was a genius at self-promotion. He had various henchmen around him who masterminded the campaign for office – the archetype of the Führer with which Hitler became synonymous – so it is not true that all the effects of Hitler's promotion to pre-eminence originated in his own fertile and evil mind. But yet Hitler would not have managed to achieve the notoriety he did, and the space in his people's imagination at the time, if he had not himself been blessed/cursed with a genius for self-promotion.

One has only to read that infamous book of his, *Mein Kampf* ('My Struggle'), still banned in Germany even today, to realize the power of his ability to force himself upon other people's dreams and romantic aspirations. In concrete and most practical terms, here was a man who had been imprisoned for the political equivalent of football hooliganism. He was not widely admired, he was not a victim of some repressive Gulag out to get the enlightened thinking people to like him. He was a violent, small-minded bigot who had been put in jail for orchestrating various unsavory campaigns, including random violence. He was not Nelson Mandela (of course, himself having been involved in violence of a very, very different kind and motivation); he was certainly not Martin Luther King in a Birmingham jail.

He was Hitler – the figure to history known as little more than the most evil dictator ever, and yet at the time little less than a pathetic, though dangerous, pipsqueak.

But he starts to boast – or self-promote – and he does it with genius. Following his outlandish and outspoken goal of telling 'the big lie' because people are more willing to believe a big lie than a small lie, he positions himself as some champion of the people. He taps into all the fears of the time (the Jewish takeover, the Soviet spies, the knife in the back during World War 1, the unfair treaty of Versailles, and on and on), playing on those fears like an expert pianist at a concert. A little here, a little there, a touch on the pedal now, a quick crescendo, but not too much. He pushes himself forward on the crest of the wave of what people want. They want a strong leader figure, a Führer, to rescue them. He will become that figure for them. They want someone to bring to justice all the evil no-hopers who have attacked the people. He will round up a series of unlikely victims, throw at them mythical caricatures from deep within the psyche of the history of the people, and sacrifice them, cheered on by the mob. They get the economy back on the road. He will take the easy way out. He will simply stop paying reparations. He will default. They want the glory days back again. He will give them late night marches and parades and tell them that they will expand for the glory of the people once more.

Each boast or self-promotion is done with maximum effect. As is well known, Hitler never actually achieved a democratic mandate or a majority vote, but once he had slid into power or close enough to it, he exercised his other area of genius – unflinching, vicious political manoeuvring to get rid of his opponents, blame a fictitious enemy, and so have an excuse for gathering sovereign power in his own hands. All this boasting, all the pamphlets, the shows, and the late meetings, all carefully done to achieve the end desired.

People are more susceptible to believing what is presented to them later at night than in the morning or in the afternoon. Therefore, the meetings took place at night, in the gloom surrounded by nocturnal fire and orchestrated drama. People at the time wanted their leaders looking like military heroes. He dressed like a military hero. People then wanted to know that the future was going to be better than the past. He did everything he could to present a vision of a glorious future and to make it a reality, come what may, and whatever cost to his person and to the lives of countless individual millions.

The strain on Hitler must have been immense. Given that he too had an immortal soul, however tortured, given that he too had loves and intimates (his famous girlfriend), what must it have been like to so wound himself for the sake of this larger infamy that he sought? Hell on earth, surely. In fact, Hitler so drove himself into the ground that during the war, he had his doctor inject him daily with amphetamine ('speed') to enable him to continue to function at the levels of performance that he felt he needed to attain to keep up the whole charade. Self-promotion, boast, genius, evil, and more self-promotion, all the big lie, all to gain the attention, power and influence, and create the effects for the people, for him, and for the glory of the Reich. And all for not nothing, but for worse than nothing, pure evil, and the devastating destruction of millions and millions of Jews, homosexuals, malcontents in the eyes of the state, and innocent children and soldiers fighting to preserve freedom for future generations.

And all it came crashing down on him. The most bitter description of an individual in modern history came in Allan Bullock's portrayal of the last days of Hitler in his bunker in Berlin, surrounded by armies inexorably marching on him, playing his hand to the end, still self-promoting (boasting) even as no one is looking. Of course, Hitler was an extreme. By no means is all self-promotion and boasting as extremely evil as Hitler's. For that we can be glad. But in the extremity of his actions, we see the full blown tree that is the possible end result of the smaller seed of an individual's own less genius, less evil, but still real negative boasting. It is like inflating a balloon. You pump and you pump, and at some point it will burst. Depending on the size of the balloon and the extent to which it is inflated will depend the resulting bang (destruction) of the over-inflated balloon. But all negative boasting is like that balloon being over-inflated.

For some it appears merely ridiculous – like the evident commercial failure, living on the street, boasting of how if things had just gone differently for him he could have been a Nobel prize winner. Or like the commercial success, boasting of his own success as if it was all his own work and ignoring all the supporting components that were not in his own control that went towards giving him the opportunities that others did not have. We self-promote, we boast. We try to gain attention. We do it through Facebook, Twitter, social media. We live lives that are a pastiche of truth, pasting together photographs that we think tell a good story about who we are and what we are trying to do. We live in many ways in the age of the negative boast.

None of us wants to think that what we are doing is what Hitler was doing. Surely not? And in many ways the comparison is absurd. What does the person who puts up innumerable pictures of their cat have in common with the man who puts up innumerable pictures of himself as the all-conquering Führer who will rid the people of the vermin of their opponents in the vilest racism ever known to man? There is no comparison. They are different in so many respects. But are they different qualitatively (in essence) or quantitatively (in scale and impact)? As we create images of ourselves for others to see, the danger is not so much to our privacy itself, but to our ability to create a real self that represents the true self, rather than the self-promoted self, the boast self, which is picked for impact rather than for genuineness.

Is there a better way than this kind of self-promotion or negative boasting? Do we just stay quiet and not say anything much, keep our heads below the parapet, and not engage in the public sphere of promotion at all? Are we who follow Jesus to be mice, or is there a way for us to be lions – not to devour, but to defend and protect the weak and vulnerable? The choice is not between negative boasting and no boasting at all, but between negative boasting and positive boasting. Of the impact of that positive boasting, there are plenty of historical examples that show us its huge potential for kingdom growth and change – three of which I will pick by way of illustration.

A brief history of positive boasting

Charles Spurgeon

In some ways, the most colourful example of positive boasting in relatively recent church history is that of Charles Spurgeon. Often dubbed 'the prince of preachers' for his finesse and effectiveness in the pulpit, Spurgeon also had, for most of his life, an unvarnished association with depression. The effects of this black mood would encapsulate him so thoroughly that it would immediately impinge on everything with which he was related. Whether he always had a tendency this way is not clear, but it seems that the ongoing ramifications were kicked into gear after the infamous event when a man yelled 'Fire!' at a packed church meeting when Spurgeon was preaching. In this building and without modern fire safety regulations, the sudden shout of the word 'Fire' caused mayhem. People jumped from the balcony, and there was a mass panic to exit the building. People were crushed to death. As Spurgeon looked on from the pulpit, helpless to intercede, he kept on preaching away, trying to offer counsel and comfort of things spiritual and eternal. The vision of people under his preaching so quickly and violently being ushered into eternity must have haunted his dreams and his thought processes ever after. He was certainly plagued with dark moods and a melancholic disposition afterwards. He described his own experience in 'When a Preacher is Downcast':

> Fits of depression come over the most of us. Cheerful as we may be, we must at intervals be cast down. The strong are not always vigorous, the wise not always ready, the brave not always courageous, and the joyous not always happy.
>
> There may be here and there men of iron to whom wear and tear work no perceptible detriment, but surely the rust frets even these; and as for ordinary men, the Lord knows and makes them to know that they are but dust.
>
> Knowing by most painful experience what deep depression of spirit means, being visited therewith at seasons by no means few or far between, I thought it might be consolatory to some of my brethren if I gave my thoughts thereon, that younger men might not fancy that some strange thing had happened to them when they became for a season possessed by melancholy; and that sadder men might know that one upon whom the sun has shone right joyously did not always walk in the light.[1]

He went on to describe how Martin Luther, surely one of the greatest and toughest preachers ever to have lived, was himself subject to such depressive moods, even though also he could be exulted later and in other times, and even his deathbed was a struggle with such terrible darkness of temperament and being downcast.

In addition to the one event of the fire, there were many other reasons why Spurgeon might have had a tendency

---

1   http://www.haventoday.org/spurgeon-on-depression-gd-434.html

towards depressive moods from time to time. For instance, he was, inevitably, as a public figure subject to much criticism and public railing against him and misunderstanding. He kept, it is said, a book of the clippings of all the criticisms he had received – as a way of being able to look back and see how God had brought him through all of these criticisms and more. He also had physical ailments, gout, and other maladies as he aged. In short, Spurgeon, famed for his good humour, quick wit, and sparkling rhetorical style, was actually subject to another side of the same coin: depression.

What makes Spurgeon's examples so apropos for this discussion about historical examples of positive boasting is that he was also able to triumph over these attacks through means of 'boasting in the Lord', among other techniques. In the same discussion about his depression cited above, Spurgeon noted that he had discovered that use to which God gave depression in his own life:

> This depression comes over me whenever the Lord is preparing a larger blessing for my ministry. The cloud is black before it breaks and overshadows before it yields its deluge of mercy.
>
> Depression has now become to me as a prophet in rough clothing, a John the Baptist heralding the nearer coming of my Lord's richer benison.

Depressive moods had a purpose, a preparatory purpose for a larger usefulness. In that larger usefulness, Spurgeon was pre- eminent with his tendency to be bold for God. So many stories are told of this side of Spurgeon's life – humorous, witty anecdotes – that it is tempting to tell them all simply for the sheer joy of them. Enough will suffice to make the point that Spurgeon was not a melancholic man only, but striving with such occasional moods, he was able to be lifted to joyful (even playful) exultation. Spurgeon would drive to church when he was preaching, puffing on a cigar – claiming that such smoking was a necessary preparation for the hard work of preaching. The very act of his driving through the streets of London in a carriage to go to preach, announcing the coming sermon by this act, and in doing so with such public (boastful!), playful cigar chomping was a kind of positive boasting.

Spurgeon was once accosted by a critic for using too much humour in his sermons. 'Madam,' he replied, 'if you only knew how much I restrain myself.' On and on the stories go. Spurgeon publicly chastised a man on a Sunday School outing: 'Aren't you ashamed to be smoking on the Sunday School outing?' The man put out his cigar. Right afterwards, Spurgeon ostentatiously lights up his own cigar. When the man protests at what Spurgeon is doing, Spurgeon replied, 'You obviously were ashamed. But I am not!'

But these anecdotes only tell half, less than half of the story. Read Spurgeon's sermons; read them again and again. I am fortunate enough to have been given a manuscript of one of Spurgeon's sermons being prepared for print with Spurgeon's own handwriting on it. It shows the care that he took with each word. This was no flamboyant fly-by-mouth windbag. Every term mattered for Spurgeon. And each term was designed to be confidently, boastfully, blessedly exulting in God and doing good thereby to God's people. The sermons throb with life, energy, passion, and also good humour, gospel clarity, and simple practical counsel for the everyday man or woman.

All this energy had its cost, another reason for his down days. It is hard to live with such output without later sucking in wind, desperately trying to replenish the soul to be ready for another great outpouring of effort in a few days to come. But also, all this effort of boasting positively in the Lord is a historical example of the sort of brave, audacious confidence that Spurgeon had because of the grace of God.

One of my favourite stories is of the young Spurgeon who used to wear a colourful pocket square in the front-facing pocket of his jacket. The deacons, however, informed him that it would be better if he didn't wear that colourful pocket square. Spurgeon – wise as well as exuberant – desisted! He was a man who, in Christ, despite his melancholic episodes, was able to exude a vibrant and audacious, confident boasting of a positive kind in the Lord. Consider this passage from a sermon called 'Harvest Joy' on Isaiah 9:3:

> The joy that we ought to have tonight, the joy of any growing church, will be joy such as God gives. That is the kind of joy we desire to have. If anybody wishes to see the church grow that we may excel other churches, that is not the joy that God gives. If we like to see converts because we are glad that our opinions should be spread, God does not give that joy. If we crave converts that we may steal them from other people, God does not give that joy, if it be a joy. I do not think God is the lover of sheep-stealers, and there are plenty of such about. We do not desire to increase our numbers by taking Christian people away from other Christian communities. No, the joy which God gives is clear, unselfish delight in Christ being glorified, in souls being saved, in truth being spread, and in error being baffled. God give us a joy over those who are added to us, which shall be pure, and Christlike, and heavenly! Oh that he might increase such joy! I think that he *has* increased it.[2]

If the prince of preachers is a worthy example of positive boasting, especially given his personal and temperamental tendency to go in the reverse direction to melancholy, not vivacious, confidence in God, he is also inevitably an ecclesiastical example. What would it mean for us to boast in the Lord outside of a church gathering, a church meeting, a church planning session, or a church prayer meeting? Clearly boasting in the Lord in these kind of scenarios is important – it can add to the group of Christians those that

---

2   Spurgeon, Sermons, vol. 38, p. 340.

God is calling, and encourage His people already so called – but it does not answer the question of what it would be like to boast in the Lord in non-religious situations. Is that even possible? Is it possible in the (post)modern, secularistic Western world, which limits us to not speaking in favour of any one particular religion, if we are to gain the approval of the dominant ideology of our day? By its nature, historical examples of faithfulness and positive boasting, in this context, are hard to come by because the situation today is so different from the situation of previous decades.

William Wilberforce

One clear example of the power of positive boasting is the life of William Wilberforce. Another great evangelical hero figure, Wilberforce was never operative within the strictly-speaking religious realm, but was a politician and an aristocrat who had a distinct passion and calling for fairness and justice. He was famous at the time for his care for animals. He would not allow creatures to be treated as poorly as they were typically treated during his lifetime. But where he became famous was not in environmental care per se, but in the long-running campaign he waged against the slavery trade. After innumerable efforts, the slave trade was first banned throughout the British empire, and then slavery itself was banned. He is a hero because he stuck to the vision of justice for slaves, fought tooth and nail to make it happen, and succeeded in large part.

What is sometimes less frequently discussed is the extent to which he employed positive boasting for his campaigns. One effort in this regard was to take a ship of elites, without their initial knowledge, past a slave ship in harbour in London so that they could have a close-up and personal smell of the stench of imprisoned humanity. In other words, Wilberforce did not just talk about it quietly, he did not just campaign about it in speeches, he found a way (in this and in many other instances) to take the issue above the politeness of normal human conversation to another level. They were confronted by the reality. They knew that this was not right. Even if they did not immediately do anything about it, they knew that something was not happening in accordance with normal human concerns. It would be harder for these people to sleep right afterwards without smelling that stench again and hearing the wailing of the suffering fellow humans. Their consciences would be forever stirred. Is it right that men be treated this way in a so-called Christian country? The unanswerable question would have rallied in their mind like no mere lecture on the economic injustices of slavery could ever have done. He put himself out-there, as it is said today, in such a way that the cause that he was championing was boasted about – but in a positive way, in a way that was not about himself but was about the cause, and ultimately about God's cause of justice.

He utilized the efforts of a man who had been a slave, too. Showing his scars and his whippings, he would move up and down the country stirring the consciences of anyone who dared look. He was bringing home to the country the ills of the slave trade, the immorality of it, in such a way that made it harder and harder to ignore.

He was, in other words, not meek in the way that that word is often misunderstood. Actually, in Jesus' teaching, meek does not mean weak or mousey. It means strength under control, like a wild horse that has been trained for battle. In that sense Wilberforce was meek. But in the more normal use of the word today, as someone who is bashful and does not put himself forward and quietly waits his turn, Wilberforce was not meek at all. He was quite willing to turn the tables over in the temple if that was the only way to get the people's attention – even knowing that in the long run that might not work. He would cry out, proclaim, shout out, and make much of the cause of justice for which he felt so passionately. He was no one's pushover. But he also did not wait to be pushed! He pushed other people! He used all the resources and connections that he had as a member of the ruling elite of the time to advance the cause that he felt was right.

Slavery was the most prominent issue against which he campaigned, but it was not the only one. His convictions as a Christian led him to campaign against a wide-range of social ills, including the Society for the Suppression of Vice (designed to champion morality); British missionary work in India (to help open up opportunities for missionary work in that country); creating a free colony in Sierra Leone (where African slaves could find a free zone in which to live); the Church Missionary Society (to champion mission work around the world); and the Society for the Prevention of Cruelty to Animals (whose title is self-evident as to its focus). In all these and other instances of passion for justice and good causes, Wilberforce was able to put the trumpet to his lips and blast out a note of strong warning, calling, or boasting of the importance of the matter under consideration.

It was the gospel that gave Wilberforce this confidence. Before his conversion, Wilberforce's life was driven by a very different set of concerns. After he gave his life to Christ, he was forever given over to a life of caring for the disadvantaged and using his own connections and power to help those who needed his and others' help. To do that, he had to do what we are calling boast positively. He had to take the cause and write it in letters a mile high so that no one could miss it, and even if people refused to join in with the cause, they could not miss the choice that was being presented to them.

Often today, people who serve in public life are viewed with suspicion because many believe they are only after power or influence and only want what they can get out of being as close as possible to the seat of power in government. To avoid such criticism, it is only possible not to have influence or to have as little influence as possible.

Wilberforce found a different path. Much criticized as he was (for ignoring social justice issues in his own country, for instance), Wilberforce nonetheless kept a laser-like focus on what his contribution could be. And he made that cause as loud and as obvious and as in-your-face as it could be, so that the cause itself would be noticed and would confront everyone with its need to be addressed.

Behind all this positive boldness was a deep conviction regarding the prevailing truth, power, and influence of the real gospel in real Christians throughout contemporary society. Wilberforce's famous little book *Real Christianity* (the full title: *A Practical View of the Prevailing Religious System of Professed Christianity in the Higher and Middle Classes in this Country Contrasted with Real Christianity*) makes his views clear in many ways regarding both the nature of real Christianity, the biblical doctrines to which he espoused, the difference between that and the prevailing 'good old boy' nominal Christianity of the classes to which he belonged in England at the time, as well as the power of real Christianity to influence social action. Towards the end of this book he said this:

> But it would be an instance in myself of that very false shame which I have condemned in others, if I were not boldly to avow my firm persuasion, that *to the decline of Religion and morality our national difficulties must both directly and indirectly be chiefly ascribed; and that my only solid hopes for the well-being of my country depend not so much on her fleets and armies, not so much on the wisdom of her rulers, or the spirit of her people, as on the persuasion that she still contains many, who, in a degenerate age, love and obey the Gospel of Christ; on the humble trust that the intercession of these may still be prevalent, that for the sake of these, Heaven may still look upon us with an eye of favour.*[3]

---

3   William Wilberforce, *Real Christianity*, p. 353.

His life was marked by a conviction, drawn out of a compassion, rooted in a faith, that he was justified before God, had received His Holy Spirit, and was therefore commissioned by God towards a great task of representing Him in the world. This he did with maximum energy, wisdom and boldness, or what we are calling, positive boasting.

Wilberforce stands as a powerful example of the necessity of connecting doctrine and biblical truth with practical social action. It is often thought or claimed that doctrine has no real implications for practical action, and indeed (even by some) that doctrine, or too much emphasis on Bible teaching, can prevent getting down and taking action against present evils in society. Such people who emphasize the truth of Christ are so heavenly minded they are no earthly good; they emphasize pie in the sky ideas that have no real positive or practical impact on the day-to-day life of suffering people today.

Wilberforce, if anyone, stands as a powerful counter-example to that claim. He was a fully committed member of the Church of England, an evangelical, and the recipient of one of the last letters ever written by John Wesley, urging Wilberforce to campaign against slavery, and encouraged to do so also by the great evangelical minister and former slave-trader John Newton. He knew his Bible, believed it, and practiced it. And not just in public, but at home too. He was a devoted and indulgent father, even paying for all the losses that one of his children suffered later in life, to the extent that the father had to spend his days going from home to home, family friend to friend of family, relying on their hospitality.

He also gives the lie to the idea that a commitment, or submission, or humility before God means lack of bold action. If anyone was bold, it was Wilberforce. If anyone was willing to take a stand, it was Wilberforce. He saw all this coming out of what he thought was the key aspect of Christianity: a present, humble attitude towards the living

God; that is, living a life not bound by arbitrary regulations to a distant deity, but a life of abundant gratitude for what Christ has actually done for the believer. All this truth was transformative for the life of William Wilberforce, as he became bold and audacious, in positive boasting for the Lord, and for the cause for which the Lord had called him – the abolition of the slave trade.

Dr Martin Luther King, Jr

Our final and more recent example from the history of positive boasting comes from what is normally referred to as the civil rights movement. In many ways, some historians think there were in reality at least two civil rights movements in the mid-century of American history. There was the more well-known movement that predominated in the Southern states, employed biblical overtones for its rhetoric, and was led by the famous Dr Martin Luther King, Jr. But there was also a movement that predominated more in the Northern states, and while also employing biblical rhetoric, had a slightly more genteel tone, and was more likely to think in terms of gradual education and slow glacial transformation than a confrontation with the powers that be through civil protest and non-violent demonstration.

The movement that is familiar to us, based in the South, had a realistic – some would say negative – view of human nature. They understood their own fallibility, their own tendency towards self-aggrandizement, and called themselves as well as others to live with strict internal discipline and a stringent, passive, and non-violent approach to the authorities, even in the face of the gravest provocation. They would not fight back when beaten, not retaliate when shamed in public arrests. Their weapon was the word and the non-violent protest that they inherited from Gandhi's protests against British Rule in India.

One of King's pithy, quotable sayings encapsulates the way in which he was able to boast positively in God in such a fashion that it had a transformative effect on those around. He would say, 'Jesus Christ was an extremist for love, truth, and goodness.' This was no callow view of Jesus 'meek and mild', in the sense of passivity in the face of evil. He was an extremist, radical even, but radical for the love of God and the love of fellow man. This attitude pervaded all that King aspired to be: a man of love, a transformative love, that would impact those around him. He did not keep his 'light under a bushel' but stood out and stood up for what he believed was right, fair, and true. He said, 'Do to us what you will, and we will still love you.' That kind of attitude was compelling, as well as deeply annoying for those who were trying to shut down the civil rights movement at the time. He was insistent on constantly taking the high moral route, keeping himself above the fray, even when in jail writing letters of love, and truth, and justice.

This neighbour-love of King's could not be quiet, or unassuming, or unwilling to take initiative in action. As the Book of Exodus was a frequent go-to resource for the civil rights movement, so was Jesus' unparalleled example of neighbour love, of self-sacrifice for the good of others – even those who persecute you. The Good Samaritan is not just a sweet story for kids; it is a technique for transforming enemies into friends. King said, 'The true neighbor will risk his position, his prestige, and even his life for the welfare of others. In dangerous valleys and hazardous pathways, he will lift some bruised and beaten brother to a higher and more noble life.' It was this initiative, this love, this action which had such a profound impact on so many people.

The civil rights movement was, of course, not perfect. The leaders were human like you and I, and there were elements of it, like any other movement, that were less sanguine than other components. But despite these contradictions and false notes, the overall sound of the movement was of a loud, clear clarion-call to change for the sake of truth and, for many of them, for the sake of God. It was a kind of social-justice positive-boasting, an initiative that took place on the part of God and for God's creation – for the sake of God's name – to rescue that 'bruised and beaten brother' and to set him up on a high place.

It was non-violence that allowed them to find a way to assert themselves without becoming arrogant or sliding into negative boasting. Again, King put it like this, 'Non-violence could symbolize the gold badge of heroism rather than the white feather of cowardice.' Such statements and bold contrasts raise the stakes immeasurably. You are either with us or you are not, you are either heroic or cowardly, the rhetoric implicitly suggests. But while the stakes are raised, the options are also held out for us in a way that provides a ladder to attain that heroic status: non-violence. There is a method, a call to action with an executable plan, that can make all the difference, and bring someone to live in a way that makes all the difference. It can turn a potential coward into an actual hero for a higher cause, by enlisting that brother into the ranks of an army of love for non-violence for justice.

King's most famous moment was, of course, his great 'I have a dream' speech. There in Washington D.C., in front of thousands and thousands of peaceful, non-violent protesters, he uttered a brief, simple declaration. It was worded with beauty and spoken with that gorgeous, resonant eloquence that King's voice had the power to imbue, and it was as clear a message of hope as we are likely to hear.

> With this faith, we will be able to hew out of the mountain of despair a stone of hope. With this faith, we will be able to transform the jangling discords of our nation into a beautiful symphony of brotherhood. With this faith, we will be able to work together, to pray together, to struggle together, to go to jail together, to stand up for freedom together, knowing that we will be free one day.

All our heroes have feet of clay, and the historical figures we have surveyed briefly above are likewise far from perfect. Some had more glaring and obvious weaknesses than others. But what made them stand out was their ability, desire, and competency to be able to present their cause, the cause of Christ, in a way that captured the imagination of those around them, and yet was not negative boasting. They were not marketing themselves, or promoting themselves, in a self-aggrandizing, Facebook-stream of misrepresentation of the perfect vacation (which was really pretty awful, if truth be told). They were speaking of that which had gripped their hearts and minds, and speaking of it loudly and clearly, with a clarion call to others to see what they saw.

In other words, they did not eschew the prize virtue of the Christian: humility. Dr Gregory Thornbury, in his chapter in *Essential Evangelicalism: The Enduring Influence of Carl F. H. Henry*, tells a remarkable story about Carl Henry in this regard. According to Henry's editor, Marvin Olasky, when Henry was writing for *World Magazine*, he had a particularly humble attitude towards works that he submitted for publication. With each article, he would include a return-addressed, stamped card marked with two options for Olasky: 'Accept' or 'Reject'. That Henry, by then one of the most famous and influential evangelical leaders of his generation, should still want feedback, and submit himself overtly to editorial review, is a remarkable testament to his ongoing humility.[4]

But it was more than a simple mousey attitude; none would call Henry a wallflower. He was at the forefront of the evangelical movements of his day, championing biblical Christianity against the winds or currents of prevailing thought in his time. What it showed was a dependence upon the empowering of Christ, of the Holy Spirit. It led to

---

4   *Essential Evangelicalism: The Enduring Influence of Carl F. H. Henry*, Matthew J. Hall and Owen Strachan, Editors, (Wheaton, IL: Crossway, 2015), p. 135.

a kind of positive boasting because the strength was not his, but was Christ's alone. In the same volume on Henry, John Woodbridge records Henry's closing comments of a 1966 address 'Facing a New Day in Evangelicalism':

> Let me note in closing, however, that without the Great Commissioner we can do nothing at all. If we take the great Commission seriously, we must take the Great Commissioner just as seriously: 'He that believeth on me, the works that I do shall he do also .... Abide in me, and I in you. As the branch cannot bear fruit of itself, except it abide in the vine; no more can ye, except ye abide in me .... Without me ye can do nothing' (John 14:12, 15:4-5). It is tragic when men who profess to serve Christ, in effect forsake the duty of evangelicalism; it is equally tragic when disciples who proclaim a devotion to the Great Commission try to 'go it alone'.[5]

The sort of confidence that we can see in Spurgeon, Wilberforce, and Martin Luther King Jr – a confidence that was enough to preach Christ in the capital city of an empire, despite the mockery of the emerging secular elite, to great effect and impact, or to campaign against millions for the cause of the African being freed from slavery, or to stand in front of thousands upon thousands and talk of a dream – that kind of confidence had to come from somewhere. It was not from within, in the sense of that much-lampooned song, *I Did It My Way*. It was from without, in the sense of that Great Commissioner, empowering within, but as an alien force, from an alien righteousness, that gives those who receive it the kind of audacious courage that rocks empires.

This section on the history of boasting – both negative (which we have discussed referring to one notorious individual) and positive (which we have illustrated with three instances) – cannot appropriately be brought to a

---

5   *Ibid.* page 99.

close without reference to perhaps the greatest instance of this kind of audacious confidence known to church history. I refer to Polycarp, in whose martyrdom, faced with an immediate and impending death, and of a most painful kind, managed to utter words that were so captivating (and infuriating to his persecutors) that they have been reliably transmitted down through history.

Polycarp was brought into the place of his doom, surrounded by a crowd baying for his blood, and asked once again to recant. Would he give up his faith even at this last moment? Would he give up Christ? He was threatened with increasingly serious, devastating and disgustingly painful consequences if he did not recant Christ. Each time his answer became more audacious, more clearly positive boasting, even in the face of death.

> Then, the proconsul urging him, and saying, *'Swear, and I will set you at liberty, reproach Christ.'* Polycarp declared, *'Eighty and six years have I served Him, and He never did me any injury: how then can I blaspheme my King and my Saviour?'*...
>
> The proconsul then said to him, *'I have wild beasts at hand; to these will I cast you, unless you repent.'* But he answered, *'Call them then, for we are not accustomed to repent of what is good in order to adopt that which is evil; and it is well for me to be changed from what is evil to what is righteous.'* But again the proconsul said to him, *'I will cause you to be consumed by fire, seeing you despise the wild beasts, if you will not repent.'* But Polycarp said, *'You threaten me with fire which burns for an hour, and after a little is extinguished, but are ignorant of the fire of the coming judgment and of eternal punishment, reserved for the ungodly. But why do you tarry? Bring forth what you will.'*[6]

---

6   From Philip Schaff, *Ante-Nicene Fathers, Volume 1. The Apostolic Fathers with Justin Martyr and Irenaeus*, https://www.ccel.org/ccel/schaff/anf01.iv.iv.ix.html#fnf_iv.iv.ix-p1.2

To quote Bob Dylan, writing about a very different kind of martyr, 'How could the life of such a man be in the palm of some fool's hand?' But there he was, and in the midst of that attack and vilification, and foolishness and pain, he was able to stand tall and give witness, be brave and have confidence, with positive boasting.

Lessons from this brief history of boasting

Multiple lessons could be drawn from this brief history of boasting, but most prominent among them would be that boasting itself is not value neutral. Boasting is not like money – a medium of exchange – which can be used for good or ill depending on the motivations of the person with money, the aims to which it is utilized, and the effects of its employment. There appears to be little middle ground with respect to boasting. It is like the call of Joshua, at the end of the biblical book of his name, saying 'Choose this day whom you will serve' (Josh. 24:15, ESV). There is little likelihood that someone can boast and it have no good, or no ill effect either. Boasting is not a mild middle-ground. If one boasts, the causes and motivations, effects and results will either be for good or for ill, for positive or for negative impact.

But while it appears likely from this brief history that the effects of boasting are never going to be in all probability neutral, another lesson would be that there are no doubt many who do not boast at all. If we have chosen only a few lives who have lived large, built impact, and made a difference, there are surely countless thousands who, even by their own lights, and according to their own opportunities, circumstances, and gifts, have done little if any boasting. Perhaps if the choice is between no boasting at all and negative boasting, then it is better not to boast at all.

Would it not have been better for the world if Hitler had kept his views to himself, lived a life of quiet bitterness, drowning his sorrows in some beer hall in Austria? The answer to that can only be that it would have been much better had Hitler not boasted at all. And so, assuming that the answer to whether to boast or not predicates the assumption that boasting must be negative (the way boasting is normally thought to operate), then it is no wonder that many people do not boast. Why would they? Who wants to be known as arrogant? Who wants to push forward their own ideas at the expense of other people's: not just ideas, but even (in the case of Hitler) very lives?

There are some denizens of even refined financial districts who live by this vicious, extreme version of the survival of the fittest; perhaps as there are in any career. But many normal people would eschew such a kill-or-be-killed approach to life, and given the option between no boasting at all and negative boasting, with massive negative consequences on other people, would choose no boasting at all.

It is worth pausing here to ponder accurately the true effects of this false dichotomy. Assuming, as most people do, that the only choice is between a life of quiet and little impact, or feasting on the lives of others in a negative boasting way – that it is a zero-sum game where what you have can only be won at the expense of what someone else has, and to get that requires trampling on the faces of other people and pushing yourself forward at the expense of others. If so, then the logical consequence is a vicious few surrounded by a quietly acquiescing multitude. In short, the results are what we see in many societies, where it takes bravery (of a malicious kind) to rise to the top and trample down the others beneath you. And the rest of the society prays for such people to get their just deserts in due course – as indeed they will.

But think of the wasted talent and opportunities, gifts and contributions, of all those countless hordes of people who live quiet lives – lives of little impact, no real contribution, no dramatic breaking down the walls of injustice – going about their lives trying not to step on anyone else's toes. All that raw material, all those aspirations, going to little future benefit for others, all those quiet ones kept down by the boasting few lording it over the others. What a difference it would make if there was some better alternative! If there was a way of formulating a life that made a massive impact, of thinking about your own gifts and talents, and contributing to the needs and desires of the world, in an appropriately, but loudly, boasting kind!

It takes a certain chutzpah to stand up to the evil dictator; it takes a certain confidence to live life in a way that makes a real difference; it takes risk, and it takes a mental concept that there is a way of living like this that does make a difference. This way is not restrained by class consciousness or a sense of place that keeps you in your place – a quiet place beneath the place of others who are rising above, sometimes by negative boasting.

So then, building upon this false dichotomy, we have the true choice that this brief history of boasting presents to us. That there is a way of living for us all that gives us a kind of *noblesse oblige* – the obligation of nobility – to live large, to give back, to make a difference, to be a champion for justice and for Christ in our world, in our village, in our town, in our own school and home. It is to be active in positive boasting: to seize the bull by the horns; to confront the wickedness of our day and in our streets, and to cry out, 'It shall not be so, not on my watch.' This is because we are freed, by Christ, to live lives of consequence: to live life to the full and make a real difference, and not be pushed down by the negative boasting of the charlatan; nor give in to the false dichotomy that there is no other alternative except either that negative boasting or being mild and letting things be as they are, and trying to keep your head down and stay out of trouble. Instead, it is to lift our heads above the parapet, to go over the trenches, and not just with bravery, but also with wisdom (the subject for another book) to confront the powers that be; to do battle with the principalities and powers of this dark age, without fear or favour, for no purpose other than to honour God and to love neighbour, to grow the kingdom, and to advance the gospel, and to do so with exuberant, confident, audacious boasting – of a positive kind.

This is surely the primary lesson from this brief history of boasting, that choosing to live a life of positive boasting can make a real difference. With that lesson from as wide a range of personalities as a Spurgeon, a Wilberforce or a Martin Luther King Jr, there is an opportunity for those who are in Christ also to live lives of this kind of boasting confidence – all based on our assurance in Christ, no longer anxious for eternity, and so spending our lives now living with full-on confidence here and now, for the future, for the good of others, and for the glory of God. With passion, zeal, and positive boasting.

Like all historical accounts, it is only a narrative of the past, not a prediction of the future. It only points to a trajectory; it does not point to its necessary conclusion, but with the predicative insight of learning from the past, so that we do not repeat its mistakes, but benefit from its lessons, so we are to be those who live lives of positive boasting too.

8.
THE FUTURE OF BOASTING

In this book we have considered the biblical trajectory with relation to the concept and actual wording of boasting. We have considered it along two main themes, that of positive boasting and that of negative boasting. In each case we have found that there are correlations as well as distinct differences; there is an overlap, but at the same time there is a quite different endpoint, motivation, and characteristic – depending on which kind of boasting we are talking about – that tends to dominate and shape that boasting. We have applied this biblical discussion about boasting to a history of boasting, its psychology, and various other matters of practical significance as we wrestle with what it might mean to boast in the Lord in a real and contemporary, current and actionable manner.

What we have not done is considered what the future of boasting might be. That is, what might it actually look like for someone to proactively determine to boast in the Lord? (We shall leave aside for the moment the possibility that someone else might decide that they actually want to proactively indulge in negative boasting; we certainly don't want to make that aspect of the possible trajectory easier for anyone to accomplish.) What would this sort of boasting, of a 'positive boasting' kind, look like in the present and – given that by the time this book is completed and published, it will no longer be the present from the vantage point of the author as he writes these words – the future?

What would it look like, in a future sense also, actually to build a reliable, realistic, and concretely practical mode of living and interacting with other human beings, that was definitively boasting in the Lord?

Are we talking only about singing worship songs in church with particular vim and zest? Is this only about being particularly enthusiastic about preaching or leading Bible studies or doing church planting or the like – specific ministry activities – or is it something that encompasses the non-religious aspects of life too? And is this boasting inevitable, non-related to intelligence, or to put it a different way: is the trajectory of boasting likely to be a little brainless, thoughtless, lacking in prudent wisdom and careful consideration? Can we really, with abandon and audacity, boast in the Lord at the same time as also giving careful weight to our viewpoints, not asserting beyond what the evidence dictates, being judicious in our assessments of potential risks, and generally having wisdom that also biblically is greatly praised – certainly the wisdom that has its foundation in the fear of the Lord?

The answers to those questions could easily be another monograph, putting into practical action the tendencies that have been discovered in this book. But for the sake of space, and the patience of the reader who may well have skipped – understandably enough, I have done it often enough myself when reading – from the introduction of this book to now the conclusion, we will summarize the future of boasting in the following five axioms of praxis:

First, think rightly. There is no point in generating enthusiasm for a particular activity if it is not surely grounded on a right and solid foundation in truth. It is not by accident that the key text we considered comes at chapter five in Paul's letter to the Romans, not in chapter one, right at the beginning of the book. We need to understand and know, internalize and have our minds and our hearts shaped with the truth, in order for us to be zealous about the truth. God's people have before had zeal but without knowledge. And it is essential that if boasting in the Lord is at least, in some way or other, a subset of zeal, that this kind of zeal is one that is genuinely, truly and profoundly, rooted and established in the truth of God, in His Word, and in what He says about any particular matter as it correlates to the truth of the world, His universe and His creation.

Second, do rightly. If thinking is important – thinking truly and accurately, carefully and profoundly, and in accordance with what is real and biblical – it is also important that we do not stay stuck in our minds. Right thinking leads to right action; otherwise, there is no right thinking. To think rightly about poverty will lead to action about poverty; otherwise, we have not thought rightly about poverty. Or to put it as Jesus put it, by their fruits you will know them (Matt. 7:20). A good tree produces good fruit. We need to live morally, to live with Christian holy charity, humble love, godliness and Christ-likeness, and to take this character invested in us by God's Spirit and apply it to the real issues of our day and our age, and genuinely and actively make a difference.

Third, speak rightly. Those who think will do, and those who are thinking and doing rightly, though, need also not undermine the power of speech. The word, the spoken word, the written word, has a life of its own. If the underpinning of the universe is *logos*, the Word of God, and if all that is, everything that exists, actually is held up and sustained by the word of His power, then we are wise to make sure that our words are impactful rationally and biblically, affectionally and passionately, and in a positive boasting sense. The words we choose with our children and our friends, with our parents and our spouse, with our colleagues at work and our boss, and with our employees – all these words can either build up or tear down. To positively boast is to apply these words with passionate care, and glorious attention to the precise nuance of what we write – yes, even what we write in the blogosphere, or in the comments sections of posts on Internet forums – and therefore not only be thinking and doing truth, but also speaking truth.

Fourth, love rightly. While in some sense love and its constituent thoughts and feelings, actions and interactions, could be summarized under one of the previous three points, if we take Scripture seriously, it deserves its own separate point and emphasis. Love is the greatest, according to Paul in 1 Corinthians 13, and if we act or speak without love, then those actions and speeches mean I gain nothing, and I am nothing. We must pray for the love that God has for those around us, to sense it, reflect and embody it, yes also feel it, and be moved by that love – not in a soppy, sentimental way, but in a generous and kind, compassionate and Christ-like (there is no better descriptor), humble love. Humility in love is an ingredient without which love becomes patriarchially or matriarchally dominant, loving the other for the sake of how wonderful is love for the person doing the loving; not for the person on the receiving end of the love. But Christian love frees, does not dominate or overlord; it is a genuine and open-handed, seamless and guileless, love for the other – and for God most of all.

Fifth, sacrifice rightly. To truly have a passionate boasting in the Lord, engagement with the world around us requires that we actually engage with that world in the same way that Christ did, and in the way that He insisted was necessary for us to follow in His footsteps. To follow Jesus at all, and certainly to do so with positive boasting such that there is an impact on the world, simply requires Christ-like sacrifice, picking up our cross and following Him. What this will mean in each of our situations will have its own particularities, and cannot be generalized beyond the principle: the man nursing his sick wife will have a different kind of self-sacrifice than the pastor facing persecution. Each, though, is following the same call, and in the self-sacrifice for the sake of redemption is having a profound, enormous story-worth-telling kind of impact on society, church, and the world.

In short, and in summary, if you know Jesus, if you love Him, don't be quiet about it.

Also available from Christian Focus Publications ...

JOHN
PERRITT

YOUR **DAYS**
ARE NUMB3RED

A CLOSER LOOK AT HOW

WE SPEND OUR TIME

& THE ETERNITY BEFORE US

Your Days Are Numbered

A Closer Look at How We Spend Our Time & the Eternity Before Us

JOHN PERRITT

Wasting time might not seem like a big deal to some, except for the fact that our time really isn't ours, but God's. Not only that, but it is a limited resource. You can be the richest person in the world and you still can't buy more time.

If we want a heart of wisdom, according to the psalmist, we must number our days. *Your Days are Numbered* takes a biblical look at the way in which we spend our time to cultivate this mind-set of seeing each day as a vital opportunity to live for the glory of God.

Of all the gifts God gives to us, few are more precious and few are more fleeting than the gift of time. Your days are numbered and you are responsible to faithfully steward each one of them for the good of others and the glory of God. This book will teach and encourage you to make the most of the time God gives you.

TIM CHALLIES
Blogger at www.challies.com

… Your Days Are Numbered *succeeds in addressing it with simplicity and practicality. If heeded, John Perritt's common sense proposals grounded in scriptural principle will enable us to 'redeem the time'.*

DAVID STRAIN
Senior Minister, First Presbyterian Church, Jackson, Mississippi

978-1-7819-1744-2

JOSH MOODY

How the Bible Can
Change Your Life

ANSWERS TO THE TEN MOST COMMON
QUESTIONS ABOUT THE BIBLE

How the Bible Can Change your Life

Answers to the Ten Most Common Questions about the Bible

Josh Moody

Christians are Bible people. We believe that God speaks to us through His inspired Word. And yet many Christians and churches don't actually open their Bibles. Josh Moody asks the question: Why should I read the Bible?

Following on from How Church Can Change Your Life, Moody tackles the next great challenge for contemporary Christians: faith in and practice of the Bible, answering 10 of the most common questions about the Bible:

Is the Bible True?
Is the Bible Relevant?
Is the Bible Interesting?
Is the Bible Authoritative?
How Do You Read the Bible?
When Do You Read the Bible?
Does it Matter if We Use the Bible in Church?
Does the Bible Make You Stupid?
Does the Bible Prevent a Tolerant Society?

Moody's book will greatly help a wide range of readers—the beginner, the Bible-hungry believer, the confused—and will minister particularly to the brilliant thinker who needs strong but succinct arguments dipped in supernatural realities. The great need of the modern church is confidence in and affection for the Word of God. How the Bible Can Change Your Life *is just the book for times like ours.*

Owen Strachan
Associate Professor of Christian Theology, Midwestern Baptist Theological Seminary, Kansas City, Missouri

978-1-5271-0151-7

How Church Can
Change Your Life

ANSWERS TO THE TEN MOST COMMON
QUESTIONS ABOUT CHURCH

How Church Can Change Your Life

Answers to the Ten Most Common Questions about Church

Josh Moody

Google books on church, there will be no shortage of choice! Some will be helpful, others less so. So why another book on church? Josh Moody, is, in fact, asking a very different question: why should I go to church at all? Filled with practical advice, this book will help you answer questions you maybe should have known the answer to and other questions you never knew to ask!

This book answers questions about the church that your friends are asking! ... Read this book and be encouraged by his answers, and then pass it along to a friend who has considered church attendance to be optional.

Erwin Lutzer
Senior Pastor, Moody Church, Chicago, Illinois

... a powerful and needed reminder of the central role the local church should play in the life of every Christian.

R. Albert Mohler
President, The Southern Baptist Theological Seminary,
Louisville, Kentucky

...presents a compelling case for why we must be part of a healthy local church ... ideal for new Christians, seekers who are unsure about the church, and for all those who have lost sight of the glorious truth that the church is God's agency for changing the world.

John Stevens
National Director, Fellowship of Independent Evangelical
Churches, Market Harborough, Leicestershire

978-1-7819-1611-7

Christian Focus Publications

Our mission statement –

STAYING FAITHFUL
In dependence upon God we seek to impact the world through literature faithful to His infallible Word, the Bible. Our aim is to ensure that the Lord Jesus Christ is presented as the only hope to obtain forgiveness of sin, live a useful life and look forward to heaven with Him.

Our Books are published in four imprints:

CHRISTIAN
FOCUS
popular works including biographies, commentaries, basic doctrine and Christian living.

CHRISTIAN
HERITAGE
books representing some of the best material from the rich heritage of the church.

MENTOR
books written at a level suitable for Bible College and seminary students, pastors, and other serious readers. The imprint includes commentaries, doctrinal studies, examination of current issues and church history.

CF4•K
children's books for quality Bible teaching and for all age groups: Sunday school curriculum, puzzle and activity books; personal and family devotional titles, biographies and inspirational stories – Because you are never too young to know Jesus!

Christian Focus Publications Ltd,
Geanies House, Fearn, Ross-shire,
IV20 1TW, Scotland, United Kingdom.
www.christianfocus.com